P9-DWX-947

NATIONAL COUNCIL OF TEACHERS OF ENGLISH
English Monograph No. 10

AMERICAN ENGLISH GRAMMAR

NATIONAL COUNCIL OF TEACHERS OF ENGLISH
Research Monograph No. 15

AMERICAN ENGLISH GRAMMAR

American English Grammar

THE GRAMMATICAL STRUCTURE OF PRESENT-DAY AMERICAN ENGLISH WITH ESPECIAL REFERENCE TO SOCIAL DIFFERENCES OR CLASS DIALECTS

by

CHARLES CARPENTER FRIES

Professor of English
The University of Michigan

The Report of an Investigation Financed by the National Council of Teachers of English and Supported by the Modern Language Association and the Linguistic Society of America

APPLETON - CENTURY - CROFTS, INC.

NEW YORK

670-10

PRINTED IN THE UNITED STATES OF AMERICA

To

A. C. F.

Preface

The National Council of Teachers of English has come more and more to realize that in order to avoid the futile and even harmful teaching practices which have resulted from ignorance, satisfactory programs for teaching the English language in the schools must rest upon essentially sound views of language and a knowledge of the facts.[1] It has also realized that, in respect to the English language in America, the necessary facts have not yet been gathered and made available. To be sure, the great *Oxford English Dictionary* contains much valuable material, but it was the very deficiencies of the Oxford Dictionary in respect to American English that led Sir William Craigie to undertake, at the University of Chicago, the production of an *Historical Dictionary of American English.* When finished, this dictionary (together with the American Dialect Dictionary which we hope will eventually be pushed to completion) will provide the facts concerning our vocabulary and its development. In addition, the facts concerning American pronunciation have received considerable attention in Professor G. P. Krapp's *The English Language in America,*[2] and in Professor J. S. Kenyon's *American Pronunciation.*[3] In general, however, those who have dealt with American English have slighted or neglected grammatical matters.[4] The National Council of Teachers of English has, therefore, given generously of its funds in order to make possible the collecting of some materials upon which to base a preliminary sketch of the inflections and syntax of American English with especial reference to social class differences.

[1] See the report on "Training in English Language for English Teachers" published in the *English Journal,* XVII (December, 1928), pp. 825–835.

[2] Published for the Modern Language Association by the Century Company, 1925.

[3] Published by George Wahr, Ann Arbor, Michigan, 1924, and subsequent editions. *The Linguistic Atlas of the United States and Canada* will eventually furnish the important details concerning the pronunciation of American English. See *Linguistic Atlas of New England,* Hans Kurath, director and editor. Three volumes and a Handbook, 1939+.

[4] Of Professor Krapp's 730 pages given to the *English Language in America,* but fifteen are devoted to the discussion of inflections and syntax. Mr. H. L. Mencken, in his *The American Language* does treat grammatical matters, but his use of sources and evidence is such that it would be very difficult to use the material for the determining of a program for the schools. See below, page 35, note 2.

This work was begun in a tentative fashion in the summer of 1926 and more seriously attacked during the three months from June to September of 1927. Some additional materials necessary to complete the study were gathered during the summer of 1930. The writing of the report has been unavoidably postponed because of the interference of other matters, but the study of the collected materials has proceeded steadily if leisurely. A number of graduate students in English language at the University of Michigan have contributed to that study, and these contributions, especially the more important ones, will be acknowledged separately at the places in which their materials appear.

It may seem to some that the attempt to explain the significance of the facts presented is unnecessarily simplified and that a chapter such as the first is out of place in a report like this. It must be remembered, however, that the report here presented is written for the many English teachers in the schools and not primarily for the comparatively few who are well trained in the scientific approach to language. I hope the latter will overlook the elementary matters to view with good-natured but searching criticism the new material here gathered and that the former will be patient with the linguistic detail necessary to a sound approach to such a problem.

In a work of this kind it is difficult to record the sources of all the suggestions and the aid that I have received, but special acknowledgment must here be made for some particular contributions. A number of language scholars read portions of the manuscript and made helpful criticisms. Among the most important of these were the comments of W. F. Bryan, W. Cabell Greet, A. G. Kennedy, Roland Kent, J. S. Kenyon, Hans Kurath, R. J. Menner, Louise Pound, R. L. Ramsay, Stuart Robertson, L. L. Rockwell, J. M. Steadman, E. H. Sturtevant, and C. K. Thomas. In typing the manuscript and especially in dealing with the proof sheets and in making the index I have had invaluable assistance from Miss Aileen Traver who gave to the book many things of extreme value. Throughout all the work, however, from the collecting of the materials, through the long processes of recording the instances of each grammatical category examined and of analyzing the evidence, to the writing of the finished book I have had the constant help of my wife, Agnes Carswell Fries, whose devoted assistance made the work possible.

C. C. F.

Contents

AMERICAN ENGLISH GRAMMAR

II

THE SOCIAL SIGNIFICANCE OF DIFFERENCES IN LANGUAGE PRACTICE AND THE OBLIGATION OF THE SCHOOLS

"English" maintains its place as the most frequently *required subject* of our school and college curriculums because of the unanimous support given it both by the general public and by education authorities. This support rests upon the general belief that the mastery of *good English* is not only the most important asset of the ambitious, but also an obligation of every good citizen. There is, however, in many quarters, a very hazy idea of the specific elements which make *good English.* A great deal of vigorous controversy ignores all the larger problems of effective communication and centers attention upon the criteria to be applied in judging the acceptability of particular words and language forms. All of this controversy is direct evidence that there do exist many differences in the language practice of English speaking people; for no controversy could arise and no choice be offered unless differing language forms presented themselves in the actual practice of English speech. It is the purpose of this chapter to set forth the general character of these differences and to analyze their significance in relation to the obligations resting upon our schools. The chapter as a whole will therefore present the principles underlying this whole investigation and the point of view which has determined its material and method.

I

Underlying many of the controversies concerning words and language forms is a very common attitude which I shall call here the "conventional point of view." Frequently stated explicitly, sometimes only implied, it appears in most handbooks and manuals of correct English, in grammars and rhetorics, in educational tests and measures, and in many editorials of the press. This conventional point of view assumes not only that there is a correctness in English language as absolute as that in elementary mathematics but also that the measures of this correctness are very definite rules. The following quotations are typical:

"A college professor rises to defend 'ain't' and 'it is me' as good English. The reed upon which he leans is majority usage. . . . 'Ain't,' as a legitimate contraction of 'am not,' would not require defense or apology if it were not for widespread misuse. Unfortunately the same cannot be said of 'it is me.' This solecism could not be given the odor of good English by a plurality as great as Warren G. Harding rolled up in 1920. . . . A vast amount of wretched English is heard in this country. The remedy does not lie in the repeal of the rules of grammar; but rather in a stricter and more intelligent enforcement of those rules in our schools. . . . This protest against traditional usage and the rules of grammar is merely another manifestation of the unfortunate trend of the times to lawlessness in every direction. . . . Quite as important as keeping undesirables out of the vocabulary is the maintaining of respect for the rules of grammar, which govern the formation of words into phrases and sentences. . . . Students should be taught that correct speaking is evidence of culture; and that in order to speak correctly they must master the rules that govern the use of the language." [1]

"Grammar consists of a series of rules and definitions. . . . Since . . . ninety-five per cent of all children and teachers come from homes or communities where incorrect English is used, nearly everyone has before him the long, hard task of overcoming habits set up early in life before he studied language and grammar in school. . . . Such people are exposed to the ridicule of those who notice the error, and the only way in which they can cure themselves is by eternal vigilance and the study of grammar." [2]

"This is a test to see how well you know correct English usage and how well you can select the *rule or principle in accordance with which a usage is correct*. In the left hand column a list of sentences is given. In each sentence there are two forms in parentheses, one correct, and the other incorrect. In the right hand column a list of rules or principles is given, some one of which applies to each sentence. . . ."

[1] From an editorial in *The Detroit Free Press,* December 9, 1928.

[2] W. W. Charters, *Teaching the Common Branches* (New York, The Macmillan Co., rev. ed., 1924), pp. 96, 98, 115.

Sentences	Principles
( ) 1. (Whom) (Who) did you meet?	*a.* The indirect object is in the objective case.
( ) 2. He told John and (I) (me) an interesting story.	*b.* The subject of the verb is in the nominative case.
	c. The object of a verb is in the objective case.

". . . Read the first sentence in Section I; then mark out the incorrect form. Read the rules in Section I, until you find one that applies to this first sentence. Place the letter of this rule in the square preceding the first sentence. . . ." [3]

"One purpose of this report is to describe and illustrate a method of constructing a grammar curriculum upon the basis of the errors of school children. . . . it is apparent that the first step is *to ascertain* the rules which are broken and to determine their relative importance." [4]

The point of view expressed in these quotations, assuming as it does that certain definite rules [5] are the necessary standards by which to measure language correctness, also repudiates *general usage* as a valid guide to acceptability, even the usage of the so-called "educated." The following quotation represents dozens of similar statements:

"The truth is, however, that authority of general usage, or even of the usage of great writers, is not absolute in language. There is a misuse of words which can be justified by no authority, however great, and *by no usage however general.*" [6]

From this, the "conventional point of view," the problem of the differences in our language practice is a very simple one. Only two kinds of forms or usages exist—correct forms and mistakes. In general, the mistakes are thought to be corrupt forms or illegitimate meanings derived by carelessness from the correct ones. In some cases a grudging acquiescence accepts some forms which are contrary to the rules when these forms are sanctioned by an over-

[3] T. J. Kirby, *Grammar Test,* University of Iowa Standard Tests and Scales.

[4] "Minimal Essentials in Language and Grammar," in *Sixteenth Yearbook* of the National Society for the Study of Education (Bloomington, Ind., Public School Publishing Co., 1917), pp. 86, 87.

[5] For a statement of the development of this point of view see C. C. Fries, *Teaching of the English Language* (New York, Thomas Nelson and Sons, 1927), Ch. I, "The Rules of Grammar as the Measure of Language Errors."

[6] R. G. White, *Words and Their Uses* (Boston, Houghton Mifflin Co., rev. ed., 1899), p. 14.

whelming usage, but here the view remains that these forms, although established by usage, are still *incorrect* and must always be incorrect. To this point of view these incorrect forms sanctioned by usage are the "idioms" of the language. In all the matters of differing language practices, therefore, those who hold this point of view regard the obligation of the schools as perfectly clear and comparatively simple—the schools must root out the *mistakes* or *errors* and cultivate the language uses that are *correct according to the rules*.[7]

Opposed to this "conventional point of view" is that held by the outstanding scholars in English language during the last hundred years. I shall call it here "the scientific point of view." Typical expressions of it abound.

"In considering the use of grammar as a corrective of what are called 'ungrammatical' expressions, it must be borne in mind that the rules of grammar have no value except as statements of facts: whatever is in general use in a language is for that very reason grammatically correct."[8]

"The grammar of a language is not a list of rules imposed upon its speakers by scholastic authorities, but is a scientific record of the actual phenomena of that language, written and spoken. If any community habitually uses certain forms of speech, these forms are part of the grammar of the speech of that community."[9]

"It has been my endeavor in this work to represent English Grammar not as a set of stiff dogmatic precepts, according to which some things are correct and others absolutely wrong, but as something living and developing under continual fluctuations and undulations, something that is founded on the past and prepares the way for the future, something that is not always consistent or perfect, but progressing and perfectible—in one word, human."[10]

"A Grammar book does not attempt to teach people how they ought to speak, but on the contrary, unless it is a very bad or a very

[7] "Some better reason than a custom arising from ignorance . . . is needed for changing the English language. It would seem to be still the part of the schools to teach the language *strictly according to rule,* and to place emphasis on such teaching, rather than to encourage questionable liberties of usage." From an editorial in *The Christian Science Monitor,* Boston, February 23, 1923.

[8] Henry Sweet, *New English Grammar,* Vol. I (Oxford, Clarendon Press, 1891), p. 5.

[9] Grattan and Gurrey, *Our Living Language* (London, Thomas Nelson and Sons, 1925), p. 25.

[10] Otto Jespersen, *A Modern English Grammar* (Heidelberg, 1909), I, Preface.

old work, it merely states how, as a matter of fact, certain people do speak at the time at which it is written." [11]

In these typical expressions of "the scientific point of view" there is, first of all, a definitely stated opposition to the fundamental principle of the "conventional attitude." All of them insist that it is unsound to take the rules of grammar as the necessary norms of correct English and to set out to make all usage conform to those rules. In these expressions of the scientific view there is, also, a clear affirmation of the fundamental principle of the attitude that usage or practice is the basis of all the *correctness* there can be in language.[12] From this, the scientific point of view, the problem presented by the differences in our language is by no means a simple one. Instead of having to deal with a mass of diverse forms which can be easily separated into the two groups of *mistakes* and *correct language* according to perfectly definite measures, the language scholar finds himself confronted by a complex range of differing practices which must be sorted into an indefinite number of groups according to a set of somewhat indistinct criteria called "general usage." [13] Those who hold this scientific point of view insist, therefore, that the first step in fulfilling the obligation of the schools in the matter of dealing with the English language is to record, realistically and as completely as possible, the facts of this usage.

This investigation and report assumes as its first principle this scientific point of view with its repudiation of the conventional attitude toward language errors. We shall, therefore, ignore the conventional classification of *mistakes* and *correct forms,* and attempt to outline the types of differences that appear in our American language practices.

[11] H. C. Wyld, *Elementary Lessons in English Grammar* (Oxford, Clarendon Press, 1925), p. 12.

[12] This statement must not be taken to imply that *mere correctness* is to be considered the ultimate ideal of language. The scientific point of view does not in any way conflict with the artistic view of *good English.* See the discussion of "The Scientific and the Artistic Points of View in Language," in C. C. Fries, *The Teaching of the English Language,* pp. 102–121.

[13] One should, perhaps, call attention at this point to the fact that the great *Oxford English Dictionary* is the outstanding document in this "scientific view of language." The principle underlying the production of the *Oxford Dictionary,* the very foundation of its method, was the insistence upon use or practice as the sole criterion of the legitimate meaning of words. Compare, for example, the treatment of the word *nice* (especially sense 15) in this dictionary with the usual statements concerning it as given in the conventional handbooks.

II

All of us upon occasion note and use for the purpose of identification the many differences in the speech of those about us. By differences in pitch of voice, for instance, we can usually tell whether the person talking to us over the telephone is a man, or a woman, or a child. By certain characteristic differences of pronunciation and of grammar, the speech of "Amos and Andy" as it comes over the radio makes us visualize two uneducated negroes. Through the speech of "Clara, Lou, and Em," we see three women of little education who have had a very limited range of social contacts. In similar fashion we should with little difficulty recognize the speech of a Scot like Harry Lauder as differing from that of a native of Georgia or Alabama. If one could conjure up Shakspere or Spenser or Milton, he would find their English strange to his ears not only in pronunciation but in vocabulary and in grammar as well. The speech of Chaucer and of Wycliffe would sound even less like English. In other words, even if one ignores such details as separate the speech of every single person from that of any other, there are at least four large types of differences to be noted in our discussion here.

First, there are historical differences. Chaucer used, as we do, *they* as the nominative plural of the pronoun of the third person, but he did not use *their* as the genitive and *them* as the dative-accusative form. Instead, he used the forms *her* or *hir*, for the genitive plural, and *hem* for the dative-accusative or objective forms. In Chaucer's language it was still the practice to distinguish carefully between the singular and plural forms of the past tense of many verbs. He would say *I rood* (rode) but we *ride(n)*, *he sang* but they *sunge(n)*. In the late sixteenth century it was no longer the practice to distinguish between the singular and plural in the past tense, and Shakspere therefore used *we rode* as well as *I rode*. For him, however, *learn* was often used with the meaning we give to *teach*, and *thou* was frequently used to address those of inferior rank or intimate friends. Thus the language forms of each age have differed in some respect from those of any other time. Constant change is the outstanding characteristic of a live language used by an intellectually active people. The historical changes do not come suddenly, nor do they affect all the users of a language equally. Thus at any time there will be found those who cling to the older methods and those who use the newer fashion. Many of the differences we note in the language of today find their explanation in this process of historical change. These older forms constitute a fairly large proportion of the materials usually called errors by those who maintain the conventional point of view. The so-called double negative, as in "They didn't take no oil with them," is thus a perpetuation of an old practice exceedingly common in the English language for centuries. It was formerly the normal way of stressing a negative. The form *foot,* in such expressions as "He is six foot tall," "The height of the bar is now six foot and two inches," is again the perpetuation of an old practice in the English language which the modern fashion has abandoned. It is an old genitive plural following the numeral. A few other examples out of dozens of such historical differences are *clomb,* usually spelled *clum,* as the past tense of the verb *climb,* instead of *climbed; wrought* [14] as the past tense of the verb *work,* instead of *worked; stang* as the past tense of the verb *sting,* instead of *stung.* Such differences belong not only in this group called "historical differences" but often also to some of the other three groups to be explained below. In fact, the four types of differences are not by any means mutually exclusive classifications but merely loose divisions with convenient labels.

Second, there are regional differences. In the south of England, in early Modern English, the inflectional ending of the verb in the third person singular present indicative was *-eth,* as in "God *loveth* a cheerful giver." In the north of England this inflectional ending was *-es,* as "God *loves* a cheerful giver." Late Modern English has adopted the form that was used only in the northern region. In the language practice of the United States, *gotten* as a past participle form of *get* is fairly general; in England it seldom appears. *You all* as a plural of *you* is especially characteristic of southern United States. In some colleges one takes a course *under* a professor; in others it is *from* one or *with* one; in still others it is *to* one. Some of the differences we note in the language practices of those about us find their explanation in the fact that the fashions in one community or section of the country do not necessarily develop in others. Regional or geographical differences show themselves more

[14] One should note that in the case of *wrought* the old form has not the flavor of "vulgar" English as have the other examples here given but suggests super-refinement.

clearly in matters of vocabulary. That part of an automobile that is called a *hood* in the United States is called a *bonnet* in England. That which they call the *hood* in England we call the *top*. *Lumber*, to most of us in the United States means *timber;* in England it still means *rubbish*. In some sections of the United States a *paper bag* is usually called a *sack*, in others a *poke*. Such regional differences become especially noticeable when a person from one section of the country moves into another bringing with him the peculiar fashions of the district from which he comes. In the new community these language differences challenge attention and give rise to questions of correctness and preference.

Third, there are literary and colloquial differences. The language practices of conversation differ in many subtle ways from those used in formal writing. Most apparent is the abundance of contractions in the language of conversation. Thoroughly unnatural would sound the speech of those who in conversation did not constantly use *I'm, you'll, isn't, don't, aren't, they'd better, we've,* instead of the fully expanded *I am, you will, is not, do not, are not, they had better, we have*. And in similar fashion the formal writing that habitually employed such contractions would seem equally unnatural because of the impression of very informal familiarity which they would create. Apparent, too, although less obvious are the differences between conversation and formal writing in the matter of sentence completeness. Conversation abounds in groups of words that do not form conventionally complete and logical sentences. Many verbs are omitted; clauses are uttered which are to be attached to the whole context of the conversation rather than to any particular word in a parsable sentence; single words stand for complete ideas. In formal writing the situation demands much more logical completeness of expression, and most of the sentences appear to satisfy the demands of a conventional grammatical analysis. Less apparent but not less real are the differences which arise out of the fact that many perfectly familiar expressions occur practically only in conversational situations and are found very seldom in literary English unless they appear in attempts to report conversation in writing. Occasions seldom arise in anything except conversational situations to use *Who* (or *whom*) *did you call?* or *It is me* (or *I*).

Many assume that the language practices of formal writing are the best or at least that they are of a higher level than those of colloquial or conversational English. When, therefore, they find an expression marked "colloquial" in a dictionary, as is the phrase *"to get on one's nerves"* in Webster's *New International Dictionary,* they frown upon its use. As a matter of fact, thus to label an expression "colloquial" is simply to say that it occurs in good conversation but not in formal writing.[15] Unless one can assume that formal writing is in itself more desirable than good conversation, the language practices peculiar to conversation cannot be rated in comparison with those of formal writing. Each set of language practices is best in its own special sphere of use; one will necessarily differ from the other.

Fourth, there are social or class differences. Despite the fact that America in its national life has struggled to express its belief in the essential equality of human beings and to free the paths of opportunity from arbitrary and artificial restraints, there still do exist some clear differences between the habits and practices of various social groups. It is, of course, practically impossible to mark the limits of any social class in this country. It is even extremely difficult to describe the special characteristics of any such class because of the comparative ease with which one passes from one social group to another, especially in youth, and the consequent mixture of group habits among those so moving. Our public schools, our churches, our community welfare work, our political life, all furnish rather frequent occasions for social class mixture. All that can be done in respect to such a description is to indicate certain facts which seem generally true for the *core* of any social group, realizing that these same facts may also be true separately of many who have connections with other groups. There are, for example, those who

[15] The word *colloquial* as applied to English words and structures is frequently misunderstood, even by teachers of English. Some confuse it with *localism,* and think of the words and constructions marked "colloquial" as peculiarities of speaking which are characteristic of a particular locality. Others feel that some stigma attaches to the label "colloquial" and would strive to avoid as *incorrect* (or as of a *low level*) all words and phrases so marked. The word *colloquial,* however, as used to label words and phrases in a dictionary like Webster's *New International Dictionary* has no such meaning. It is used to mark those words and constructions whose range of use is primarily that of the polite conversation of cultivated people, of their familiar letters and informal speeches, as distinct from those words and constructions which are common also in formal writing. As a matter of fact, even the language of our better magazines and of public addresses has, during the last generation, moved away from the formal toward the informal.

habitually wear formal dress clothes in the evening and those who never wear them. Many of the former frequent the opera and concerts of the best music; many of the latter find their entertainment solely in the movies. The families of the wealthy, especially those whose wealth has continued for several generations, ordinarily mix but little with the families of unskilled laborers; and the families of college professors even in a small city have usually very little social life in common with the families of policemen and firemen.

Just as the general social habits of such separated social groups naturally show marked differences, so their language practices inevitably vary. Pronunciations such as "*ketch*" for *catch* and "*git*" for *get;* and grammatical forms such as "He *seen* his mistake as soon as he *done* it" or "*You was*" are not the characteristic modes of speech of university professors, or of the clergymen who preach from the pulpits in our large city churches, or of the judges of the supreme court, or of the presidents of our most important banks, or even of those who habitually patronize the opera. Such language practices, therefore, if used in these particular social groups attract as much attention as a pair of overalls might at an evening gathering where custom demands formal dress clothes. In fact, part of the significance of the social differences in language habits can well be illustrated by a comparison with clothes. Fundamentally the clothes one wears fulfill the elementary practical functions of comfort by keeping one warm and of modesty by avoiding indecent exposure of one's person. These two practical purposes could just as well be accomplished by rather shapeless simple garments produced over a standard pattern for every one and worn upon all occasions. Such clothes could be made to fulfill their primary functions very efficiently with a minimum of cost. In such a situation, however, aside from the significance of differing degrees of cleanliness, the clothes would show us very little concerning the individuals who wore them. With our present habits of dress the clothes connote or suggest, in a broad general way, certain information concerning the wearers. Among other things they suggest the *circumstances in which we usually see them worn.* A dress suit suggests an evening party (or in some places a hotel waiter); overalls suggest a piece of dirty work or possibly a summer camp. In like manner language forms and constructions not only fulfill a primary function of communicating meaning; they also suggest the circumstances in which those particular forms and constructions are usually employed. If, then, one uses the pronunciations and grammatical forms given earlier in this paragraph, they may serve to communicate his meaning unmistakably, but they will also suggest that he habitually associates with those social groups for whom these language forms are the customary usage and not with those for whom they are not characteristic. We must, therefore, recognize the fact that there are separate social or class groups even in American communities and that these groups differ from one another in many social practices including their language habits.

As indicated earlier the four kinds of differences in language practice here outlined are by no means mutually exclusive. Many historical differences and some sectional differences have become also social differences. For our purpose here the social or class differences are of most concern; other types of differences will be treated only as they bear upon these social or class dialects.

III

In order to grasp the significance of these social differences in language practice for the obligation of the schools one must under stand clearly what is meant by "standard" English, and that can perhaps best be accomplished by tracing the course by which a particular kind of English became "standard." As one examines the material written in England during the twelfth and thirteenth centuries—a period from one hundred to two hundred years after the Norman Conquest—he finds a situation in which three things are of especial note:

1. Most of the legal documents, the instruments which controlled the carrying on of the political and the business affairs of the English people, were not written in the English language but in French or in Latin. This fact was also true of much of the literature and books of learning familiar to the upper classes.
2. Although some books, especially historical records and religious and moral stories and tracts, were written in English, there was no single type of the English language common to all English writings. The greatest number used what is called the Southern dialect. This particular kind of English had been centered in Winchester, which was the chief city of King Alfred and his successors until the time of the Norman Conquest.

3. There was, therefore, no "standard" English in twelfth and thirteenth century England, for no single type of the English language furnished the medium by which the major affairs of English people were carried on. Instead, English people used for these purposes French, Latin, and at least four distinct varieties of English. The particular kind of English spoken in southern England came nearest to fulfilling the function of a "standard" English because more writings and more significant writings were produced in this type of English than in any other.

In the fourteenth and early fifteenth centuries, however, this situation changed. London had become the political and in some respects the social head of English life in a much more unified England. Many of the major affairs of the realm had to be handled in London. More and more the English language, the English of London, was used in the legal documents of politics and business. Solely because of the fact that more of the important affairs of English life were conducted in this London English rather than in Winchester English, London English became "standard" English. Naturally, then, the growing use of this particular type of English for the important affairs of English life gathered such momentum that even writers to whom other types of English were more natural felt constrained to learn and to use the fashionable London English. Gower, for example, a Kentishman, did not write his native kind of English but practically the same forms, constructions, and spellings as Chaucer, a Londoner born. Naturally, too, this London English gained a social prestige because of the fact that its use connoted or suggested relations with the center of affairs in English life, whereas the inability to use London English suggested that one did not have such social contacts. "Standard" English, therefore, is, historically, a local dialect, which was used to carry on the major affairs of English life and which gained thereby a social prestige.[16]

Many changes occurred in this dialect of English and these changes especially affected the usage of the younger rather than of the older generations in the centers of fashionable social life. Thus the continued use of the older forms rather than the newer changes

[16] "Standard" French, "Standard" Italian, "Standard" Dutch, etc., have similar histories.

always suggested a lack of direct contacts with those who were active in the conduct of important matters. In this connotation lay the power of "standard" English to compel the ambitious to conform to its practices.

In America, however, we have had no one recognized center for our political, business, social, and intellectual affairs. More than that, the great distances between various parts of the United States made very difficult frequent actual social contacts in the earlier days. Our coast cities, Boston and New York, maintained direct relations with London long after the earlier settlers had moved west, but the middle western settlements had practically no relations with Boston and New York. This fact can probably explain the differences between our middle-western speech and that of nineteenth century Boston and New York. Because of the fact that New England so long dominated our intellectual life there has been a good deal of feeling in many parts of the United States that the language usages of New England connoted a connection with a higher culture than did the language of the Middle West. Hence the rather widespread attempt to imitate certain New England speech characteristics. On the whole, however, if we ignore the special differences that separate the speech of New England, the South, and the Middle West, we do have in the United States a set of language habits, broadly conceived, in which the major matters of the political, social, economic, educational, religious life of this country are carried on. To these language habits is attached a certain social prestige, for the use of them suggests that one has constant relations with those who are responsible for the important affairs of our communities. It is this set of language habits, derived originally from an older London English, but differentiated from it somewhat by its independent development in this country, which is the "standard" English of the United States. Enough has been said to enforce the point that it is "standard" not because it is any more correct or more beautiful or more capable than other varieties of English; it is "standard" solely because it is the particular type of English which is used in the conduct of the important affairs of our people. It is also the type of English used by the *socially acceptable* of most of our communities and insofar as that is true it has become a social or class dialect in the United States.

IV

With this analysis it is not difficult to understand the nature of the obligation assumed by our schools in respect to the teaching of the English language. Long have we in our national life adhered to the principle that no individual in his attempts to rise to the highest positions should be disqualified by artificial restraints. Our people have been devoted to education because education has furnished the most important tool of social advancement. Our public schools have therefore held to the ideal that every boy and girl should be so equipped that he shall not be handicapped in his struggle for social progress and recognition, and that he may rise to the highest positions. In the matter of the English language it is clear that any one who cannot use the language habits in which the major affairs of the country are conducted, the language habits of the socially acceptable of most of our communities, would have a serious handicap. The schools, therefore, have assumed the burden of training every boy and girl, no matter what his original social background and native speech, to use this "standard" English, this particular social or class dialect. To some pupils it is almost a foreign language; to others it is their accustomed speech. Many believe that the schools have thus assumed an impossible task. Certainly the widespread and almost unanimous condemnation of the results of their efforts convinces us that either the schools have not conceived their task adequately or they have chosen the wrong materials and methods to accomplish it. We shall find, I think, that seldom have school authorities understood the precise nature of the language task they have assumed and very frequently have directed their energies to teaching not "standard" English realistically described, but a "make-believe" correctness which contained some true forms of real "standard" English and many forms that had and have practically no currency outside the classroom.[17]

A few brief statements will serve both to summarize the preceding discussion and to bring into a single view the principles which underlie this investigation and report.

[17] See, for example, H. B. Allen's article "The Standard of Usage in Freshman Textbooks," in *English Journal* (college ed.), Vol. 24, 1935, pp. 564–571; and R. C. Pooley, *Grammar and Usage in Textbooks on English,* Bulletin 14, Bureau of Educational Research, University of Wisconsin, 1933.

1. All considerations of an *absolute* "correctness" in accord with the conventional rules of grammar or the dicta of handbooks must be set aside, because these rules or these dicta very frequently do not represent the actual practice of "standard" English but prescribe forms which have little currency outside the English classroom. We assume, therefore, that there can be no "correctness" apart from usage and that the *true* forms of "standard" English are those that are actually used in that particular dialect. Deviations from these usages are "incorrect" only when used in the dialect to which they do not belong. These deviations suggest not only the particular social dialect or set of language habits in which they usually occur, but also the general social and cultural characteristics most often accompanying the use of these forms.[18]

2. It is the assumed obligation of the schools to attempt to develop in each child the knowledge of and the ability to use the "standard" English of the United States—that set of language habits in which the most important affairs of our country are carried on, the dialect of the socially acceptable in most of our communities.

3. The first step in fulfilling that obligation is the making of an accurate and realistic survey and description of the actual language practices in the various social or class dialects. Only after we have such information in hand can we know what social connotations are likely to attach to particular usages.

[18] See note 14 on p. 24.

II

OTHER ATTEMPTS TO DETERMINE WHAT LANGUAGE MATTERS TO TEACH

In the course of the preceding chapter we have attempted to indicate the general principles which should determine the matters of English language to be taught in the schools. Before proceeding to give the details of the language program arrived at by an investigation controlled by these principles, we shall briefly describe the more important of the previous efforts to determine the materials of an effective English language teaching program in order to indicate the precise place which this study holds in the development of such efforts, and its essential difference.

Anxiety concerning the kind of English spoken and written by English people seems to have had its most vigorous early expressions in the eighteenth century as an outgrowth of the striving for "elegance," and especially attending the rise of the commercial middle classes into more prominence socially.[1] Several quotations from eighteenth century publications will reveal clearly enough the important aspects of the attitude of this time.

a. From Swift's letter to the Lord Treasurer in 1712.

"My lord, I do here, in the name of all the learned and polite persons of the nation complain to your lordship, as first minister, that our language is extremely imperfect; that its daily improvements are by no means in proportion to its daily corruptions; that the pretenders to polish and refine it, have chiefly multiplied abuses and absurdities: and that in many instances it offends against every part of grammar. . . . and these corruptions very few of the best authors in our age

[1] See H. C. Wyld, *History of Modern Colloquial English* (New York, E. P. Dutton and Co., 1920), p. 18.

C. C. Fries, "Rules of the Common School Grammars," *Publications of the Modern Language Association,* Vol. 42, March, 1927, pp. 232–236.

S. A. Leonard, *The Doctrine of Correctness in English Usage, 1700–1800,* University of Wisconsin Studies in Language and Literature, Vol. 25, 1929.

have wholly escaped. . . . Besides the grammar part, wherein we are allowed to be very defective, they will observe many gross improprieties, which, however authorized by practice, and grown familiar, ought to be discarded."

b. From the preface of Robert Lowth's *Grammar* in 1762, referring to Swift's letter.

"But let us consider how, and in what extent, we are to understand this charge brought against the English Language. . . . Does it mean that the English Language, as it is spoken by the politest part of the nation, and as it stands in the writings of our most approved authors, often offends against every part of grammar? Thus far, I am afraid, the charge is true. Or does it further imply, that our Language is in its nature irregular and capricious; not hitherto subject, nor easily reducible to a System of rules? In this respect, I am persuaded, the charge is wholly without foundation."

c. From the preface of Thomas Sheridan's *Dictionary* in 1780.

". . . Yet so little regard has been paid to it [the English language] . . . that out of our most numerous array of authors, very few can be selected who write with accuracy; . . . nay it has lately been proved by a learned prelate in an essay upon our grammar, that some of our most celebrated writers, and such as have hitherto passed for our English classics, have been guilty of great solecisms, inaccuracies, and even grammatical improprieties, in many places of their most finished works."

d. From William Ward's *Grammar* in 1765.

"This piece is excellent [referring to the work of Lowth] on account of the notes, in which are shown the grammatic Inaccuracies that have escaped the Pens of our most distinguished Writers . . . If your Scholars are Natives of England, . . . false English pointed out to them may be of the greatest use. For they are apt to follow Custom and example, even when it is faulty, till they are apprized of their Mistake. And therefore by shewing where Custom is erroneous, his Lordship has well deserved the Thanks of everyone who values the English Language and Literature . . . In short a very blameable Neglect of grammatic Propriety has prevailed amongst the English Writers, and at length we seem to be growing generally sensible of it; as likewise of the Use which may be made of a Knowledge of the English Grammar, towards assisting children to comprehend the general Import and Advantage of Rules concerning Language."

e. From Richard Johnson's *Grammatical Commentaries,* 1706.

"I cannot but think it would be of great Advantage, both for the Improvement of Reason in general . . . and also for the exact use of our own Language; which for want of Rule is subject to Uncertainty and the Occasion of frequent Contentions. And upon this account, it has been the Practice of several wise Nations, such of them, I mean, as have a thorough Education, to avoid that Confusion, that must needs follow from leaving it wholly to vulgar Use."

f. From James Buchanan's *Syntax* of 1767.

"Considering the many grammatical Improprieties to be found in our best Writers, such as Swift, Addison, Pope, etc., a Systematical English syntax is not beneath the Notice of the Learned themselves. Should it be urged, that in the Time of these Writers, English was but a very little subjected to Grammar, that they had scarcely a single Rule to direct them, a question readily occurs. Had they not the Rules of Latin Syntax to direct them?"

g. From J. Newberry's *Grammar Made Easy,* 1745.

"This [English Grammar] ought to be taught children as soon as they have a Capacity for it, which is generally very early: for 'tis a Shame we should be ignorant of our own Tongue: . . . For want of an early Acquaintance with *English* Grammar, there are many grown Persons, and those of good natural Abilities, who not only express themselves very improperly in common Discourse, but who cannot so much as write a Letter of a moderate Length to a Friend or Correspondent, without trespassing a hundred times either against the Rules of Orthography or Syntax."

The point of view revealed in these quotations from the eighteenth century may be briefly described in the two statements following:

a. The *English* used by most English people, even by the learned and the best authors, is deplorable because of its grammatical incorrectness and inaccuracy.

b. The only remedy for this deplorable use of English will be for English people, young and old, to set out to learn *correct* English by means of a study of grammar rules.

The first attempts, therefore, to determine what English language matters to teach in the schools grew out of this eighteenth century point of view and naturally resulted in the great stress that was laid upon the study of systematic or formal grammar. This emphasis upon formal grammar as the necessary material in an effective program of teaching good English lasted well through the nineteenth century.[2] Even today many schools continue the former practice and its advocates are by no means few.

Throughout more than half of the nineteenth century, however, the opponents of formal grammar insisted that there was no necessary connection between a knowledge of systematic grammar and a practical control of good English; but the study of grammar was not only deeply intrenched in the traditional prejudices of the public, it was also supported by the "mental discipline" theory of psychology as well as by the teachers of Latin and of the modern foreign languages.

Formal or systematic grammar continued to provide the most important material of the English language program until the coming of the measurement movement in education brought the first really effective challenge of the asserted connection between grammar and good English. The results of the tests administered seemed to demonstrate "the absence of any relation between knowledge of English grammar and the ability either to write or to interpret language." [3] Then too, repudiation of the older "faculty" psychology with its grosser conception of the "transfer of training" and the acceptance of a psychology of learning which emphasized the need

[2] In the United States especially, with its great middle class gaining control of affairs and striving for social acceptability, the speller and the school grammar became the most important instruments of the accepted marks of culture, so that in this country the study of systematic grammar received an additional emphasis. This fact probably accounts for the present attitude toward grammar in our schools, an attitude phrased by Professor J. H. G. Grattan, of the University of London, as follows:

"Now the attitude of the American schools is, so far as the English language is concerned, ultra-conservative. Eighteenth-century ideals of 'correctness' are not yet dead in the United States.

"Indeed, by American standards, many idiomatic usages long sanctioned in Great Britain are still 'bad grammar.' Such are the construction of the collective noun with plural verb, the use of *their* referring back to *every one*, the compound pronoun *these kind of*, the employment of *who* as object and of *me* as predicative. Without attempting to justify this rigid formalism, we can recognize in it a sign of the strength of tradition in the United States."—"On Anglo-American Cultivation of Standard English," *Review of English Studies*, October, 1927, p. 437.

[3] See especially the study by Franklin S. Hoyt in *Teachers College Record*, Vol. 7, November, 1906, pp. 467–500. Other such studies are indicated in R. L. Lyman's *Summary of Investigations Relating to Grammar, Language, and Composition*, Chicago, 1929.

of specific training for each specific ability in every activity helped to make necessary a new approach to the problem of teaching good English. The second attempts, therefore, to determine what English language matters to teach in the schools grew out of this emphasis put upon specific training and showed itself in the many efforts to discover the particular items of English forms and structure which should furnish the materials of drill in the various school grades. These attempts led to the demand for "functional" grammar as distinct from "formal" grammar. The following quotation provides a statement of this particular point of view:

"The reaction against English grammar arose from the knowledge that the formal work in the subject that was being done was of small practical value. A further influence resulted from investigations tending to show that grammar provides little mental discipline of a general character. The movement in favor of simplifying the school course and concentrating on essentials did the rest. . . . A sane attitude toward the teaching of grammar would seem to be to find out what parts and aspects of the subject have actual value to children in enabling them to improve their speaking, writing, and reading, to teach these parts according to modern scientific methods, and to ignore any and all portions of the conventional school grammar that fall outside these categories." [4]

Many methods were employed in the effort to determine just what aspects of the material taught as English language would adequately serve the needs of both children and adults. Language error counts became popular under the assumption that the details of a grammar curriculum should be selected "upon the basis of the errors of school children" and therefore, "that the first step is to ascertain the rules which are broken." [5] In most of these studies the investigation took for granted that frequency of occurrence meant importance for teaching. In a few there was some attempt to evaluate the items selected in relation to the frequency of their use in contemporary writing.[6] Others have depended on the opinions of

[4] *Reorganization of English in the Secondary Schools,* Department of Interior, Bureau of Education, Bulletin, Vol. 2, p. 37.

[5] Summaries of the studies of language errors appear in the *Sixteenth Yearbook* of the National Society for the Study of Education, Part I, pp. 85–110; R. L. Lyman, *Summary of Investigations Relating to Grammar, Language, and Composition,* pp. 71–133; Henry Harap, "The Most Common Grammatical Errors," *English Journal,* Vol. 19, June, 1930, pp. 440–446.

[6] See Stormzand and O'Shea, *How Much English Grammar?* Baltimore, 1924.

teachers, or on opinions of the general public, or on opinions of the members of the various professions; all gathered by questionnaire and statistically summarized.[7] All these efforts, however, assumed as the infallible measure of good English the conventional rules of the common school grammars. They have been concerned solely with *selecting* the particular items out of the mass of traditional material which has all along constituted the English language program, but they have emphasized mastery by drill upon these items rather than knowledge of rules as the end of teaching. In the higher grades they have been responsible for the appearance and widespread use of "handbooks" of usage. Most of the programs in English language in the more progressive schools of today are in accord with the point of view just outlined.

The attempts to challenge the traditional material and the conventional rules as valid measures of correctness, can be set off as the third group of efforts to determine what English language matters to teach. These attempts start from the knowledge that many of the rules inherited in our grammars are either the result of striving to apply to the English language formulas of Latin or those which were products of eighteenth century reasoning concerning what English people ought to say,[8] and they assume that usage is the sole criterion of correctness. They have grown out of the attempt to interpret, for practical teaching, the more scientific approach to language. On the whole, however, most of the stress here has been directed toward eliminating from the teaching program those matters which have not a validity based upon usage,[9] but very little attention has been given to the problem of a constructive program of English language teaching. Two important examples of this particular kind of effort are J. Leslie Hall's *English Usage* and

---

E. L. Thorndike and others, "An Inventory of English Constructions with Measures of Their Importance," *Teachers College Record*, Vol. 17, February, 1927, pp. 580-610.

[7] See Bibliography in Lyman, *op. cit.*, pp. 256–292.

[8] C. C. Fries, "Rules of the Common School Grammars," *Publications of the Modern Language Association*, Vol. 42, March, 1927.

S. A. Leonard, *Doctrine of Correctness in English Usage, 1700–1800*, University of Wisconsin Studies in Language and Literature, Vol. 25, 1929.

[9] "It should hardly need to be said that if we really intend getting down to fundamentals it is necessary first to stop teaching a great mass of valueless distinctions and untrue dicta about usage: the usual distinctions between *shall* and *will;* the arbitrary condemnation of *was* in all *if* and *as if* clauses, or *have got*, and of *get* for *receive, have, become, grow;* . . ."—"Report of the Committee on Economy of Time," *English Journal*, Vol. 8, March, 1919, p. 185.

S. A. Leonard's *Current English Usage*.[10] The former bases its challenge of the handbooks upon the actual usage of eminent and reputable authors in literary works that are above question.[11] The latter depends primarily upon a summary of the opinions expressed by some thirty of the recognized scholars in English language. These opinions were also compared with the opinions expressed by six other groups of judges.[12] The opinions asked for in S. A. Leonard's

[10] *Current English Usage,* a monograph published by the National Council of Teachers of English in 1932, is a development of an earlier study by Leonard and Moffett, reported in the *English Journal,* Vol. 16, May, 1927, pp. 345–359, under the title "Current Definition of Levels in English Usage."

Another presentation of similar material from these sources and from the *Oxford Dictionary* which has much the same purpose is R. C. Pooley's "Handbook of Current English Usage," *Colorado State Teachers College Bulletin,* Series 30, June, 1930, No. 3.

[11] "In the ensuing sections, the author will take up a number of locutions at issue in our language, most of them burning questions in the best grammars and rhetorics. Evidence *pro* and *con* will be given, the opinions of the best grammars, rhetorics, and dictionaries cited, and the reader left to draw his own conclusions. In many cases the word or phrase will be traced through the literature for centuries. . . . About two hundred authors, either 'reputable' or eminent, will be cited or quoted. Those who believe in the authority of a few supreme writers will find that these have been emphasized. Those who prefer to find their authority in a majority or a large number of reputable authors will no doubt be satisfied. . . . One prime object of this volume is to show the continuous use of certain words and phrases in the literature. If a locution can be so traced from early periods down to recent or present days, there is every reason to regard it as good English. On the other hand, a new word, or phrase, if found in enough standard writers, ought to be given a fair chance to spread through the language. . . . The tables, or lists, in the ensuing pages are, of course, not exhaustive: they simply show how often the various locutions have been found in over 75,000 pages of English and American literature. If a statement such as 'Found in 65 reputable authors 453 times' does not carry conviction to the reader, it might at least entitle the word to a fair chance and help to mitigate any attacks made upon it by purists and pedants. . . . The author of this volume relies mainly upon usage to establish a locution. . . . 'Custom is the most certain mistress of language.' "—J. Leslie Hall, *English Usage* (Chicago, Scott, Foresman and Co., 1917), pp. 23, 25, 26.

[12] "The conclusions arrived at in the following pages were derived from a study of the results of two ballots. The first contained 102 expressions . . . of whose standing there might be some question. This ballot was submitted to a number of groups of judges whose standing qualified them to indicate what seemed to them to be the norm of usage among educated people generally. . . . The first group of judges comprised a number of the foremost linguistic experts in the world—lexicographers, philologists, and grammarians. As trained observers of language ways, they were naturally qualified above all others to estimate the standing in actual cultivated use of the various items on the ballot. Therefore, in the following discussion of the separate items, their comments are given special prominence. . . . Where the other groups show any significant divergence from the judgment of the linguists, the fact is noted. The second group consisted of active members of the National Council of Teachers of English. A third group was composed of well-known authors; a

study were not the opinions of "what usage *should* be," but the judgments arising from an "observation of what *is* actual usage." Both studies should be helpful in eliminating from the teaching program the drill upon many language practices that have no validity outside the classroom. Unfortunately, however, the items that make up the traditional material of the drills and the formal tests most frequently given, are so firmly supported by the textbooks and practice pads, to say nothing of the inertia of much teaching routine, that these efforts to challenge the handbooks, rhetorics, and grammars have thus far had but little effect.

The various attempts to determine the material of an effective English language program for the schools can thus be roughly arranged in three groups. The first used the study of systematic or formal grammar, aimed at a knowledge of rules, and demanded much practice in classification, analysis, and parsing. The second used the rules of the conventional grammars as the criteria of good or correct English and set out to determine the common errors of language used by school children and adults. Adopting the psychology of specific training for each specific ability and assuming that frequency of error argued importance for teaching, they built up an English language program of teaching and tests made up of a large number of items for drill. The third group has tried to sift the items for drill and center attention in teaching upon driving out of the language of pupils, practices which are not *used* by "educated" people. They refuse to adopt the rules of the conventional grammars as the necessary standard of good English, and assume that only usage by the writers of literature or usage in the speech of those whose education is above question guarantees the satisfactory correctness of any item. They also assume the psychology of specific training, and their program consists therefore of a large number of items for drill and mastery.

The study here presented in this report, in its attempt to arrive at the details of a sound program for the teaching of the English

fourth, of the editors of influential publications; a fifth, of leading business men; a sixth, of members of the Modern Language Association; and a seventh, of teachers of speech. Returns were received from 229 judges altogether. They should constitute a significant sampling of cultivated usage. . . . Ballot II consisted of 130 additional expressions of the same nature as those in Ballot I."—S. A. Leonard, *Current English Usage* (Chicago, National Council of Teachers of English, 1932), pp. 95, 96, 97.

language, differs fundamentally from any of those described above, in three respects.

a. It assumes that the only method to attain really good English—effective language nicely adapted in both denotation and connotation to the circumstances of the occasion and the needs of both the speaker and the hearer—demands constant observation of the actual practice of the users of the language together with *a sensitiveness to the suggestions inevitably attached to words and constructions.* Any procedure, therefore, which makes one conscious of the "rules of grammar" or which centers attention solely on particular facts to be learned as such, rather than on actual observation of usage, serves to deaden this sensitiveness to one's speech environment and to turn the student away from the only path to real knowledge.

b. This study, therefore, does not attempt to set forth a closed handbook or authority of usage. It does not aim at a series of details judged to be "established" or "disputed" or "illiterate" which can be mastered by drill. It strives to present the material so organized as to provide the tools for further observation, classification, and interpretation; to show certain tendencies and patterns with the details that deviate from them; to provide a method and outline for *continual* filling in on the part of the reader and the student.[13]

c. It assumes that the most important facts concerning any words, forms, or constructions of language are the circumstances in which they are usually used, because these words, forms, or constructions will inevitably suggest these circumstances.[14] As indicated in the preceding chapter, there are language forms and constructions that are somewhat limited in their constant use to particular social groups. To use any such forms seriously, whether they be those customary to the "vulgar" or those customary only to precise "school mistresses," helps to give the impression that the common social contacts of the user are with that particular group. This study, therefore, has attempted to find the important matters of American English that thus have distinct social class connotations. Unlike any of the former studies it has not been limited to an examination of the so-called "disputed" constructions and phrases; it has been concerned with a first-

[13] See Chapter IV for an explanation of the method here indicated.

[14] "A part of a complex stimulus, recurring by itself or in some foreign context provokes a complete reaction previously made to the total situation of which this detail was a part. . . . The fundamental fact underlying all these associative processes is perhaps a tendency for brain patterns to be reinstated more or less completely when any of their parts are excited."—H. L. Hollingworth, *The Psychology of Thought* (New York, D. Appleton-Century Co., 1926), pp. 92, 94.

hand examination of the grammatical matters that appeared in a large number of carefully selected specimens of the language of several social groups. A description of these materials and the scope of the examination to which they were subjected will be the subject of the next two chapters.

III

THE MATERIALS HERE EXAMINED AND THE SCOPE OF THE INVESTIGATION

Through the efforts of the Modern Language Association of America [1] with the support of the Linguistic Society [2] there were made available for this investigation certain files of informal correspondence in the possession of the United States Government. Access to these materials has, indeed, been a great privilege, and the government officials have most courteously aided the work in every possible way. In order to avoid the possibility of any embarrassment, all names or other items of identification were removed from whatever material was copied as specimens for study and our own serial numbers substituted. Each quotation will therefore have attached to it the number of the letter in which it may be found. At the conclusion of our studies [3] copies of these letters will be deposited in the University of Michigan Library so that they will be

[1] "This is to certify that at the annual meeting of The Modern Language Association of America, held at Columbia University, New York City, December 31, 1924, the following resolution was adopted by unanimous vote:

'Resolved: that the Modern Language Association of America officially requests the Bureau of Education of the Department of the Interior, United States Government, to aid this association in a Survey of American English by using its influence to make available for this purpose correspondence materials now on file in the . . . Bureau.' . . .

Carleton Brown, Secretary."

[2] "I take pleasure in sending you this official transcript of a minute formally adopted by the Linguistic Society of America, on December 27, 1926, at Cambridge, Mass., on the recommendation of the Executive Committee:

'The Linguistic Society of America, recognizing the scientific value of a survey of the inflections and syntax of American English, hereby expresses its approval of the plans formulated by the Committees of the National Council of Teachers of English, for this purpose, and joins these organizations in urging the United States Government to make available for such a scientific study correspondence in its possession.'

Roland G. Kent, Secretary."

[3] We plan later to study these materials in respect to local or geographical differences.

available to any one who wishes either to verify the conclusions here offered or to make further studies in the same material.

The ideal material, of course, for any survey of the inflections and syntax of Present-day American English would be mechanical records of the spontaneous, unstudied speech of a large number of carefully chosen subjects. The practical difficulties in the way of securing a sufficient number of records of this kind from each of a large number of subjects, sufficient to make possible the kind of study necessary in charting the field, seem to make it prohibitive as a preliminary measure.[4]

The use of any kind of *written* material for the purpose of investigating the living language is always a compromise, but at present an unavoidable one and the problem becomes one of finding the best type of written specimens for the purpose in hand. The stenographic reports of evidence given in our courts are usually worthless for linguistic study, for almost invariably the stenographers, in transcribing their notes, not only use their own spelling but normalize the language forms as well. Business correspondence is much too limited in respect to its range of situation. Informal letters, if carefully handled, can, at least, provide the basis of a valuable tentative sketch to serve as a chart to guide methodical observation in the field. Certainly to check and to verify the conclusions of such a tentative sketch is a much more feasible undertaking than to make an original study without such a chart.

Any letters that are to be made the basis of an acceptable preliminary study of the social differences in our inflections and syntax must satisfy certain definite requirements. Some of these matters are quite obvious, but they are recorded here in order to list the considerations that guided the choosing of the materials collected for this study.

1. It must be certain that the language used in the particular letter or letters is really the language of the subject whose usage we are attempting to investigate. For that reason we included no typewritten letters; we took only those in the original handwriting of the persons selected as suitable subjects. At the time of examination we tried to make certain that there was always some item of evidence in con-

[4] It is hoped that the survey of local differences in the language of certain communities of rural New England, now being conducted by the Linguistic Atlas of New England with the aid of the American Council of Learned Societies, will find it possible to lead the way in the use of such mechanical records.

nection with the letter that would justify the conclusion that the language used was actually that of the writer.

2. It must be possible to procure sufficient and reliable information concerning the writer. In respect to the writers of the letters here gathered we had at hand the following information:

a. Place and date of birth of the writer
b. Place and date of birth of both father and mother
c. Present address of each
d. A record of the writer's schooling
e. A record of the occupations in which he had been engaged
f. In some cases (not in all, and chiefly in those classed in the "vulgar" or "popular" English group) a confidential report on the family [5]

3. There must be enough material from each subject to be a fair sample of his language; not, of course, of his vocabulary, but of the language forms and structures.

4. The correspondence must cover a wide range of topics. The material here used was largely made up of intimate descriptions of home conditions (family activities, family needs, domestic troubles, financial difficulties, sicknesses, ambitions, accidents) all offered as reasons for appeals of one kind or another. This material was limited, however, by the fact that all the letters were very serious in tone. Nowhere was there anything of a light or humorous feeling.

[5] Two specimens of such reports follow. The first is a report on 8062.

"This young man was born and raised in Callahan County, Texas, . . . virtually all his life he and his parents lived within a few miles of Baird, County Seat of Callahan County, where I live, and I have known his parents and this boy all their lives. He has a splendid father and grandfather. . . . The young man was raised on a farm, and has a good knowledge of cows, horses, etc., also all products that are generally raised on a farm. He applied himself well to his school and has made a success in that line and after the close of the schools he attended Normal school and became a school teacher in this county . . . this places him at about twenty or twenty-two years old. . . ."

The second is a report on 8072, a family living in southern Ohio. It consists of three pages, typewritten in single space.

"The . . . family consists of . . . . This family lives in a four-room house for which they pay $20 a month rent. The house is in poor condition. The neighborhood is composed of old and rather dilapidated houses. The . . . home was dirty and in disorder. The mother and the three younger children whom we saw, were all dirty and their clothing was ragged. . . ."

(Then follow first a paragraph on the sicknesses in this family during the last two years and some doctor's reports, and next, four paragraphs on the family income, giving the employment of each, their education and the possibilities for employment, and the bills outstanding.)

"The family's only income consists of about $20 per week, which is earned by the father and brother together. The father does paper hanging for . . . . Their work has been satisfactory, but according to . . . their employer, they work very slowly and therefore make very little money."

Altogether we have used for this particular study some two thousand complete letters, and excerpts from about one thousand more. They were all from native Americans for at least three generations.[6] These were arranged in social or class groups in accord with the information available concerning the writers of the letters. Because of the nature of the material used, there is in this study no evidence of what may be termed "literary" language. These were all personal letters written to accomplish an immediate purpose with presumably no thought that they might ever be read by any one other than the particular person to whom they were directed.[7] On the other hand, there is nothing from the distinctly "illiterate," for, of course, the language of those who cannot read and write must be studied by other means. There remain then three groups or social classes concerning whose language we sought information through these letters. In order to reduce to a minimum the subjective element in classifying our subjects into social or class groups, we have set up some definitely specific criteria and have tried to apply them rigidly. It is perhaps needless to insist that we classified the writers of the letters, not the letters themselves, and ***then*** studied the language of the specimens from each class.

At the lower level are those we classified in the group for "vulgar" [8] English, the nearly illiterate, hereafter called Group III. For inclusion in this group we depended upon three types of evidence. No one of these three types of evidence was regarded as sufficient to place a subject; he had to qualify under all three to be classified in Group III.

a. The record of the schooling. We included in Group III no one who had passed beyond the eighth grade in the schools. Most of our subjects in this group had not attained that level. This statement must not be taken to mean that all who had had only seven or eight years of schooling were included. This was simply a negative stand-

[6] In order that the materials could also be used for the study of geographical differences, only those subjects were chosen for whom the available information revealed the facts that the present address of the subject was also the locality in which he had been born and raised.

[7] We hope later to publish a study of the language of the locally written material in 3,500 newspapers covering two weeks' issues from some three hundred carefully selected localities.

[8] "Vulgar" as here applied to English must not be taken to mean "offensive to good taste"; it stands simply for a type of English that is as nearly "illiterate" as writing may become and still fulfill the function of communication.

ard; no one who had had more than this amount of schooling was included.

b. The general information concerning the family circumstances. Only those whose occupations were strictly manual and unskilled were included; clerical workers of every sort were ruled out, even those merely clerking in stores. Even strictly manual workers were excluded if their wages amounted to more than ninety dollars a month.

c. Certain definite, formal, non-linguistic matters in the letters themselves. These were matters of spelling, capitalization, and punctuation which clearly demonstrated that the writer was not accustomed to writing at all, that he was semi-illiterate. For this purpose mere accidental misspellings were not considered, but the habitual misspelling of eight or ten simple words was regarded as significant when joined with the evidence from capitalization (lower case letters for the pronoun *I* and the initial letters of the names of towns and persons), and with the evidence from punctuation (no sentence end punctuation of any kind in a letter of more than two hundred words). Such, for example, was the situation in a letter from 8005. The word *know* was spelled *"no"* all six times it was used; *"rote"* for *wrote,* three times; *"rong"* for *wrong,* twice; *"crect"* for *correct; "prade"* for *parade; "hu"* for *who; "anoff"* for *enough; "parence"* for *parents; "nervice"* for *nervous.*

Using these three types of evidence together we found specimens from more than three hundred subjects whom we classified in Group III.

At the upper end of the scale were those whom we have classified in the group for "standard" English, the socially acceptable, called hereafter Group I. For inclusion in this group the information available concerning the subject must show that he qualified in all three of the following points:

1. The record of his formal education must show that he is a graduate of one of our reputable colleges after having had at least three years of college life.

2. That his present position must be one of recognized standing in the community in which he lives. These positions were usually those which are regularly classed as *professions* and included college professors, physicians, lawyers, judges, clergymen, commissioned officers of the United States Army above the rank of lieutenant, and,

from cities of more than 25,000 inhabitants, the superintendents of schools and the editors of newspapers.

3. It is perhaps unnecessary to add that no subjects were put into Group I if the formal, non-linguistic matters in their letters did not conform completely to the usual conventions of written material. As in choosing the subjects for Group III, these non-linguistic matters included spelling, capitalization, and the uses of end punctuation.

No one was accepted as a subject for either Group I or Group III whose record did not meet all the requirements here laid down. The letters of border line cases were not included in the material to be examined. The purpose of such rigid *exclusion* from these two groups was to make sure that no serious objections could be raised against the results obtained for either Group I or Group III on the ground that the specimens came from some subjects that might just as well be classified in some other group.

Whether the reader will agree with the names applied to each of these groups does not matter. All will agree, at the very least, that we have here for examination specimens of the language of two very distinct social groups of subjects chosen by the rigid application of certain perfectly definite standards.

Between these two ends of the social scale lies a third class—the great mass of the people in most of our communities—whom we shall call Group II, the users of "common" English. The specimens chosen for examination here come from subjects who may be said to make up the *central core* of this class which includes the majority of our people. They are those whose record meets the following requirements:

1. They have had a formal education ranging from at least one year of high school to a single year in college or technical school.

2. They are substantial citizens of a community, with occupations that are neither professional on the one hand nor strictly manual and unskilled on the other. They include business men, electricians, foremen of large shops, superintendents of mills, heads of police departments, undertakers, Red Cross workers, nurses, and non-commissioned officers of the army of the grade of sergeant. Qualified representatives of other similar occupations would have been included in this group had there been specimens from such subjects in our material. Those listed include all that make up our Group II.

3. In the formal, non-linguistic matters, considered for other groups, the subjects accepted for Group II all conformed with the conventional practice in respect to ordinary capitalization and the end punctuation of sentences. In respect to spelling none were included who like those of Group III habitually misspelled any of the very common words, but occasional misspelling of the common "problem" words or of unusual words did not exclude a subject from this group as it did from Group I.

We have then a fairly large number of specimens of the language used in intimate personal letters by each of these three classes of American people. The language used by Group I we have called "standard" English; that used by Group II, "popular" or "common" English; and that used by Group III, "vulgar" English.[9] There is no doubt that there is a large body of the language which we call English which is common to all three groups. More than that, Group I and Group II have language habits in common which do not occur in Group III, and Groups III and II have common characteristics that do not occur in Group I. Finally there are some language practices which occur predominantly in Group I and others which occur predominantly in Group III. It is these distinctive forms which carry the connotations of social contacts with the particular group in which they are used. It is because these distinctive forms thus suggest the social circumstances in which they usually occur that the use of language forms characteristic of Group III or of those common only to Group II and Group III becomes a handicap to the socially ambitious. This study therefore started with the careful classification of subjects into the groups indicated above in order to attempt to discover what language forms and constructions were really thus distinctive and characteristic of each of these three classes of our people. The study is obviously limited by the fact that the letters examined do not by any means cover all the situations of our complex life. The material deals only with the

[9] The reader must be warned against supposing that all people can be classified in one of the three groups here named or even in the five groups made with addition of "literary" and "illiterate" classes. Many subjects investigated in connection with this study could not be put into any of the groups here indicated; they seemed to stand between them. We took no specimens from such subjects. Here we have attempted to analyze only the specimens taken from those subjects that could be isolated in accord with the definite standards set up, assuming that these standards would serve to select those who could be convincingly classed as the *core* of each group.

serious aspects of family life and its relationships. More than that, even three thousand letters can yield only incomplete returns concerning the actual usage of the great mass of native Americans. This study, therefore, cannot pretend to any completeness or finality; it offers a tentative sketch and chart to guide observation, an outline to be filled and corrected as new evidence is examined. It has the merit, however, of resting upon a recording of actual usage rather than upon opinion, and of using a procedure as objective as possible in sorting the subjects into social groups. There are nearly the same number of subjects representing each group and these come from nearly every state in the United States. The method of dealing with the language matters in these letters will be set forth in the next chapter.

IV

THE METHOD OF EXAMINATION, A CLASSIFICATION OF THE GRAMMATICAL PHENOMENA

In the attempt to gather, analyze, and record the significant facts from any such mass of material as the specimens here examined, one cannot depend upon general impressions and note only the special forms that attract attention. If he does, the unusual forms and constructions or those that differ from his own practice will inevitably impress him as bulking much larger in the total than they really are. Those forms and constructions that are in harmony with the great mass of English usage will escape his notice. This seems to me to be a fundamental difficulty with the earlier editions of Mencken's *The American Language* and accounts in part for the difference between his representations of "The Common Speech" and the results given here. Mencken, for example, prints in the 1924 edition of his book the "Declaration of Independence in American," as one of his "Specimens of the American Vulgate" or, as he says, "translated into the language they use every day." [1]

"When things get so balled up that the people of a country have to cut loose from some other country, and go it on their own hook, without asking no permission from nobody, excepting maybe God Almighty, then they ought to let everybody know why they done it, so that everybody can see they are on the level, and not trying to put nothing over on nobody.

"All we got to say on this proposition is this: first, you and me is as

[1] H. L. Mencken, *The American Language* (New York, Alfred A. Knopf, 3rd ed., 1924), p. 398. See, however, the following quotation from the 4th edition, 1936, Preface, p. vii: "I have also omitted a few illustrative oddities appearing in that edition [the 3rd edition]—for example, specimens of vulgar American by Ring W. Lardner and John V. A. Weaver and my own translations of the Declaration of Independence and Lincoln's Gettysburg Address. The latter two, I am sorry to say, were mistaken by a number of outraged English critics for examples of Standard American, or of what I proposed that Standard American should be. Omitting them will get rid of that misapprehension. . . ."

good as anybody else, and maybe a damn sight better; second, nobody ain't got no right to take away none of our rights; every man has got a right to live, to come and go as he pleases, and to have a good time however he likes, so long as he don't interfere with nobody else. That any government that don't give a man these rights ain't worth a damn; also, people ought to choose the kind of government they want themselves, and nobody else ought to have no say in the matter."

In the 176 words here quoted there are, for example, five uses of the multiple negative. Every negative statement except one has two or three negative particles. This excessive use of the multiple negative construction cannot be found in any actual specimens of Vulgar English. Even in Old English, where the use of the double negative was normal, less than 35 per cent of the total negative statements occur with multiple negative particles. Such a complete use of the multiple negative construction as Mencken displays will only be heard from those who consciously attempt to caricature Vulgar English. Most of the comic writers produce their language effects in similar fashion by seizing upon a few such especially noticeable or spectacular forms and expressions of Vulgar English and then working them excessively. Such representations of Vulgar English become grossly inaccurate both because the amount of deviation from the standard forms is greatly exaggerated and also because many of the forms characteristic of Vulgar English that are not sufficiently picturesque to be funny are completely ignored.[2]

In order to avoid errors of this kind we have in the study of this material tried first to record *all* the facts in each category examined. For example, every preterit and past participle form was copied on a separate slip of paper in order that we might determine not only

[2] See also Professor Robert J. Menner's comments in his article "The Verbs of the Vulgate," *American Speech*, January, 1926, pp. 230–231. Concerning *The American Language* he says, "but Mencken seems to have gathered his forms from all kinds of sources, oral and written; it is impossible to distinguish those he has observed personally from those he has found in contemporary writers of comic stories. Furthermore, he gives the impression of preferring to record as characteristic of the common speech whatever is furthest removed from the language of literature. . . ."

Part of Professor Menner's remarks concerning the accuracy of the writers of comic stories follows: "Ring Lardner . . . employs only forms of the verb which are familiar, or at least conceivable, in colloquial speech. But he besprinkles the conversation of his characters with barbarisms much more plentifully and consistently than they occur in actual life. This is the inevitable exaggeration of comic art. 'He win 10 bucks,' is funnier than 'He won 10 bucks,' and Mr. Lardner now uses the preterite *win* almost consistently, though, according to my observation of oral practice, it is used, even in class D, only once out of ten times."

the kind of variety that existed in actual usage but also something of the relative amounts of that variation. In similar fashion all instances with forms expressing number in verbs and in demonstratives used attributively as well as in substantives were gathered to form the basis of the summaries we offer concerning concord in number. We do not assume that the absolute frequency of occurrence of particular forms in the limited material here examined is in itself significant; we have simply tried to make sure of the *relative* frequency of the language usages appearing here in order to give proportion to our picture of actual practice and to prevent a false emphasis upon unusual or picturesquely interesting items.

This approach to the gathering and analysis of the language facts to be observed in our material made necessary some system of classification by which those facts of essentially similar nature should be inevitably brought together. We were seeking to record as completely as possible the methods used by the English language to express grammatical ideas and to discover the precise differences in these methods as employed by the various social dialects. The outlines of our grouping quite naturally settled themselves. The facts gathered in an early preliminary study of our material all fitted into a classification made up of three general types of devices to express grammatical ideas.

First of all there were the *forms* of words. The way in which the word *tables* differs from the word *table* indicates one grammatical idea; the way in which *roasted* differs from *roast,* or *grew* from *grow* expresses another; and the way in which *harder* differs from *hard* shows another. These examples illustrate the expression of grammatical ideas by the *forms* of words. Other ideas, however, are also shown by word forms as *truth* differing from *true,* or *kindness* from *kind,* or *rapidly* from *rapid,* or *stigmatize* from *stigma,* or *national* from *nation,* or *writer* from *write*. These latter derivational forms will not be included here although it is difficult to draw an exact line between them and the grammatical forms with which we are especially concerned. It is enough for our purpose to point out that most of these derivational forms are, in Present-day English, chiefly vocabulary or word-formation matters rather than inflectional matters and that we have limited our study to grammatical structure and have excluded vocabulary. But these "forms of words" as we shall use them are interpreted broadly to include even entirely different words as *we* or *me* or *us* in relation to *I*, *went* in relation to *go*, and *worse* in relation to *bad*.[3]

Second, there were the uses of *function* words. These words frequently have very little meaning apart from the grammatical relationship they express. Examples are *of* in "A house *of* stone," or *with* in "He struck the animal *with* a rod," or *more* in "A *more* important battle," or *have* in "They *have* had their reward," or *going* in "He is *going* to go to New York." Many of the grammatical ideas formerly expressed by the *forms* of words are now expressed by such function words.

Third, there were the uses of *word order*. Word order is often an important item of the idiom of a language, but it is not always a grammatical device as it is in English. In Latin, for example, the periodic structure with the verb at the end occurs very frequently, but the word order in such a sentence as "Nero hominem interfecit" has nothing whatever to do with indicating the so-called "subject" and "object." The basic meaning of the Latin sentence remains unchanged with every possible order of these three words. In English, however, "Nero killed the man" and "The man killed Nero" express very different ideas and that difference comes to us solely through the order in which the words are placed. Some of the grammatical ideas formerly expressed in English by the forms of words are now expressed by *word order*.

All the language facts gathered from the letters here examined were classified in one of these three groups—the uses of the forms of words, the uses of function words, or the uses of word order—

[3] For a thorough analysis of the problem involved here see Leonard Bloomfield, *Language* (New York, Henry Holt and Co., 1933), pp. 207–246. On pages 222 and 223 occur the following statements: ". . . The structure of a complex word reveals first, as to the more immediate constituents, an outer layer of *inflectional* constructions, and then an inner layer of constructions of *word-formation*. In our last example [the word *actresses*], the outer, inflectional layer is represented by the construction of actress with [-ez], and the inner word formational layer by the remaining constructions, of *actor* with *-ess* and of *act* with [-r]. . . . Another peculiarity of inflection, in contrast with word-formation, is the rigid parallelism of underlying and resultant forms. Thus, nearly all English singular nouns underlie a derived plural noun, and, vice versa, nearly all English plural nouns are derived from a singular noun. Accordingly, English nouns occur, for the most part in parallel *sets of two;* a singular noun (*hat*) and a plural noun derived from the former (*hats*). Each such set of forms is called a *paradigmatic* set or *paradigm*, and each form in the set is called an *inflected form* or *inflection*. . . . It is this parallelism also, which leads us to view entirely different phonetic forms, like *go: went*, as morphologically related (by suppletion): *go* as an infinitive (parallel, say, with *show*) and *went* as a past-tense form (parallel, then, with *showed*)."

and there studied. In respect to each group the description will first set forth the practice of Group I or "standard" English and then indicate the deviations from that practice, characteristic of Group III, or of Group II and Group III combined. Some of the significance of these language facts will, however, be best revealed by showing them in relation to similar situations as they appeared in older stages of the English language, for even complete statistics of the relative frequency of two alternative forms in any single period of language history can never give us a guide as to the relative importance of those forms or the direction of change. For such purposes the statistics must be viewed in relation to the situation in a previous or in a later period. For example, if we were living at the close of the first quarter of the fifteenth century, the bare fact that the alternative pronoun forms *them* and *hem* were used with a relative frequency of approximately 20 per cent of *them* to 80 per cent of *hem* would tell us little without the knowledge that *hem* was the form that was being superseded and that the tendency to use *them* in its place had already progressed one fifth of the way along which the forms *they* and *their* had already gone much farther. In the effort therefore to make clear the significance of the records of contemporary English which formed the basis of this study it will frequently be necessary to picture the present usage against the background of the practice in older stages of the language. We shall try always to deal with the patterns of the language to which particular forms belong and to show the path along which these patterns have developed.

It will be clearly evident as we proceed that the three general types of grammatical processes in accord with which our language material has been classified are not now and have not been in the history of the English language thoroughly coördinate or of equal value. As a matter of fact any one of the three could have served quite adequately all necessary grammatical needs. Instead, they overlap in the expression of grammatical ideas and in some respects may be said to compete for the expression of the same ideas. The function-word method and the word-order method of expressing dative and accusative relationships have, for example, almost entirely displaced the inflectional method. In the early stages of the language there is no doubt that the use of the forms of words as a grammatical process was much more important than the grammatical uses of either word order or of function words. Some of the problems of usage in Present-day English arise where there is such a so-called conflict between two types of grammatical processes for the expression of a single grammatical idea. While, therefore, we shall classify and describe our language details in accord with the demands of each of the three types of grammatical processes indicated above, it will be necessary to discuss them in relation to the historical patterns with which they are connected and sometimes to refer to the use of a competing type of grammatical process for the expression of the same idea. The next two chapters will deal with the language facts that belong to the first of these three grammatical devices, the uses of the forms of words.

V

THE USES OF THE FORMS OF WORDS: TWO MAJOR OR LIVE INFLECTIONS

We are concerned here with describing the grammatical uses of the forms of words, or inflections, found in our letters. As indicated above, our method has been to record all the forms that appeared and then to group them in accord with the grammatical ideas expressed. The study of each group has centered upon (1) the pattern most commonly used to express a particular idea, (2) the exceptions to the pattern or the less usual forms indicating the same grammatical idea, (3) the significance of both the usual pattern and the less frequent forms in relation to the older forms in English and the direction of change in the language, (4) the common and the divergent practices of the social classes from which the letters were gathered.

As one surveys our recorded instances of the uses of inflections in comparison with the instances of the uses of the other processes to indicate the same grammatical ideas, he cannot help being impressed with the fact that only two of these uses of inflections stand out as alive and vigorous today and that all the others have been more or less replaced by the devices of function word and word order. The two uses of the forms of words that show no signs of losing their importance for Present-day English are those to distinguish the plural number from the singular and those to distinguish the preterit tense from the present.

I. THE FORMS FOR NUMBER

Although, on the whole, the forms for number may be said to have retained a vigorous life in English, yet the number inflections of modern English differ in many ways from those that existed in the older stages of the language. Most important of these differences is the fact that in Present-day English the number forms are *almost entirely confined to substantives.* Formerly the definite article, all the adjectives, and, of verbs, all persons of the present and preterit tenses in both the indicative and subjunctive moods had forms for number. These forms have now almost entirely disappeared. The few that remain will be discussed a little later in relation to the matter of number concord.

Of almost equal importance is the fact that the number forms of substantives—at least of nouns—are *more distinctive* in Present-day English than they were in the older stages of the language. They are *more distinctive,* first, because the forms now used are clearly number signs and in general do not have to do duty as case symbols as well. In Old English, for example, the form *menn* was both the dative singular and the nominative-accusative plural. The *-an* ending of the weak declension, as in *oxan* (MnE *oxen*), served not only for the plural number but also for the genitive, dative, and accusative singular. Many neuter nouns had the same form for both the nominative singular and the nominative plural. In Present-day English, on the other hand, the plural inflection is used for number only, except for the identical sound of the few inflected genitives still used. The number forms of substantives in Present-day English are more distinctive, also, because the forms now used have become a clear pattern. In Old English each kind of noun had a different ending for the plural number. Masculine *a*-stems used the ending *-as;* feminine *o*-stems ended in *-e* or *-a;* neuter *a*-stems had no ending or *-u;* weak nouns used *-an.* In Present-day English, however, all our nouns except a very few form their plurals by use of the so-called *-s* ending. Ever since the thirteenth century this particular type of plural ending, which in Old English belonged only to the masculine *a*-stems, has become more and more the pattern upon which the plural inflections of the other groups of substantives were modelled. As a result, not only have native English words which earlier had other plural endings or none at all taken on the *-s* ending but borrowed foreign words have usually adjusted their plural forms to this *-s* ending even to the extent of adding the *s* to forms already plural.[1]

[1] The following are examples of native English which have adopted the regular plural *s* ending:

OE Plural	*has become*	*MnE Plural*
word	"	words
hors	"	horses

(*Continued on next page*)

In substantives, therefore, (nouns and such pronouns as *one* and *other*) the one important use of word forms to express any grammatical ideas is this use of an *-s* ending to indicate plural number.

A

In the letters examined for this study the actual situation in respect to the number inflections of substantives may be summarized in the following statements:

1. In all three social groups the so-called *-s* ending is the regular pattern of the plural inflection for nouns. Out of a total of more than three thousand plural nouns only 153 (5 per cent) appeared with any other form.

2. The variations from this pattern which appeared regularly in the usage of Group I (Standard English) are the following:

a. Some remnants of older English patterns still persisting in very common and much used words.

men, feet, teeth—old umlauted plurals
children—now with the plural ending of the old weak declension.
sheep—old neuter without inflectional ending in the plural.
year, foot, acre, in such expressions as "my three *year* old daughter" (9054), "a 420 *acre* farm" (8298), a "five *foot* pole" (7421)—nouns for periods of time or measures of distance after numerals.[2]

OE Plural	*has become*	*MnE Plural*
hus	"	houses
gear (*sometimes* gearas)	"	years
cwene	"	queens
glofa, glofe	"	gloves
monaþ	"	months
bec	"	books
tungan	"	tongues
eagan	"	eyes
naman	"	names

The following borrowed words are typical of the great mass of foreign words for which we use the regular *-s* ending plural rather than the form the foreign language would use: *circus, crocus, chorus, premium, medium, gymnasium, serum, vacuum, atlas, specimen, item, folio, opera, idea, plus, minus, bonus.*

[2] These words were the only ones appearing in such a form in our materials for Group I. In all other cases the plural form was used. We have, for example, "a five *year* old child" but "a six *months* old baby." Other instances from Group I which should be compared with the examples of the practice of Group III (see statement No. 3 in the text) are the following:

"a four *year* high school" (9065)
"a three *year* course" (9064)

million, in "over three *million* members" (9036)—the larger numerals without *-s*.

b. Some foreign words still maintaining the inflectional forms of the language from which they come.

data,[3] *alumni, phenomena*

3. The variations from the usual pattern in which the usage of Group III (Vulgar English) differed from the practice of Group I (Standard English) are the following (in some cases these forms appear also in the practice of Group II, Common English):

a. The *s*-less form of nouns for periods of time or measures of distance after numerals appears in a wider range of constructions in Group III than in Group I. The following examples are typical of uses that do not appear in the Standard English of Group I.

"he has been in . . . 18 *month*" (8168)
"my husband left me 3 *month* ago" (8012)
"he only served about 3 *month*" (8401)
"havnt herd from him for two *month*" (8118)
"he is only 16 *year* of age" (8040)
"a 8 *month* old baby" (8211)
"from 5 to 10 *gallon* of water" (8455)
"about five *foot* away" (8402)
"five *foot* eight inches tall" (8460)

---

but

"had ten *years* service" (6418)
"several *years* experience" (8403)
"a six *months* course" (9024)
"four *months* leave" (9024)
"the three *months* school" (9027)
"a three *weeks* training" (6514)
"a ten *days* leave" (9065)
"He received a five *days* pass" (7415)

but

"an eight *day* furlough"

Even after the numeral *one* an *-s* is used, sometimes with and sometimes without an apostrophe.

"a one *day's* leave" (9007)
"each *days* delay" (6500)
"the *month's* time that I have lost" (9027)

It seems evident that, in most cases, the nouns in this construction with numerals have come to be felt as plurals, hence the *s*-forms without apostrophe. The uninflected forms have tended to disappear from Standard English. The *s*-forms with apostrophe, especially in such context that the noun of "extent" is clearly singular, continue as genitives of measure. (See below, Ch. VI, p. 76, and Ch. X, pp. 274–275, for the use of noun adjuncts.)

[3] The word *data* is sometimes regarded as a singular form, as in "This *data* has been gathered by the Red Cross office."

Even in Group III, however, this wider and older use of the *s*-less form after a numeral is not very frequent, for it appeared in only 11 per cent of the situations in which it was possible. In Group II it is even more rare; only two instances were found.

b. The Vulgar English of Group III differs sharply from the Standard English of Group I in respect to the form of the word *regard* in the expression *in regard(s) to*. The letters from Group I used only *in regard to*. Those from Group III used *in regards to* much more frequently than *in regard to*, the exact proportion being 69.5 per cent of *regards* to 30.5 per cent of *regard*.[4] Those from Group II also used both *in regard to* and *in regards to* but the form *regard* predominated slightly; the exact proportion was seven of *in regard to* to six of *in regards to*.[5] There may be some connection between this *regards* and the verbal form *regards* in "as regards his ——" which appeared once in the materials of both Group I and Group II but not in those of Group III.

c. Group III differs from Group I in its treatment of the form *lot* meaning "many, a large number." Group I uses only *a lot* as in "thirty letters and *a lot* more" (6514). Group III has *a lots* as in "save *a lots* of lives and money" (8063), or *a lot* without the *of* as in "and *a lot* other things." (8186). Several instances occur without the *a* as "there has been *lots* of sentence cut" (8039) and "you have *lots* of mothers asking for . . ." (8187).

d. Group III seems to be alone in furnishing examples of a distinct form for the plural of the pronoun of the second person except for the very few instances of *you all* and *you folks* in letters of Group I from the southern United States. In Group III appear *youse* as in "I am writing *youse* this letter" (8243), *you people* (8074, 8133), *you folks* (8038), *you men* (8038), and many cases of *you all* (8244, 8045, 8244, 8097). Whether the *youse* in (8243) is indeed a plural in this letter addressed to one man or the *you all* in (8045) "I writ sevel days ago to *you all*," or in (8097) "I want *you all* to send him back to me," in each case also addressed to one man, is perhaps impossible to decide.

e. The plural written form with the apostrophe before the *s* in words other than letters and numbers (A's, B's, 1's, 2's) appears only in Group III. Examples are "4 month's" (8147), "5 younger brother's" (8143), "what the Doctor's testified" (8153), "4 little one's" (8154), "no paper's" (8190), "for the employee's only" (8274), "in regard's

[4] Examples of *in regards to* are found in the following specimens: 8084, 8120, 8135, 8136, 8153, 8168, 8270, 8259, 8255, 8249, 8238, 8230, 8229, 8035.

[5] Examples of *in regards to* are found in the following specimens from Group II: 8256, 8221, 8105, 8068, 8007.

to" (8259, 8255, 8249, 8238, 8230, 8229). In Group II there is this one possible instance of the same practice, "the Dr's say there is no cure" (8131). This method of writing or printing plural forms was considerably used in the late sixteenth and early seventeenth centuries.

From the evidence here presented, concerning the number inflections of substantives, four matters of language usage and one of writing form seem to be distinctly Vulgar English:

a. s-less forms of nouns for periods of time or measures of distance after numerals, other than *year* in such expressions as "a four *year* old child," *foot* in "a twelve *foot* pole," *acre* in "a 420 *acre* farm," and *mile* in "a 200 *mile* trip." Typical of Vulgar English are "3 month ago"; "16 year of age"; "2 mile down the road"; "ten gallon of water."

b. in regards to

c. a lots of

d. youse, or with less distinct vulgar connotations *you folks.*

e. the writing of plurals other than those of letters, numbers, or other symbols, with an apostrophe before the *s* as in *4 month's.*

B

In English the number inflections of words other than substantives have been gradually disappearing ever since the beginning of the twelfth century. As a result, concord or agreement of number has been reduced to very low terms in the present-day language, for this concord depends solely upon the presence of grammatical forms for number in such secondary words as the article, adjectives, and verbs. An inspection of the following examples will make this statement clear:

Modern English	1. The good man wrote.	2. The good men wrote.
Old English	1*a*. Se goda mann wrat.	2*a*. Þa godan menn writon.

These two sentences differ only in *number.* In the first there is but *one* man who did the writing; in the second *several* men wrote. These facts are indicated by the difference between the forms of the substantive; in (1) the word *man* is singular, in (2) *men* is plural; in (1*a*) *mann* is singular, in (2*a*) *menn* is plural. But in the Old English sentences (1*a*) and (2*a*) the forms of the other words in the two sentences also differ. The definite article in the first sentence is *se,* singular, in the second it is *þa,* plural. The adjective in the first is *goda,* singular; in the second it is *godan,* plural. These distinctions, however, in the number forms of the article, adjective, and verb have no significance for the *meanings* of the words to which they are attached. The plural form of the adjective does not mean that the man was *good* in several respects, nor does the plural form of the verb mean that the man *wrote* several times. These forms simply *repeat* the grammatical idea of number already expressed by the form of the noun. In the first sentence they each express the grammatical idea that but one man was doing the writing; in the second they each support the idea that several men wrote. In other words, concord or agreement in number means simply that by means of distinct forms in such secondary words as articles, adjectives, or verbs there is a *repeating* of the number idea already expressed by the form of the substantive. It must be clearly evident then that there can be no such repetition of the grammatical idea unless the secondary word has a distinction of form for number. In the Modern English equivalents of the Old English sentence given above there is no *agreement* or *concord* of number, for the forms of the article, of the adjective, and of the preterit verb do not differ in the two sentences. Without such distinct forms for number in secondary words there can be no concord or agreement.

In Modern English, therefore, the definite article *the* does not agree with the substantive to which it is attached. It has lost completely the means it had in Old English to differentiate the form of the article to be used with a singular noun from that to be used with a plural noun. In Modern English the adjective also has lost its distinctive forms for singular and plural and the word *good* remains unchanged whether attached to the singular *man* or to the plural *men*. It is true that the demonstrative pronouns *this* and *that* are also used attributively and are thus sometimes called adjectives. These two words, probably because of their use as substantives, have maintained separate forms for singular and plural in this attributive use and do, therefore, show concord or agreement with the substantives to which they are attached. These are the only cases, however, of words which may be classed with the adjectives and which in Present-day English have the forms to maintain any number concord.[6]

[6] One should call attention here to the fact that the word *other*, which took on an *-s* plural in the sixteenth century, does not use this plural form when it is used attributively. As a substantive it is *the other*, singular, and *the others*, plural. As an attributive (or adjective) it is *the other man* and *the other men*.

The verb also has gradually lost the many number distinct forms it had in Old English. In early Middle English the general levelling of the unstressed vowels made the present indicative plural form like that of the third person singular. The plural *ridað* became *rideð,* which was also the third person singular form. The loss of *n* made the plural of the preterit indicative of weak verbs identical with the first and third person singular forms. This loss of *n* also reduced to a common form the singular and plural of both the present subjunctive and the preterit subjunctive. Later the analogical reduction to a single stem of the separate forms for singular and plural in the preterit indicative of strong verbs removed another of the possibilities of concord in verbs. Today, therefore, except for the verb *to be,* we have in verbs but the one form which can indicate any trace of inflection for number. This form is the so-called *s*-ending which has, since the sixteenth century, been attached to the third person singular of the present indicative. This is the only form, aside from those of the verb *to be,* that can lend any support to a subject-verb concord of number. It is the only number distinctive form left out of the thirteen that existed in the Old English verbal inflection. In the verb *to be,* out of the fourteen such forms in Old English, there are five remaining in Present-day English: *am, is, are,* for the present indicative and *was, were,* for the preterit indicative.

The personal pronouns of the third person are often used to refer to substantives already mentioned and, inasmuch as they still retain their number distinctive forms without loss, they can and do repeat whatever number idea attached to their antecedents.

As we have said above, the English language has shown a marked tendency to eliminate all number distinctive forms in secondary words but to continue them in substantives. Concord or agreement in number has, therefore, nearly passed out of the language. The

One other matter of adjective form should receive comment here. Many insist that the comparative degree form, not the superlative, should be used when only two things are considered and that the superlative implies more than two. They prefer "of the two cars the Ford got the *worse* of it." This use of the comparative form for two and the superlative form for more than two seems to me to be the last remnant of the old distinction between a dual and a plural number which was set off by many clear forms in the older stages of Indo-European languages. Examples are abundant in classical Greek and in Gothic. In Old English, however, most of this dual inflection and concord had already disappeared. Standard Present-day English sometimes uses the comparative degree in this way, but the superlative form is more frequent by far. See below pages 99, 100, especially footnote 45.

only possibilities for a number concord in Present-day English are (1) in the use of *this, that, these,* and *those* as attributives; (2) in the use of *am, is, are, was, were* of the verb *to be,* and of the present indicative third singular *-s* of other verbs; and (3) in the use of the pronouns of the third person when they refer to substantives already mentioned.

The question of concord or agreement in Present-day English, therefore, is limited to that of the use of these particular forms. In the great majority of instances there is no chance for *concord* or *agreement,* for the secondary words—the adjectives and the verbs used—have no special form to distinguish the singular form from the plural.[7]

More than that, there are many situations in Present-day English when even the very few number forms that still survive in verbs are not used in accord with the demands of a formal concord of number. A collective noun like *family,* for example, may be followed by a plural verb as in "The *family were* all present" whenever the meaning stresses the individuals that make up the group. The difficulties or problems of concord or agreement in number have arisen primarily in situations in which there is a conflict in the substantive between the form and the number idea implied in that meaning. In most instances, there is no such conflict, for the form of the substantive coincides with the meaning; *book* is singular and *books* is plural both in form and in meaning. The words *family, nation, government, audience, committee, class, crowd, multitude, herd, dozen, enemy, people, troop, folk, crew, party,* however, are singular in form, with *families, nations, governments, audiences, committees, classes, crowds, multitudes, herds, dozens, enemies, peoples, troops, folks, crews, parties,* as plurals.

But the singular forms of all of these and similar words may be used when the attention clearly centers upon the plural idea of the several individuals included in the kind of group named. In such cases modern grammars, rhetorics, and dictionaries all agree that

[7] It seems a mistake to insist upon the generalizations usually made that

1. "Adjectives agree in number with the substantives they modify" when the only forms to support such an agreement are *this, these, that, those;*

and that

2. "Verbs agree with their subjects in number" when the only forms to support that statement are the *-s* of the third person singular present of all verbs except those of the verb *to be.* Approximately one fifth of the verbs in the materials examined here had number distinct forms. See page 103.

verbs plural in form are used.[8] It will be worth while to examine the history of this practice in English in order, if possible, to make clear the direction in which usage has been moving and to describe what might be called the pattern of that use.[9]

Even in Old English, collective nouns singular in form sometimes appeared with a plural verb or were referred to by a pronoun of plural form. In these Old English instances, however, the plural form practically never *immediately* followed or *immediately* preceded the collective noun of singular number. Several words (very rarely only one) intervened between the collective and the plural verb or pronoun.

"þæt Iudeisce folc gewat fram Gode forsewen þurh heora upahefednysse" *Aelfric.*
"þæt folc sæt . . . and arison" *Exodus* XXXII:6.
"þin ofspring sceal agan heora feonda gata" *Genesis* XXII:17.
"Se here swor þæt hie woldon" *Anglo-Saxon Chronicle* 921.

It was not until the Middle English period that the collective noun singular in form appeared with any frequency *immediately* followed or preceded by a plural verb form. Collective nouns have ever since, however, had in English a concord of number which depended on the meaning emphasized rather than on the form of the noun.

[8] See, for example, Otto Jespersen, *A Modern English Grammar,* Vol. II (Heidelberg, 1914), 4, p. 813.

"According as the idea of plurality is more or less prominent in the mind of the speaker, there is in all languages and at all times a tendency to forget the fact that collectives are grammatically singular, and we often find plural constructions, partial or total. . . . In Modern English the tendency is perhaps stronger than in most languages, because so few verb forms and hardly any adjectives show any distinction at all between the two numbers. . . . And then also distance plays some part, the plural construction occurring more easily at some distance from the singular substantive (*they* in the next sentence, etc.) than in immediate contact with it."

Also E. H. Sturtevant, *Linguistic Change* (Chicago University Press, 1917), p. 140.

"In addition to the ordinary plural nouns most languages have a number of collective nouns which are singular in form. That Latin *multitudo,* English *crowd,* etc., are virtually plural appears from the fact that they tend to govern plurals, as when Shakespeare writes, 'The army of the queen mean to besiege us,' . . . The change from specific meaning to collective involves but a shift of emphasis."

Also Webster's *New International Dictionary* (2nd ed., 1934), lxxxvii, p. 49.

"Collective nouns, of course, take a plural verb when the individuals of the group are thought of."

[9] For the evidence and conclusions concerning the history of collectives and indefinites in English see especially the two following dissertations:

Ernst Liedtke, *Die numerale auffassung der Kollektiva im Verlaufe der englischen Sprachgeschichte,* Königsberg, 1910.

Florence G. Beall, *Concord of Number in Modern English with Special Reference to the Indefinites* (unpublished dissertation), University of Michigan, 1932.

Some of the indefinite pronouns—*none, any*—reached during the Middle English period the stage of number concord that collective nouns held during the Old English period. *None* was frequently followed by a plural verb form but only when words intervened between the *none* and the verb. *None* was not immediately followed or preceded by a plural verb form until the end of the Middle English period and the beginning of Early Modern English.

Our present practice concerning number concord in respect to the other indefinite pronouns of later formation—*everyone, everybody, nobody, anyone, anybody,* etc.—parallels that of collective nouns in Old English and of *none* in Middle English. We never use a plural verb or plural pronoun form immediately following or immediately preceding the singular form of these indefinites, but when other words intervene, especially when these intervening words serve to emphasize the plural idea contained in the indefinite, a plural verb form or a plural pronoun is common. In other words the pattern concerning the use of number forms in secondary words that has emerged in the development of English is a concord based primarily on the number idea emphasized in the primary word rather than on its form.[10] In nearly all cases, form and meaning coincide and no problems arise. In these instances, however, in which form and meaning conflict, Modern English tends to give meaning the right of way. Collectives and some of the indefinite pronouns such as *none* have now no restrictions in their use with plural verb forms in accord with the idea uppermost in the speaker's mind, but most of the other indefinites (*everyone, everybody, nobody, anyone, anybody,* (*n*)*either*) that may be singular in form with plural idea take a plural reference pronoun or a plural verb only when other words intervene between the indefinite and the verb or reference pronoun.[11]

This statement concerning the practice of number concord in

[10] Compare the development of the use of logical gender with reference to the pronouns *he, she, it,* out of the older grammatical gender.

Samuel Moore, "Grammatical and Natural Gender in Middle English," *Publications of the Modern Language Association,* Vol. 36, 1921, pp. 79–103.

[11] Typical examples are:

a. "I hold no malice toward *anyone* for my arrest and prosecution. I think *they* acted in good faith. . . . "—*American Mercury,* July, 1930.

b. "FITLER: Has *anybody* been saying anything to you about me, Antoinette? MISS LYLE: What could *they* say?"—George Kelly, *Behold, the Bridegroom.*

c. "[War] is not a game to the conscript, or the pressed sailor; but *neither* of *these* are the causes of it."—Ruskin, *Crown of Wild Olive* (London, 1904), p. 125.

Present-day English applies in its details to the Standard English of our letters (Group I) but not to that of Group III or Vulgar English. The precise situation revealed in the letters is as follows:

1. This, These, That, Those

In Group I, the letters of Standard English, *this, these, that, those* as attributives usually agree in form with the form of the noun following. This agreement in form applies even to collective nouns, as "*This throng* of people was gathered to pay *their* tribute to the heroes" (8066). With two words, however, *kind* and *sort* (which may also be considered collectives)[12] the plural forms *these* and *those* very frequently appear in those cases in which a plural noun follows the *of*, as in "*These* kind of letters." The use of *these* and *those* with *kind of* and *sort of* appears here in Group I, the letters of Standard English, but *not once* in Group III, the letters of Vulgar English. The one example in Group III that comes nearest to this use is the sentence "I suppose you get all kind of letters the same as this" (8005).

One other exception to the usual practice of agreement in form of *this, these, that, those,* with the nouns they modify shows itself in those situations in which a plural word is taken as a unit, as in "This eleven days was consumed in . . . ." (9043), and "That twenty-five dollars I had to borrow . . . was . . ." (8288). In this construction the singular form *this* or *that* does not *immediately* precede the plural noun; some other word or words, including a numeral, stand between the singular demonstrative and the plural noun. This practice is not limited to any one of the classes of English examined. It appears equally in all three.

The distinct Vulgar English plural demonstrative form, which, however, appears only four times in the letters, is *them* as in "*them* nice little boys" (8187). Paralleling the Standard English use of *these* and *those* it also is used with the words *kind of* and *sort of,* as in "*them* kind of books."[13]

2. Verb Forms

a. In Group III or Vulgar English there are frequent instances in

[12] See *Oxford English Dictionary,* s.v. *sort,* sense 7, and *kind,* sense 14*b.* Also G. O. Curme, *Syntax* (Boston, D. C. Heath and Co., 1931), pp. 544, 545.

[13] For literary examples of *them* as a demonstrative attributive = *those,* see OD *them* III, 5, *a, b.*

which a plural subject (plural both in form and in meaning) is followed immediately by a verb with singular form. Examples are

"my *children is* too small" (8037)
"my *children is* on starvation" (8037)
"but *births was* not recorded when James was born" (8016)
"the dirt *floors requires* continual work" (6413)
"all my *uncles was* in the civil war" (8154)
"and *times is* so hard" (8293)
"so the *Letters* that i have send to him *has* been opened by others" (8106)
"my *Wife and 2 children has* got the Plegleory" (8179)

Some few examples can be explained on the ground that the plural has been grasped as a single unit, as in

"the doctor's at . . . claim that *5 yr's is* his limit to live" (8153)
"to hear from you before six *months expires*" (8215)

Three instances occur in Group III in which a singular subject (singular both in form and in meaning) is followed immediately by a verb without the *s*-form that is characteristic of the singular.

"i hope *it make* a man of him" (8097)
"they said his *licence*[14] *were* in the paper and it was" (8186)
"*he has* not been in good health and *have*[15] been getting worse" (8072)

b. In Group III or Vulgar English there occur some instances of the singular form *was* with the plural pronoun forms *we, you, they.*

"we told them that *we was* just taking the car back" (8039)
"*you was* the one that could help" (8018)

One should call attention to the fact that no instances occurred of *we is, you is,* or *they is,* a fact which suggests that this use of *was* is a carrying through of the levelling to a single form which affected all the preterits of strong verbs in Early Modern English. As a matter of fact, the verb *to be* with its preterit singular *was* and preterit plural *were* is the only verb left out of more than a hundred that had, up to the time of Shakspere, distinct forms for singular and plural in the past tense.

c. In Group II and also in Group III the form *don't* occurs with a singular subject. No instances of this appeared in Group I; not more

[14] The final sound of this word *licence* being an [s] may account for the plural verb. See below, p. 53.
[15] Not immediately following the singular subject.

than 30 per cent of *don't* to 70 per cent of *doesn't* appeared in Group II; but in Group III *doesn't* is exceedingly rare.

Examples in Group II are

"*He don't* say in his letter" (8092)
"*Father* has not had . . . and *don't* make but a small salary" (8275)

Examples in Group III are

"the *climate dont* agree with him" (8168)
"his mind is bad untill *he dont* remember his age" (8245)
"if *he dont* get back" (8251)
"*He dont* know what it is to stay away from home" (8190)

d. A number of nouns appearing always in plural form take singular verb forms. Such words are *means, headquarters,*[16] *news, remains, whereabouts.*[17] The following examples are from Group I except the last, which comes from Group II. No examples appeared in Group III.

"The only *means* of support *is* $15.00 weekly compensation insurance" (8260)
"The only visible *means* of support of this family . . . *is* $60.00 per month" (8260)
"His *remains was* left in . . ." (8436)
"No *news has* come" (8075)
"Who's only *means* of making a living *is* selling papers" (8102)

e. When the subject consists of two or more words joined by *and,* the verb has a singular form when the several words of the subject refer to the same thing broadly understood, or when these words refer to several things that can be included in one category.

Examples from Group I are

"the organization *and* work of this office *has* increased ten foal", (9000)
"the necessary forms *and* other machinery for operation *was* furnished by" (8416)
"the discipline *and* hygiene of the . . . where the men were prepared for . . . *speaks* for itself" (8415)
"their sanitary conditions *and* the arrangement of their quarters *was* very good" (8426)

[16] *Headquarters* also appears with plural demonstratives in the following examples from Group I:

"will report to *these headquarters*" (5101)
"the early departure of *these headquarters*" (9056)

Means appears with a plural demonstrative in the following example from Group II: "I employ these *means* in seeking your kind office" (8078)

[17] In *whereabouts* the *s* is the adverbial ending, not the plural inflection.

Sometimes, of course, although infrequently, the plural verb is used, as in

> "the care *and* repair of all . . . vehicles at this station *are* under my supervision" (9052)

A plural verb also appears where the words *as well as* take the place of *and,* as in

> "The registrant *as well as* his dependents *were* given an opportunity to appear before . . ." (8417)

From Group II come the following examples:

> "The money *and* jewelry *was* found on him" (6503)
> "Please answer this as the Mother *and* Father *needs* his support" (8262)

In Group III, Vulgar English, no examples were found of a clear unification of such a double subject into a single category, but frequently the singular verb was used with a double subject which in Standard English would undoubtedly take a plural verb. This use seems to be like that illustrated in (*a*) above.

Examples are

> "after 13 days him *and* this man that was with him *was found*" (8026)
> "I wish to inform you that D—— R—— *and* R—— R—— *is* the Same Boy" (8151)
> "My Wife *&* 2 children *has* got the Plegleory" (8179)
> "The father *and* mother *is* dead" (8181)

f. A collective noun subject takes a plural verb whenever the attention centers upon the plurality of individuals embraced by the collective. Examples are abundant in Group I and in Group II; they are very rare in Group III.

From Group I,[18] examples with the plural verb are

> "The family *occupy* a house consisting of six rooms" (8303)
> "Apparently the family *have* never been in better circumstances" (8027)
> "The majority of the officers . . . *are* now so widely scattered" (9010)
> "The family *were* very fine people" (8283)

Examples with the singular verb are

[18] Other examples from Group I may be found in 8419, 8283, 8095, 8002. Examples with the singular verb may be found in 9061, 8073, 8002.

"The family *consists* of an invalid father . . ." (8260)
"Out of which number the necessary quota *was* selected" (8421)

From Group II,[19] examples with the plural verb are

"Look and see where the rest of them *are*" (8447)
"If the U.S. Army *take* men . . ." (8031)

An example with the singular verb is

"The class of men now being recruited as a whole *is* very good" (8085)

From Group III there are the following two examples; the first, one that in Standard English would probably take a plural verb, the second showing a shift of number in the second verb.

"as my familie *is* all sick" (8179)
"the court *has* a commitment for him and *are* looking for him" (8080)

g. A singular subject separated from the verb by intervening words containing plural substantives sometimes (about 30 per cent of the instances in Group I) has a verb in the plural number. The greater the distance between the subject noun and the verb, the greater the power of attraction to the plural form of the intervening substantives.

Examples from Group I are [20]

"Absence from continental United States and my home *prevent* obtaining certificates within the required time" (9065)
"The schedule of our orders *are* that officers shall . . ." (8413)

Examples from Group II are

"ability for wining wars *are* nearer attained by . . ." (8061)
"Current furnished by galvanic cells *are* directly proportional to . . ." (8066)

Examples from Group III are

"No one but God and myself *know* what I've gone through this last year" (8038)
"The feeding of public animals *consist* principly of Hay Bran and Oats and water . . ." (6413)
"the history not only of the U.S. but all others countries *prove* that a soldier must be well trained" (8063)

[19] Other examples from Group II may be found in 8452, 8146, 8008; examples with the singular verb in 8221, 8085.

[20] Examples of singular verbs in such situations can be found in 8410, 8437, 8418, 8420. Examples of plural subjects with singular verbs are in 9043, 8430.

h. The indefinite pronouns *none, any,* and the disjunctive pronouns *neither* and *either* in all examples from Group I where they are used with number distinctive verb forms, with but one exception, appear with plural verbs.

Examples are

"*None* of the married children *are* in a position to assist" (8283)
"Evidently the four men . . . did not stay to assist the injured man for there *were none* with him when he was found" (8412)
"and would like to know if *any* of the officers of . . . *are* to be given an opportunity . . ." (9027)

The one example with the singular verb is

"Numerous affidavits were brought in but *none was* sufficient to prove his claimed status" (8412)

Examples from Group II are

"has accused me of several irregular acts . . . but *none* of them *have* any foundation . . ." (8443)
"*Neither* of my parents *read or write*" (8210)

Examples from Group III are very rare. The following is the only one appearing in our material:

"with nine children . . . and *none* of these children *are* old enough to go to work" (8084)

i. The word *there* (especially when it is a mere function word without adverbial significance) is very frequently followed by a singular *is, was,* or *has been* before a plural subject. Of the examples occurring in Group I only three contain the plural verb. They are

"There *are* a good number of Negroes in our district" (8429)
"There *were* none with him" (8409)
"There *are* three married daughters" (8283)

Examples of the singular verb form are

"There *is* $200.00 in improvement assessments" (8303)
"The fact is there *is* fewer criticisms on that organization" (8427)
"There *has* been numerous times that I . . ." (8426)
"There *has* been several occasions when that was not done" (8426)
"There *has* been several lieutenants attached to . . ." (8426)

Examples from Group II provide many with the singular verb but only two with the plural form.

"There *was* soldiers inside" (8450)
"there *was* only two of us left" (8449)

"there *was* about fifteen or twenty members" (8443)
"there *was* several other men" (8446)
"there *are* no blankets in it, nor there never *has* been" (8444)
"there *are* men who will" (8069)

Examples from Group III are similarly abundant with singular verb forms. One (the last given below) has a plural verb form, but in it the subject is singular.

"there *is* three of us" (8251)
"there *was* no misleading statements made" (8251)
"there *is* also four children" (8270)
"There *is* six more children besides him" (8288)
"there *is* five or six letters on the way" (8077)
"if there *is* any grounds of him getting out" (8037)
"there *has* been lots of sentence cut" (8039)
"I want to know if there *are* a chance for me to get . . ." (8090)

3. *Reference Pronouns and Their Antecedents*

Reference pronouns are usually separated from their antecedents by at least one other word and often they stand in the next sentence. As a result, in Modern English, they usually agree in their form with the number meaning which is in the attention of the writer rather than with the form of the antecedent. Thus with singular collectives and indefinite pronouns there is very frequently a plural reference pronoun.[21]

Examples from Group I are

"and my *company* has formed a dislike for him which *they* have never forgotten" (8423)
"get in touch with the Captain of his *Company,* if *they* are still at . . ." (8424)

[21] The following examples from literary materials are significant:
"Every English *man* and *woman* has good reason to be proud of the work done by *their* forefathers in prose and poetry."—Stopford Brooke, *Primer of English Literature.*
"Our club *has* frequently caught him tripping, at which times *they* never spare him."—Addison, *Spectator,* No. 105.
"*Each house* shall keep a journal of *its proceedings,* and from time to time publish the same, excepting such parts as may in *their* judgment require secrecy. . . ."—*Constitution of the United States,* Art. I, Sec. 5, #3.
"*No one* could have made *themselves* more liked in so short a time."—Archibald Marshall, *The Old Order Changeth.*
"And with equal justice may the lexicographer be derived who being able to produce no example of a *nation* that *has* preserved *their* words and phrases from mutability. . . ."—Johnson, Preface to *Dictionary.*

"This *company* could not promise to employ him . . . If *they* do employ him . . ." (8425)

"He said he would run *anyone* out of town or he would lock *them* up and *they* would stay . . ." (6415)

Examples from Group III do not seem to employ a plural reference pronoun to accord with the number idea in the antecedent as in Group I but rather to use the *they, their,* or *them* as a form for common number. The examples from Group III are

"where if it was another *man they* would have got 1 month" (8039)

"After a Mother & Father suffer to raise a *Boy* to become the age of 17 *they* should be some help to their parents" (8074)

"I wroted to the County Health *Officer* to see if *they* had a record of his birth" (8254)

"*he* forgets . . . and joins and is shipped away from the poor old couple hu raised *them*" (8005)

"he was not baptised as we do not believe in baptizing *a child* until *they* are old enough to understand" (8067)

The facts revealed by this survey of the number distinctive forms in secondary words, as that use is represented in the letters examined here, seem to justify, at least tentatively, the following conclusions:

1. *These kind (sort) of, those kind (sort) of* are not matters of Vulgar English. They appear primarily in Group I (Standard English). The characteristic Vulgar English demonstrative of plural number is *them.* This word is also used with *kind* and *sort* as in "them kind of books."

2. *We was, you was, they was* are characteristic of Vulgar English only. These usages do not seem to be matters of number concord, for the present tense *is* does not appear with these plural pronouns. They seem rather to be a levelling of this verb to a single form in the preterit as all the strong verbs were levelled in the sixteenth and seventeenth centuries.

3. The form *don't* rather than *doesn't* with a third person singular subject (other than a collective noun or an indefinite pronoun) seems to be characteristic of Vulgar English. It appears in our Group II (Common English) but not in Group I (Standard English).

4. The gross violation of concord—the use in a verb of a number distinctive form which does not correspond with the number form of the subject when that number form is in harmony with the number meaning implied in the subject—occurs with moderate frequency *only* in Vulgar English.

5. The use of the introductory formula *There is* (*was*) (*has*), especially where the word *there* is a mere function word without adverbial significance, followed by a plural subject is not limited to any one of the three groups examined but appears in Group I as well as in Group III.

6. Such violations of a formal concord as the use of a singular collective noun with a plural verb or a plural reference pronoun; *none* with a plural verb; the indefinites *everyone, everybody,* etc., with a plural reference pronoun or a plural verb separated from the indefinite by other words; a double subject connected by *and* with a singular verb when the two substantives refer to the same thing or can be included in a single category; a singular subject with a plural verb when words intervening between the subject and verb (or other context) give a distinctly plural meaning to the subject;—these violations of a formal number concord in order to use the few number distinctive forms of verbs and those of reference pronouns in accord with the actual number in the referent rather than the formal number of the word used as subject are characteristic of Group I (Standard English) and seldom appear in Vulgar English.

II. THE FORMS FOR TENSE

The forms to distinguish the preterit (or past) tense of the verb from the present tense provide the second important use in Modern English of the forms of words to express grammatical ideas. The simple past tense is the only one of the time distinctions expressed in Present-day English that is still distinguished by inflection or the form of the words. The others are shown by function words in periphrastic combinations and will be treated in Chapter VIII. The participles (the verb in adjective functions), however, are also distinguished from the present tense form by inflections—the present participle with the ending *-ing* [22] and the past participle with a form (in most cases) like that of the simple past tense (preterit). Within the preterit there is now no distinction of form for number or for person except in the verb *to be* in which *was* is used with singulars and *were* with plurals. The preterit form, therefore, does duty as a tense form only, and in all except eighteen verbs [23] clearly distinguishes the past tense from the present.

[22] For the history of this form see H. C. Wyld, *A Short History of English*, pp. 237-258; for its use in periphrastic combinations see Chapter VIII below.

[23] These eighteen verbs are: *beat, bet, burst, cast, cost, cut, hit, hurt, let, put, rid, set, shed, shut, spit, split, spread, thrust.* Seven other verbs should perhaps also

The particular form which has become the pattern for the past tense in Present-day English is the so-called dental (alveolar) suffix, spelled *-ed* or *-t,* but (1) a voiced stop, (2) a voiceless stop, (3) a separate syllable, depending upon the phonetic character of the sounds preceding the ending. Examples of (1) are *raised, saved, dragged, played, chewed;* of (2) are *raced, coughed, walked, pushed, stopped;* of (3) are *nodded, gilded, wanted, lighted.* These, the "regular" verbs of modern English, comprise the great body of English verbs. The pattern is that of the Old English "weak" verbs, the various classes of which fell together as a result of the levelling and loss of inflectional vowels in Early Middle English and in Early Modern English respectively. In general the pull of this pattern has been so great that most of the verbs which formed their past tense by other means have lost their old forms and have adopted the dental suffix. For example, of the 195 old "strong" verbs which still last [24] in Modern English 129 or about 65 per cent have gone over to this regular pattern. It is worth noting also that in this regular pattern there is no difference in form between the past tense and the past participle. We have, therefore, in the pattern a "two form" verb—one form for the present and one for both the past tense and the past participle.

---

be included with those given above although each of them does appear with the differentiated past tense and past participle, as *knit, quit, shred, slit, sweat, wed, wet.*

[24] In all there were in Old English at least 312 strong verbs (including the class of reduplicating verbs but not compounds). Of these about one third have dropped out of use in the later stages of the language.

My lists of strong verbs show the following figures:

Class	*Original Number*	*Remaining in Modern English*	*Adjusted to Regular (Weak) Pattern*	*Retaining Strong Forms*
I	62	26	15	11
II	50	32	28	4
III	81	53	31	22
IV	14	8	3	5
V	26	18	8	10
VI	31	25	18	7
VII	48	33	26	7
	312	195	129	66

Of the 312 verbs which were originally strong in Old English, 195 or 62 per cent continue in Modern English in some form. Of those that continue in Modern English 129 or 66 per cent have been adjusted in forms to the regular (weak) pattern; only sixty six or 34 per cent still retain strong forms. Of the 195 that continue in Modern English, 153 or 78.5 per cent have a similar form for both the simple past tense and the past participle.

There are, however, several groups of verbs that have not yet adjusted themselves to the pattern of tense inflection in Present-day English. Chief among these are those "strong" verbs, some sixty six in all,[25] which still show a change of vowel within the stem instead of the dental suffix to indicate the past tense.

Two facts in the history of the "strong" verbs in English seem especially important:

1. Only the sixty six most common strong verbs have resisted the pull of the regular pattern of verb inflection for tense and still maintain the change of stem vowel rather than use the dental suffix to indicate past time. The others, 129, have been drawn into the regular pattern.

2. Of these sixty six common strong verbs only forty two still maintain a difference of form between the past tense and the past participle. The other twenty four of the sixty six verbs and the 129 that have become regular have the same form in both past tense and past participle.[26] As a matter of fact, during the sixteenth and seventeenth centuries there was a strong tendency to eliminate the distinction of form between the past tense and the past participle in all of these verbs, and every one of the forty two appears from time to time in acceptable literary writing with past tense and past participle

[25] These sixty six "strong" verbs are:

Class I		*Class II*	*Class III*					*Class IV*	*Class V*	*Class VI*	*Class VII*
abide	strike	choose	begin	sling	spin	wring	run	bear	bid	draw	fall
bite	slide	freeze	drink	slink	sting	bind	fight	break	eat	forsake	hold
drive	smite	cleave	shrink	spring	stink	find		steal	give	shake	hang
ride	stride	(to split)	sing	swim	swing	grind		tear	get	slay	blow
rise	write	fly	sink	cling	win	wind		come	lie	stand	grow
shine									see	swear	know
									sit	take	throw
									speak		
									tread		
									weave		

[26] The twenty four "strong" verbs that have become "two form" verbs in Present-day English are: *abide, shine, slide, strike, stride; cling, sling, slink, spin, sting, stink, swing, win, wring, fight, bind, find, grind, wind; get, sit; stand; hold, hang.* The forty two strong verbs that still maintain different forms for preterit and participle are: *bite, drive, ride, rise, smite, write; choose, freeze, cleave, fly; begin, drink, run, shrink, sing, sink, spring, swim; bear, break, steal, tear, come; bid, eat, give, lie, see, speak, tread, weave; draw, forsake, shake, slay, swear, take; fall, blow, grow, know, throw. Come* and *run* have distinctive forms for the present and preterit only. A very few verbs that did not originally belong to the strong verbs have been drawn by analogy to strong forms: *strive, thrive, ring, fling, wear, hide, dig, string, chide, stave.*

forms alike. In this case Samuel Johnson [27] supported by the eight-

[27] The earliest statement in the effort to halt the elimination of the distinction of form between past tense and past participle in the surviving strong verbs seems to have been the following from Samuel Johnson's *Grammar* (prefixed to the *Dictionary*) in 1755:

"Concerning these double participles it is difficult to give any rule; but he shall seldom err who remembers that when a verb has a participle distinct from its preterite, as *write, wrote, written,* that distinct participle is more proper and elegant, as *The book is written,* is better than *The book is wrote,* though *wrote* may be used in poetry."

Bishop Robert Lowth, in *A Short Introduction to English Grammar* (1762), pp. 94–98, took up this battle to prevent the passing of the difference in form between the past tense and past participle, gave a bill of particulars, and was especially effective through his influence upon following grammarians. His comments follow:

"There are not in English so many as a Hundred Verbs, . . . which have a different form for the Past Time Active and the Participle Perfect of Passive. The general bent and turn of the language is towards the other form; inclination and tendency of the language seems to have given occasion to the introducing of a very great Corruption; by which the Form of the Past Time is confounded with that of the Participle in these verbs, few in proportion, which have them quite different from one another. This confusion prevails greatly in common discourse, and is too much authorized by the example of some of our best writers. Thus it is said, *He begun,* for *he began; he run,* for *he ran; he drunk,* for *he drank:* The Participle being used instead of the Past Time. And much more frequently the Past Time instead of the Participle: as, *I had wrote, it was wrote,* for *I had written, it was written; I have drank,* for *I have drunk; bore,* for *born; chose,* for *chosen; bid,* for *bidden; got,* for *gotten;* etc. This abuse has been long growing upon us, and is continually making further encroachments; as it may be observed in those Irregular Verbs of the Third Class, which change *i* short into *a* and *u;* as *Cling, clang clung;* in which the original and analogical form of the Past Time in *a* is almost grown obsolete; and, the *u* prevailing instead of it, the Past Time is now in most of them confounded with the Participle. The Vulgar Translation of the Bible, which is the best standard of our language, is free from this corruption, except in a few instances; as *hid,* for *hidden; held,* for *holden,* frequently; *bid,* for *bidden; begot,* for *begotten,* once or twice; in which, and a few other like words, it may perhaps be allowed as a Contraction. And in some of these, custom has established it beyond recovery. In the rest it seems wholly inexcusable. The absurdity of it will be plainly perceived in the example of some of these Verbs, which Custom has not yet so perverted. We should be immediately shocked at *I have knew, I have saw,* etc.: but our ears are grown familiar with *I have wrote, I have drank, I have bore,* etc., which are altogether as barbarous."

The following material is a footnote in Lowth, pp. 94–98:

"He would *have spoke.*" Milton, P.L. x. 517.

"Words *interwove* with sighs found out their way." P.L. i. 621.

"And to his faithful servant *hath* in place *Bore* witness gloriously." Samson Ag. 1752.

"And envious darkness, ere they could return, *Had stole* them from me." Comus, 195. Here it is observable, that the Author's MS, and the First Edition, have it *stolne.*

"And in triumph *had rode.*" P.R. iii. 36.

"I *have chose* This perfect man." P.R. i. 165.

"The fragrant brier *was wove* between." Dryden, Fables.

"I will scarce think you *have swam* in a Gondola." Shakespear, As you like it.

"Then finish what you *have began,* But scribble faster, if you can." Dryden, Poems, Vol. II. p. 172.

eenth century prescriptive grammarians seems to have been the chief factor in retarding this development in verb forms.[28]

Other groups of verbs that have not yet adjusted themselves completely to the regular pattern with a dental suffix attached to the unchanged stem are

a. The "irregular" verbs *be, go, do.* The first of these verbs uses forms from three originally distinct and independent verbs to produce the present infinitive *be* and past participle *been,* the present indicative *am, is, are,* and the past tense *was, were.* The second, *go,* has used, ever since the fifteenth century, the form *went,* the old past tense of the verb *wend,* as its preterit. The forms of the third, *do,* with its preterit *did,* are explained in various ways.[29]

b. The old "weak verbs without middle vowel." Of the twenty four

---

"And now the years a numerous train *have ran;* The blooming boy is ripn'd into man." Pope's Odyss. xi. 555.
"*Have sprang.*" Atterbury, Vol. I. Serm. IV.
"*Had spake—had began.*"—Clarendon, Contin. Hist. p. 40 & 120.
"The men *begun* to embellish themselves." Addison, Spect. No. 434.
"Rapt into future times the bard *begun.*" Pope, Messiah.
And without the necessity of rhyme:
"A second deluge learning thus *o'er-run,*
And the Monks finish'd what the Goths *begun.*" Essay on Criticism.
"Repeats you verses *wrote* on glasses." Prior.
"Mr. Misson *has wrote.*" Addison, Preface to His Travels.
"He could only command his voice, *broke* with sighs and sobbings, so far as to bid her proceed." Addison, Spect. No. 164.
"No civil broils *have* since his death *arose.*" Dryden, on O. Cromwell.
"Illustrious virtues, who by turns *have rose.*" Prior.
"*Had* not *arose.*" Swift, Battle of Books: and Bolingbroke, Letter to Wyndham, p. 233.
"The Sun *had rose,* and gone to bed, Just as if Partridge were not dead." Swift.
"This nimble operator will *have stole* it." Tale of a Tub, Sect. x.
"Some philosophers *have mistook.*" Ibid. Sect. ix.
"That Diodorus *has* not *mistook* himself in his account of Phintia, we may be as sure as any history can make us." Bentley, Dissert. on Phalaris, p. 98. [Added in 1775 edition]
"Why, all souls that were, were forfeit once; And He, that might the 'vantage best *have took,* Found out the remedy." Shakespear, Meas. for Meas.
"Silence *Was took* ere she was ware." Milton, Comus.
"Into these common places look, Which from great authors I *have took.*" Prior, Alma.
"A free Constitution, when it has *been shook* by the iniquity of former administrations." Lord Bolingbroke, Patriot King, p. 111.
"Too strong to *be shook* by his enemies." Atterbury.
"Ev'n there he should *have fell.*" Prior, Solomon.
"Sure some disaster *has befell:* Speak, Nurse; I hope the Boy is well." Gay, Fables.

[28] This point seems to have been fairly well established by the material collected by Dr. Paul Royalty and presented in his dissertation *The Preterite and Past Participle Forms of Modern English Verbs* (unpublished), University of Michigan.

[29] See Streitberg, *Urgerm. Grammatik,* 329.

verbs which were of this kind in Old English seven [30] still resist the pull of the old pattern: *sell, tell, buy, teach, seek, think, bring.*[31]

c. "Weak" verbs with the usual dental suffix but with a "shortened" vowel (some have no added consonant because the stem ended in a "dental"):

creep-crept,[32] *keep-kept, leap-lept, sleep-slept, sweep-swept, weep-wept; flee-fled, hear-heard, say-said, shoe-shod;*
bleed-bled, breed-bred, feed-fed, lead-led, read-read (*red*), *speed-sped; light-lit, meet-met, shoot-shot.*[33]

d. "Weak" verbs with stems ending in a voiced consonant with a *voiceless* dental suffix instead of the usual voiced dental, a few with "shortened vowel": [34]

*bend-bent, build-built, burn-burnt,** [35] *dwell-dwelt,* gild-gilt,* gird-girt,* lend-lent, pen* (enclose)*-pent,* rend-rent, send-sent, smell-smelt,* spell-spelt,* spend-spent, spill-spilt,* spoil-spoilt;* *
bereave-bereft, cleave-cleft,* deal-dealt, dream-dreamt,* kneel-knelt,* lean-leant,* leave-left, lose-lost, mean-meant.*

The materials of Vulgar English show also the following preterits of this kind:

earnt, feart, kilt, ruint, scairt, of the verbs *earn, fear, kill, ruin,* and *scare.*

In the letters examined in this study the mere statistics of the various types of verb forms used seem to point to interesting and significant facts.

In the letters of Group I (Standard English) there were the following preterits:

[30] Eight if one counts *beseech* as a separate verb rather than as belonging to *seek.*

[31] *Catch* seems to have been attracted to this group by analogy with ME *lachen* from *OE laecc(e)an,* "to seize." The preterit *fought* of the old strong verb *fight* has probably been supported by the similar preterit forms of the verbs in this class.

[32] *Creep,* originally a "strong" verb, still has in Vulgar English a preterit *crep. Leap, sleep, sweep, weep,* were in Old English "reduplicating" verbs and the forms: *lep, slep, swep, wep,* still persist in Vulgar English.

[33] *Shoot,* a "strong" verb of Class II, developed much like *choose,* but is put here with the assumption that the preterit *shot* is the modern representation of the fourteenth-century "weak" form *schotte.*

[34] See the dissertation by Albert H. Marckwardt, "Origin and Extension of the Voiceless Preterit and the Past Participle Inflections of the English Irregular Weak Verb Conjugation," *Language and Literature,* Vol. 13 (Ann Arbor, University of Michigan Press, 1936), pp. 151–328.

[35] The verbs marked with a star have also a preterit that is in accord with the regular pattern, *burned, dwelled, gilded, girded, learned, penned, smelled, spelled, spilled, spoiled, bereaved, cleaved, dreamed, kneeled, leaned.*

TABLE I

		Number	Per cent
a. Completely regular pattern (with dental suffix)		354—	49 %
b. Strong verb (with internal change)		72—	10 %
c. "Irregular" verbs		222—	30.8%
did	10		
did (function word) [36]	38		
went	7		
was, were	167		
d. "Weak" verbs without middle vowel		25—	3.5%
e. "Weak" verbs with "shortened" vowel (*said*)		20—	2.8%
f. "Weak" verbs with irregular voiceless dental suffix		28—	3.8%
(1) with "shortened" vowel *left, kept, felt, meant*	17		
(2) without vowel change *sent, spent*	11		
g. Invariables (*let*)		1—	.1%
		722	100.0%

In the letters of Group III (Vulgar English) there were the following preterits:

TABLE II

		Number	Per cent
a. Completely regular pattern (with dental suffix)		215—	42 %
b. Strong verb (with internal change)		52—	10.1%
c. "Irregular" verbs		149—	29 %
did	8		
did (function word)	0		
went	19		
was, were	122		
d. "Weak" verbs without middle vowel		22—	4.3%
e. "Weak" verbs with "shortened" vowel, *heard, said*		21—	4 %
f. "Weak" verbs with irregular voiceless dental suffix		30—	5.8%
(1) with "shortened" vowel *felt, kept, left, lost*	21		
(2) without vowel change *sent*	9		
g. Invariables *put, let*		4—	.8%
h. Vulgar English deviation		20—	4.0%
		513—	100.0%

After recording every preterit form in all the letters both from the Vulgar English group and from the Standard English group, I

[36] See Chapter VIII below, pages 146–149.

found that the actual amount of the difference of the preterit forms of Vulgar English materials from those of the Standard English material was astonishingly little.[37]

1. In both groups, in Standard English and in Vulgar English, about half the verbs used, 49 and 42 per cent, were of the regular pattern with preterits made by the usual dental suffix phonetically adjusted to the character of the preceding sound.

2. In both groups, likewise, there were approximately the same proportions, 10 per cent, of strong verb preterits with internal change of vowel.

3. There was, in the Vulgar English materials, a somewhat greater use of the preterit with "shortened" vowel (*keep-kept, mean-meant,* etc.). Eight per cent of the Vulgar English preterits were of this kind, whereas but 5 per cent of the Standard English preterits belonged to this group.

4. Only about 4 per cent of the preterits in the Vulgar English letters had forms not used in Standard English. These are the ones that attract attention and because of that fact seem to bulk much larger in Vulgar English than they actually are.[38]

5. The following were the kinds of differences in preterit forms which appeared in the Vulgar English materials:

a. No added dental suffix. The preterit form was thus like the present except in the third person singular.

> "The firm he *work* for was after him to work" (8235)
> "Mr. . . . *ask* me to sign" (8244)
> ". . . where I *sigen* up for this boy" (8225)
> "For I just *pick* this boy up and raisd him" (8025)
> "I diten know he *Joyn* the army till . . ." (8045)
> ". . . he *slip* of from me and got in" (8045)
> ". . . officer . . . that . . . *perswaid* him" (8045) [39]

In similar fashion, verbs which ordinarily have a change from a voiced dental stop to a voiceless dental stop in the preterit appeared

[37] Mencken's lists, in his book *The American Language,* and the comic representation of Vulgar English give a very different impression. In respect to this point I should urge again Professor Menner's comments in his article "The Verbs of the Vulgate," *American Speech,* Vol. I, pp. 230–240. See above Chapter IV, page 35, note 2.

[38] ". . . It is easy to note unusual preterits and participles but hard to detect the customary ones. The person who shocks one with 'I done it' or 'I have saw' cannot compensate for his error by a dozen 'correct' forms, because the latter pass unnoticed."—R. J. Menner, "Verbs of the Vulgate," *loc. cit.,* p. 231.

[39] Other instances of this type of Vulgar English preterit appeared in 8200, 8033, 8072, 8244.

with no change. Here again the preterit differs from the present only in the third person singular.

"My boy *send* her money to help her out" (8028)

b. No vowel change in strong verbs. Here again the preterit becomes like the present form except for the third person singular.

"My son . . . *run* away" (8291)
"Will say, he *run* off from . . ." (8190)
"you can get his age that he *give* from your recruiting officer"[40] (8025)

c. A second dental suffix added to the form which already had a dental suffix. According to the pattern, this second suffix is adjusted to the form by means of an extra syllable.

"We had the officers from . . . here and they *agreeded* with all I rote you before" (8005)

d. A past participle form used for the preterit in strong verbs. This occurs especially in the verbs *do* and *see* but occasionally in other words.

"for he *done* nothing wrong" (8201)
"I *written* in or had the Red Cross to write to Captain . . ." (8028)

e. A preterit with the vowel of the old preterit plural in words in which Standard English has adopted the vowel of the old preterit singular for both singular and plural.

"I *writ* sevel days ago" (8045)

The statistics of the past participle forms are even more interesting, both with respect to the distribution of the various kinds of participle forms and with respect to the differences between Standard English and Vulgar English. In the letters of Group I (Standard English) there were the past participles that are counted and summarized in Table III.

In the letters of Group III (Vulgar English) there were the past participles for which the figures are given in Table IV.

[40] Other examples appeared in 8045, 8190.

TABLE III

Category	Subgroup	Count	Subtotal	Total		Percent
a. The completely regular pattern (with dental suffix)						
	with *have*	220				
	with *be*	606		829	—	71.7%
	with *get*	3				
b. Strong verbs (with internal change)						
	with *have*	57				
	with *be*	61		118	—	10.2%
c. Irregular verbs						
	with *have*: *done*	8				
	with *have*: *gone*	5	148			
	with *have*: *been*	135				
	with *be*: *done*	6		157	—	13.5%
	with *be*: *gone*	3	9			
d. "Weak" verbs "without middle vowel"						
	with *have*	2				
	with *be*	6		8	—	.7%
e. "Weak" verbs with "shortened" vowel						
	with *have*	9				
	with *be*	3		12	—	1.0%
f. "Weak" verbs with irregular voiceless dental suffix						
	with *have*	2				
	with *be*	24		26	—	2.3%
g. Invariables						
	with *have*	4				
	with *be*	3		7	—	.6%
				1157		100.0%

TABLE IV

Category	Subgroup	Count	Subtotal	Total		Percent
a. The completely regular pattern (with dental suffix)						
	with *have*	107				
	with *be*	59				
	with *have* and *been*	15		188	—	60.45%
	with *get*	7				
b. Strong verbs (with internal change)						
	with *have*	13				
	with *be*	16		29	—	9.32%
c. Irregular verbs						
	with *have*: *done*	6				
	with *have*: *gone*	3	63			
	with *have*: *been*	54				
	with *be*: *done*	1		67	—	21.54%
	with *be*: *gone*	3	4			
d. "Weak" verbs "without middle vowel"						
	with *have*	3				
	with *be*	1		4	—	1.29%
e. "Weak" verbs with "shortened" vowel				0		
f. "Weak" verbs with irregular voiceless dental suffix				0		
g. Invariables	with *have*	0				
	with *be*	1		1	—	.32%
h. Vulgar English deviation				22	—	7.08%
				311		100.00%

The most striking fact revealed by these statistics is the comparatively small number of participles found in the Vulgar English materials. In approximately equal amounts of writing covering much the same sorts of situations the Standard English matter contained nearly *four times as many participles as did the Vulgar English.*

Although the number of the participles was much smaller in Vulgar English, the amount of the deviation from the forms of Standard English was nearly twice that which appeared in the preterit forms. There was no very great difference in the two sets of materials in the kinds of participles used, whether of the regular pattern with dental suffix or of the strong verb, etc. Standard English had a slightly larger proportion (10 per cent) of the regular pattern. The chief differences which appeared in the participle forms of Vulgar English were the following:

a. Past participles with no dental suffix. The participle form was thus like the present without any inflection.

> "I feel that he *has change* place" (8147)
> "I *was knock* down" (8133)
> "The people *aint* never *discharge* my son" (8001)
> "Can you inform me . . . what time he *was discharge*" (8109) [41]

The participles, also, of verbs which ordinarily have a change from a voiced dental stop to a voiceless dental stop appeared with no change.

> "So the letters that i *have send* to him has been opened by others in mistake and *send* back to me" (8106)

b. A preterit form used for the past participle in strong verbs. Aside from the verbs *do* and *see* this method of eliminating the distinction of form between preterits and past participles is much more frequent than the use of a past participle form as preterit.[42]

> "the ones that *have gave* it" (8072)
> "My folks may *have wrote* you" (8198)

[41] Other examples of this form of past participle occurred in 8258, 8001.
[42] See note 27, page 62 above for the situation and tendency in Standard English of the seventeenth and eighteenth centuries.

"I hope I *haint* don any thing rong or *rote* anything rong in this letter" (8005)
"I *have broke* my health to have a home to live in" (8235)
"He was the best boy I had and *has gave* me most help" (8272)
"He liyed his self in the army and *was took* without letting me know any thing about it" (8045)
"I wish you would see what *has became* of my son" (8015)
"Everything I *have wrote* is the truth" (8026) [43]

The preterit form is also used for the past participle in the "irregular" verb *go,* but did not appear for the verbs *be* and *do.*

"That poor mother *has went* and got a job" (8005)

c. A dental suffix added to the past participle form of strong verbs

"He *was Borned* May 30—1910" (8000)
"Unless I was where he *was borned*" (8280) [44]

d. A present participle form used for a past participle [45]

"I said she didnt no What she was doing and she didnt and I *have* just *showing* you she didnt" (8005)

e. Ought *as a past participle in the sense "been obliged"*

"Maybe I *hadnt ought* to write to you" (8038)
"But was afraid I would . . . do something I *had not ought* to do" (8038)

The materials here examined seem to justify the following conclusions concerning the chief verb forms that are characteristic of Vulgar English:

1. Preterits and past participles occur without the dental suffix. These forms are like the present tense forms except for the fact that the third person singular of the preterit has no inflection.

2. Preterits of strong verbs occur without the change of internal vowel. These forms are also like the present tense forms except for the fact that the third person singular has no inflection.

3. Past participle forms of strong verbs are used for preterits and preterit forms for past participles. Here one must not include such forms as *they sung, it sunk, it shrunk,* as Vulgar English, for these

[43] Other examples of this use of the preterit for the past participles occurred in 8087, 8153.

[44] Other examples occur in 8280.

[45] There was but one example of this use and I am inclined to regard it simply as an orthographic variation of the form *shown.*

forms with the vowel of the old preterit plural which happened to be like that of the past participle are common in Standard English.[46]

4. Preterits and past participles of strong verbs occur with an added dental suffix, as *agreeded, borned.*

5. *Ought* is used as a past participle, as *had ought.*

[46] See Webster's *New International Dictionary* (2nd ed., 1934) for the forms of the past tense of *ring, sing, sink, shrink, spring.*

VI

THE USES OF THE FORMS OF WORDS: FOUR MINOR INFLECTIONS, REMNANTS OF OLDER PATTERNS

In a former chapter [1] it was pointed out that the uses of the forms of words to indicate grammatical ideas were much more important in the earlier stages of English than they are now. We have just seen, however, that the inflections for number and tense are not only still vigorously alive in the language but are even more distinctive than they were in former times. These facts will not be true in general of the other types of inflection still existing in English—the four which must be treated now. These grammatical uses of the forms of words have been largely displaced by one of the other grammatical processes which Modern English employs—function words or word order. Those four are:

I. The Genitive Inflection
II. The Dative-Accusative Forms
III. The Inflection for Comparison
IV. Person and Mood Forms

I. THE GENITIVE INFLECTION

A. The Genitive Forms of Nouns

Like the noun inflections for number in Old English, the genitive inflections of nouns in the older period of the language were of several types rather than a single pattern. The Old English word *cwen* (*queen*) formed its genitive by adding *-e*. The form *oxan* was the genitive singular of the Old English *oxa* (*ox*), as well as the nominative and accusative plural. The genitive plural usually had *-a*. Masculine and neuter *a-* stems had *-es* as the ending of the genitive singular. This *-es* ending was the source of the Modern English so-called *s*-ending of the genitive which has become the regular

[1] Chapter IV, pages 36–39.

pattern. In sound it is like the plural suffix and similarly adjusted to the phonetic character of the sounds that immediately precede. There are less exceptions to it as a pattern than there are to the plural *s*, for even those words that retain an old model plural form, as *man-men, child-children, ox-oxen,* have a regular pattern genitive form as *man's, child's, ox's*. In such words, also, the plural has the same genitive suffix, as *men's, children's, oxen's*. Orthographically, however, the suffix for the genitive ending differs from that of the plural by the use of the sign (') which we call an apostrophe.

This sign, the apostrophe, as first used in the sixteenth century, marked the omission of a letter, usually an *e,* in the writing. In this use it was equally common in the nominative plural and in the genitive singular. One frequently finds in the printed materials of this period such plurals as *two folio's*. The present use of the apostrophe to form the plurals of letters and figures, *a*'s and *b*'s, *6*'s and *7*'s, is a remnant of this practice. During the seventeenth and eighteenth centuries the apostrophe sign was gradually disused in nominative plural forms and was looked upon as a distinct mark of the genitive case. It was therefore extended to all genitive case forms, even to those in which no *e* had ever been written before a final *s* as *the men's hats* and after the *s* of the plural ending as *the ladies' hats*. This extended practice was by many considered illogical and a mistake.[2] Frequently in the writings of Vulgar English the apostrophe is omitted.[3] This genitive inflection of nouns has tended to be displaced by the use of the function word *of* until, in Present-day English, the proportion of the inflected genitive forms to the periphrastic genitive is very small indeed. The figures, page 74, give the percentages showing the increasing proportion of adnominal periphrastic genitives in large selections of English prose chosen to represent Old and Middle English.[4]

[2] T. C. Hansard, *Typographia* (1865), p. 440. "The genitive case of the singular number is generally known by having *'s* for its termination, but is not allowed in the plural."

Mason, *English Grammar* (1876), p. 29. "It is . . . an unmeaning process to put the apostrophe after the (possessive) plural *s* (as birds'), because no vowel has been dropped there."

[3] In the instances appearing in the letters of Group III nearly half did not have the apostrophe.

[4] These figures are quoted from the dissertation by Russell Thomas entitled *Syntactical Processes Involved in the Development of the Adnominal Periphrastic Genitive in the English Language* (Ann Arbor, University of Michigan, 1931), p. 88. Chapter III, gives the "Chronology of the Decreased Use of the Adnominal Inflected Genitive and the Increased Use of the Adnominal Periphrastic Genitive."

PERCENTAGE OF THE PERIPHRASTIC GENITIVE WITH "OF"

Period	Percentage
End of ninth century—Beginning of tenth	.5%
Latter part tenth—Beginning of eleventh	1.0
Eleventh century	1.2
Twelfth century	6.3
First half thirteenth century	31.4
Fourteenth century	84.4

In the materials examined here there were in Group I (Standard English) but thirty nine instances of the inflected genitive forms of nouns as against 868 instances of the periphrastic genitive with *of*, or 4.3 per cent of inflected genitive and 95.7 per cent of periphrastic genitive with *of*. In Group III (Vulgar English) there were thirty one instances of the inflected genitive forms of nouns as against 389 instances of the periphrastic genitive with *of*, or 7.4 per cent of inflected genitive and 92.6 per cent of periphrastic genitive with *of*. The actual number of the inflected genitive forms of nouns has been so greatly reduced in Present-day English that these genitives appear no more frequently than do the non-pattern plural forms without the *s* ending.[5]

On the other hand, in spite of the great decrease in the total number of inflected noun genitives, the uses of the inflected genitive continue to live in Present-day English in proportions not strikingly different from those that existed in the older periods of the language. This assertion contradicts the commonly expressed view that the inflected genitive is now confined almost entirely to but one definite function, the possessive meaning.[6]

[5] See above pp. 42–43. Five per cent of the plural nouns appeared without the *s*-ending.

[6] Typical quotations illustrating this commonly expressed view are the following: "The inflectional genitive is now nearly confined to the possessive meaning, whence it is often called the 'Possessive Case.'"—W. H. H. Kelke, *An Epitome of English Grammar* (London, Kegan Paul, Trench & Co., 1885), p. 77.

"From the fact that the genitive in the majority of cases expresses a relation of possession, it is often called the possessive."—H. Poutsma, *A Grammar of Late Modern English* (Groningen, P. Noordhoff, 1904–1917), Part II, Section I, A, p. 41.

"In the course of time we witness a gradual development towards greater regularity and precision. The partitive, objective, descriptive and some other functions of the genitive become obsolete; the genitive is invariably put immediately before the word it belongs to; irregular forms disappear, the *s* ending alone surviving as the fittest, so that at last we have one definite ending with one definite function and one definite position."—Otto Jespersen, *Language* (New York, Henry Holt and Co., 1922), pp. 351–352.

In the materials examined for this study, the inflected genitives of the Standard English (Group I) letters were distributed as follows:

TYPICAL EXAMPLES OF INFLECTED GENITIVE

Possessive Genitive (liberally interpreted)—40%
"lived at his father's home" (8064)
"My son Sam's wife" (9018)
"I am enclosing Mrs. M——'s passport" (8267)
"the enlisted man's parents" (8183)

Subjective Genitive—23%
"in support of his mother's request" (8234)
"since the soldier's enlistment" (8081)
"action regarding the boy's application" (9011)
"I have been under a physician's care" (8278)
"His parent's consent" (8242)

Genitive of Origin [7]—6%
"return the General's letter" (6415)
"the mother's affidavit" (8239)
"according to the neighbor's story" (8002)

Objective Genitive—17%
"he contributed toward the family's support" (8283)
"instructions that will affect the boy's release" (8294)
"in regard to my son's discharge" (8046)
"urging her son's release" (8027)

Descriptive Genitive (including genitive of measure) [8]—10%
"They found a woman's handkerchief as a clue" (7095)
"the month's time that I have lost" (9027)
"Unfortunately his education did not fit him to teach in a woman's college. He attended first a boys school and then a men's college" (9436)
"a one day's leave" (9007)

[7] A distinction has been made between the subjective genitive and the genitive of origin in such cases as "the man's resignation" and "the boy's application," on the following basis: when the context showed that the attention centered in the activity—the fact that *the man resigned* or that *the boy applied*—the genitive was called the subjective genitive; when the attention centered upon a resultant thing, as, for example, the *document* in which the man expressed his intention of resigning, or the *letter* by which the application was made, the genitive was called a genitive of origin.

[8] See above Chapter V, pp. 42–43, for the diversity of use in this construction with numerals: (*a*) uninflected forms; (*b*) *-s* forms without apostrophes, understood as plurals; (*c*) *-s* forms with apostrophes, especially in context in which the noun of extent is clearly singular. See also Chapter X, page 275.

There was but one example of the absolute use of the genitive; in this case the so-called "double" genitive. (Cf. page 81, note 23.)

> "He was accompanied by a friend of his father's" (7061)

One use of the genitive form needs special comment. It is the mechanical use of the *-'s* form on nouns that stand before gerunds —the English verbal [9] in *-ing*. Only one example appeared in the letters of Standard English.

> "There can, of course, be no objection to Sergeant S——'s making an application, through military channels, . . . for such appointment as . . ." (7050)

On the other hand, the uninflected noun form (singular) or the regular plural ending without the apostrophe appeared before such gerunds very frequently.

Examples are

> "due to the *instruments* being out of adjustment" (9027)
> "Nothing was said about his *mother* receiving it instead of me" (5104)
> "Did you know of the *company* coming here?" (7553)
> "There is no necessity for her *son* being with her" (8017)
> "Another reason for the *War Department* crediting my war service to West Virginia was . . ." (9053)
> "There is no record in this office of any *stone* being taken for use in . . ." (7051)
> "the announcement he had made . . . in regard to field message *blanks* being on the person of the men . . ." (7253)
> "There is no record of this *officer* having been attached or assigned to this detachment or of his ever having reported here" (7356)
> "Now you said something a while ago about *officers* being informed they should get orders from headquarters" (7501)
> ". . . a failure on their part would result in *Col. T*—— losing command of the regiment" (7052)
> "There is no trace of this *man* ever having been mustered into or discharged from the U.S. service" (7151)

Examples of pronouns that might have had the *-'s* form:

> "I did not do it myself and would not stand for *anybody else* doing it" (7430)
> "If I did, it was by *some one* glancing at my paper" (7420)

[9] See below pages 84, 85, 87, for the use of the pronouns in this construction; also Otto Jespersen, *On Some Disputed Points in English Grammar*, S.P.E. Tract No. 25, pp. 147–172.

Certainly from the evidence occurring in these materials it would be natural to conclude that the inflected form of nouns is ***not*** the normal practice before gerunds in Standard English.

The situation concerning the kinds of genitive that use the genitive inflection in Vulgar English (Group III) is much like that in Standard English. Genitives of possession make up about 40 per cent of the total number of instances. Nearly 30 per cent are subjective genitives and 12 per cent are objective genitives.

Examples of the genitive of possession are

"The *boy's* father is in the insane Asylum" (8077)
"My *Nephews'* Mother and Father died" (8084)
"this is *M—L—'s* mother writing you all" (8045)
"his *step father's* name" (8236)
"my *sons* full name is" (8038)
"and am forced from my *mothers* [10] by my step father" (8229)

Examples of the subjective genitive are

"knowing that we couldnt get along without the *Boys* help" (context shows that *Boys* is singular,—a son) (8005)
"I need my *son's* help now" (8235) (8233)
"without my or my *Husband* consent" (8033)
"his *parents* consent" (8242) (8215)
"complaining about my *sons* enlistment (8251) (8227)

Examples of the objective genitive are

"in regards to my *son's* discharge" (8259)
"towards my *Boys* discharge" (8104)
"arrange for *Earl* discharge" (8199)
"he is his *sisters* support" (8028)

In the Vulgar English materials no examples occurred of the *-'s* form of the descriptive genitive of measure. The uninflected form of the noun indicating the extent appeared in all instances.[11] This was also true of the nouns standing before the gerund—the English verbal in *-ing*. No instances of this construction occurred with the genitive form ending in *-'s*. On the other hand, as in Standard English, there were many examples of the uninflected noun in this position.

[10] This absolute use of the genitive form implying a house or place did not occur in the Standard English materials, nor did the so-called "double" genitive occur in the Vulgar English letters.

[11] See above, Chapter V, page 43.

"to tell him of his *sister and brother* dying" (8149)
"a letter telling me about this *man* saying he was his father" (8033)
"to write you about my *son* getting out of the army" (8016)
"they agreed With all I rote you before Except the *Mother* signing" (8005)
"on account of their *father* being sick" (8016)
"Sorry to hear of *Private M——* being injured" (8167)
"on account of his *Mother* being very ill" (8288)

A summary of the significant facts concerning the genitive inflection of nouns will be postponed until the matters concerning the genitive forms of pronouns can be set forth, in order that it may be possible to bring together in a single view the important matters of both.

B. The Genitive Forms of Pronouns

Although the genitive inflection of nouns has been almost completely displaced by the periphrastic genitive with *of* (4.3 per cent of inflected genitive against 95 per cent of periphrastic genitive), the genitive inflections of pronouns still persist with little decrease. As a matter of fact, in the letters of Standard English (Group I) there were 682 instances of the genitive forms of the pronouns against twelve instances of the pronouns with *of,* 98.3 per cent of genitive forms and but 1.7 per cent of pronouns with *of.* Of these twelve instances of the pronouns with *of* only one might possibly have had the inflected genitive form in Present-day English and this was not one of the so-called personal pronouns.

"The boy no doubt secured the services *of some one* falsely representing herself as his sister" (8234)

All the others were in constructions which in Present-day English invariably take the *of* function word.

"She is dependent upon him to take care *of her*" (8234)
"He feels he should be with her and take care *of her*" (8095)
"People who know the father do not think a great deal *of him* (8002)
"The man's parents are in need *of him* very much" (8183)
"I take pleasure in saying *of him* that he is a man of high moral character" (9039)
"getting the benefit *of it* part of the way" (9016)
"He could order part *of it* turned over to the new hospital" (9002)
"has made mistakes . . . many *of them*" (8296)
"and both *of them* have a personal knowledge of ——'s age" (8267)

"special orders . . . a copy *of which* is enclosed" (9058)
"some service . . . *of which* I have no definite record" (9055)

The situation in Vulgar English (Group III) parallels completely that in Standard English (Group I) although there is a slightly larger (but insignificant) proportion of the pronouns with *of* in Vulgar English. There were 718 instances of the genitive inflections of pronouns against thirty one instances of the pronouns with *of*, or 95.5 per cent of genitive forms and but 4.5 per cent of pronouns with *of*. All of these thirty one instances occurred in constructions which in Present-day English invariably take the *of* function word.

Typical examples are

"help take care *of them*" (8179) [12]
"i havent herd *of him*" (8313) [13]
"if you will kindly think *of me*" (8187)
"I am very much in need *of him* at home" (8141)
"I am now asking *of you*" (8235) [14]
"there is three *of us*" (8251) [15]
"it [his picture] all i hav *of him*" (8313)
"both *of them* cannot go" (8272)
"able to pay for all *of it*" (8072)
"I need my son's help now most *of all*" (8235)
"that is the worst *of all*" (8281)
"we have had proof *of this* in recent years" (8063)
"I cant see anyway out *of it*" (8005)
"What will become *of me*" (8219)
"it would be a Human act *of you*" (8187)
"i hope it make a man *of him*" (8097)
"old enough to know the meaning *of it*" (8067)

With pronouns the genitive forms both in Standard English and in Vulgar English appear, from this evidence, to have successfully resisted the pull of the periphrastic pattern which has almost completely displaced the inflected genitive forms of nouns.[16] In these

[12] Other examples of this construction with *me, us, them*, etc., occur in 8084, 8288, 8155, 8225, 8127.

[13] Other examples in 8281, 8049, 8030.

[14] Other examples in 8112, 8155, 8187, 8253.

[15] Other examples of this partitive use are in 8187, 8313.

[16] *Neuter* pronouns in the genitive form are very rare. In the materials here, only 1.6 per cent of the total number of genitive pronouns in Standard English were the neuter pronoun; in the Vulgar English letters only two instances of the neuter appeared out of a total of 718 genitive pronouns.

genitive forms of pronouns there have been comparatively few changes other than phonetic ones throughout the history of the English language.

The forms *my,*[17] *our, your,*[18] *his, her, whose*[19] are all historical forms from the early period of English. *Their* replaced the historical *her* for the genitive plural of the third personal pronoun during the fifteenth century, and *its*[20] was created near the close of the sixteenth century. Until the fourteenth century the same forms were used whether the genitive appeared before a noun or absolutely.

"*Our Liturgie* is the more ancient, and *our Church* the more noble."
"*Our* is the more ancient Liturgie, and *our* the more noble Church."[21]

In fact, *our, your, their* continued as absolute forms to the seventeenth century. But beginning in the fourteenth century there was an increasing use of a new form to distinguish the two uses of the genitive in pronouns. In the first and second persons *mine* and *thine* continued to be used absolutely, after *my* and *thy* were well established. It was natural, therefore, that *ourn, yourn, hern,* etc., after the pattern of *mine* and *thine,* should be created and for a time compete with *ours, yours, hers,* etc., formed on the pattern of the *s* genitive of nouns.[22] *Ourn* and *yourn* appeared in Wycliffe; *hern* appeared earlier in the fourteenth century; and *hisn* appeared in the fifteenth century. *His* and *its,* ending as they do in *s,* have not de-

[17] With loss of *n* from *mine.*

[18] Used as singular as well as plural since the sixteenth century.

[19] *Whose* in its earliest history served as the genitive for all three genders—masculine, feminine and neuter. It still continues for all three although there is some pressure to substitute *of which* in the case of neuter nouns.

[20] The neuter form of the genitive of the third personal pronoun was originally identical with that of the masculine *his.* The neuter genitive *his* continued through the sixteenth century and is the form used in the 1611 Bible. A neuter genitive, *it,* developed in the fourteenth century and lasted to the early seventeenth century. This genitive *it* appears in Shakspere and once in the 1611 Bible (Lev. 25:5). In the 1660 Bible this *it* was changed to *its. Its,* originally written *it's,* was formed upon the pattern of the *s*-genitive of nouns and became the common form during the seventeenth century. See page 81, concerning *ours, yours, hers, theirs.*

[21] "Smectymnuus," *Vindication of the Answer* (1641), ii, 38.

[22] Formed as they are on the model of the genitive inflection of nouns it would be logical to assume that all these forms, *ours, yours, hers, theirs,* as well as *its,* should use the apostrophe before the *s.* The objection frequently offered that our present practice is necessary to distinguish between the contraction of "it is" and the possessive "its" cannot be valid. Certainly there is no confusion in speech where the apostrophe sign does not function. Nor is there any in the case of nouns in which the apostrophe appears in both contractions and possessive forms. ("The *man's* been singing." "The *man's* hat hangs on the door.") In the letters of Standard English *it's* (with apostrophe) sometimes appeared, as in "that my name be placed in *it's* proper place." (9022)

veloped separate forms for the absolute use although Wycliffe used *hisis*.

As a matter of fact, however, if the materials examined here are typical, the use of the absolute forms is very little indeed.[23] In Standard English there appeared the following instances:

TABLE V

absolute		*attributive*	
mine	6	my	241
ours	1	our	14
yours	0 [24]	your	30
theirs	0	her	154
his	0	their	22
its	0	his	202
hers	0	its	8
		whose	4

In Vulgar English (Group III) the situation is practically identical.

TABLE VI

absolute		*attributive*	
mine	3	my	313
ours	0	our	30
yours	3	your	35
hers	0	her	26
theirs	0	their	3
its	0	his	303
		its	2

No examples occurred in the materials here of *ourn, yourn, hern, theirn, hisn*.

One last matter concerning form needs comment before passing to a statement of the kinds of genitive expressed by these pronoun

[23] Just as in the case of nouns (see above page 76) there is some use of the so-called "double" genitive with pronouns. Only one example occurred in Group III (Vulgar English); two were in Group I (Standard English), and two in Group II (Common English).

From Group I "a former tutor *of mine*" (9012)
"This communication *of mine*" (9056)
From Group II "So long as this great nation *of ours* lives" (8066)
"This brother *of mine*" (8051)
From Group III "in regard to a brother *of mine* who ran away" (8165)

[24] The formula *yours truly* with its variations, which appears at the close of the letters, was not included in the figures.

forms. In Middle English the dative-accusative forms of the pronouns were most frequent with *self*. From the fourteenth century on, the tendency has been to regard *self* as a noun and therefore to use the genitive form of a preceding pronoun, thus *myself,*[25] *ourselves,*[26] (*thyself*), *yourself, yourselves.*[27] *Herself* is an ambiguous form and *itself* has sometimes been taken (eighteenth century especially) as *its* plus *self*. If any word intervenes between the pronoun and *self, its* is used, as "its own self." *Himself* and *themselves* still cling to the older dative-accusative forms of the pronouns against the pressure of the more regular *hisself* and *theirselves*. As in the case of *it,* when words intervene between the pronoun and *self, his* and *their* are used, as in "his very self" and "their own selves." In the materials here examined there were but very few instances of these words and there seems to be little difference between the three groups. In Group III, Vulgar English, appeared two instances of *hisself*.

"he liyed his self in . . ." (8045)
"he named his Self R——" (8151)

There were, however, in Group III four instances of *himself*. The number of instances of each of these words was as follows: [28]

TABLE VII

	Group I	*Group II*	*Group III*
myself	21	20	11
ourselves	0	0	0
yourself	2	0	4
yourselves	0	0	0
herself	6	1	0
itself	2	0	0
himself	6	2	4
themselves	0	0	0

In the pronouns the uses of the genitive parallel those of the nouns in most respects. In the materials of Standard English there were the following:

[25] *Meself* occurs in literature as late as the sixteenth century.
[26] Chaucer uses *us selven*.
[27] This unmistakable plural developed in the sixteenth century.
[28] The nature of the material would be likely to limit the use of the plurals.

a. The Possessive Genitive—40%

"*his* name has been overlooked" (9022)
"*his* wife" (9030)
"which he held in *his* hand" (9007)
"*your* office" (9010)
"a sister *whose* husband is in" (8196)
"on *my* victory medal" (9018)
"in driving *my* car" (9064)

b. The Subjective Genitive—21%

"regarding *his* charges that" (8144)
"that *his* resignation was very reluctantly accepted" (9013)
"hearing of *his* disappearance" (8076)
"subsequent to *my* departure" (9056)
"*My* choice of a university" (9050)
"Before *my* entry into the army" (9050)
"*my* resignation from the Public Health Service" (9005)
"and *their* appeal comes to me" (8073)
"they should file *their* claims for" (9012)
"to ask *your* help" (9018)
"that this request may receive *your* favorable consideration" (9062)
"Replying to *your* inquiry of July 2nd" (8137)
"in *her* disregard of Belgium's neutrality" (9017)
"*Its* affect was far reaching" (9012)

c. The Objective Genitive—10%

"He was expecting *his discharge*" (8075)
"In the event of *my promotion*" (9022)
"to the date of *my examination*" (9022)
"Under *my present assignment*" (9062)
"did not contribute to *her support*" (8240)
"the type of *her employment* has been" (8240)
"immediately upon *its receipt*" (8299)
"in cutting timber for *their support*" (8180)
"to obtain the release of . . . from . . . in *whose service* he now is" (8273)

d. The Genitive of Origin—3%

"According to *her account*" (8240)
"her attention to *our first letter*" (8299)
"with reference to *your wire*" (9000)
"*your reports* of change" (9019)

e. The Genitive of Association, Participation, etc.—2.2%

"I have been *their family physician*" (8144) (8260)
"an affidavit from her *physician*" (8240)
"We will rejoice if the young man is honored by *your officers*" (8060)

"Until recently *our chief of staff* had some ideas with respect to . . ." (9000)
"Due to mistake either by *my banker* or myself" (9057)
"Some of *his relatives*" (8076)
"it being *my former school*" (9050)
"During *my college course*" (9058)
"In his school life he was a figure in *his classes*" (9038)

f. Some miscellaneous genitives not included in the groups named above
"a man of *his years*" (9039)
"In *her earlier years* she was employed" (8095)
"they would send him the money when *his year* of enlistment was up" (8076)
"I am not sure of *his present location*" (8075)
"to return to *my proper station*" (9050) (9036) (9052) (9053) (9057) (9029)
"a change in *my address*" (9042)
"had worked *his way* out west" (8142)
"was then on *his way* to" (8076)
"for which *his past experience* had fully equipped him" (9013)
"to take care of *her funeral expenses*" (8095)
"doing *his best* to bring honor to his" (8060) (9033)

It was clear from the evidence given on pages 76, 77, and 78 above that the use of the inflected genitive form of nouns is not the normal practice before gerunds in Standard English. Only one example occurred in all our material. On the other hand, there was an overwhelming number of cases with the uninflected noun form (singular) before such gerunds in *-ing*. In the case of pronouns, however, the situation appears to be different. Fifty two per cent of the cases in Standard English have the genitive form of the pronoun before the verbal and but 48 per cent have the dative-accusative form.

Examples of the genitive form are

"in the event of *my being assigned* to" (9043)
"correspondence concerning *my taking* an examination" (9008)
"As to *my being* on the eligible list" (9042)
"nothing to indicate *my having* received a citation" (9018)
"I have no knowledge of *my having* any chronic disease" (9026)
"She had given her consent to *his entering* the army" (8144)
"Have you known of *his* ever *being* guilty of anything that . . ." (7093)
"Because of *his being* a married man" (6416)

"concerning the matter of *your having* consulted certain notes that were of assistance to you" (7091)
"How did you come to tell . . . of *your having* done this?" (7091)
"the report about *his having* such a fight" (7094)
"we knew nothing of *his being* in . . ." (6417)

Examples of the dative-accusative form of the pronoun in this construction are

"conditions are such as would justify *you taking* favorable action" (7089)
"certain things were done without *you being* consulted" (7092)
"I have not heard any complaints about *him* not *being* punctual" (7077)
"the possibility of *them being delayed* until that hour and consequently of *them arriving* at R—— toward midnight" (7086)
"That led to *me being questioned* with regard to his efficiency" (7088)
"I never heard of *him working* hard" (7087)
"My choice of the University of . . . is made because of *it being* my former school" (9050)
"There is no doubt about *him being married*" (8130)

The Vulgar English uses of the genitive pronouns differ very little from those of Standard English.

TYPICAL EXAMPLES OF GENITIVE PRONOUNS IN VULGAR ENGLISH

a. Possessive Genitives—59%

"I am crippled in *my limbs*" (8201)
"get this boy back or break up *my home*" (8152)
"came to *my house*" (8005)
"help Save *Our Crops*" (8253)
"clerk in *her Grocerie store*" (8251)
"all of *my money* has been spent" (8224)
"he sine *his neam*" (8112)
"he is *my youngest boy*" (8067)

b. Subjective Genitives—11.3%

"upon *my return* home" (8251)
"it is *my earnest wish*" (8069)
"and kept up *his payments*" (8080)
"to get along with out *his care*" (8312)
"I need *his help*" (8280)
"nead *his suppord* to help to" (8264)
"to make amends for *his error*" (8152)
"meets with *your approval*" (8231)

c. Objective Genitives—4.4%

"for he is *my only Suport*" (8312)
"the place of *my employment* is shut down" (8079)
"He is *my only help* on the farm" (8021)
"if my son got *his release*" (8233)
"we therefore wish *his discharge*" (8067)
"or have *his sentence* remitted" (8052)
"I am *her lone support*" (8028)

d. Genitive of Origin—4.3%

"In *my first letter*" (8274)
"if *their testimony* will do" (8242)
"*his answer* was that" (8038)
"to send *my petition* to" (8157)

e. Genitive of Association, Participation—3%

"I wrote *his captain*" (8038)
"both of *his bosses* have been to see me" (8080)
"where I was apointed *his gardine*" (8025)
"he and a couple of *his class-mates*" (8251)
"sent back to *his outfit*" (8230)
"an affadavitt from *our Justice*" (8101)
"from *your recruiting officer*" (8025)
"now *My Dr and nurse* are both diad" (8242)
"*my Lawyer* advised me to" (8251)

f. Some miscellaneous genitives not included in the groups above

"will give him a clean white discharge for *his Christmas*" (8038)
"this would work out for *our future* better" (8094)
"5 yr's is *his limit* to live" (8153)
"this was *his second time* to leave home" (8218)
"he would do *his best*" (8152)
"pleas Sir for *my sake* do let him out" (8204)
"During *my ten years* in the" (8057)
"*My debts* are at a standstill" (8079)
"to pay *our Grocery Bill*" (8052)
"to work *his way* up" (8288)
"pray for the best to come *his way* some day" (8038)
"left here on *his way* back there" (8117)
"i am not able to pay *his way* here" (8005) (8097)
"set me back with *my sickness*" (8281)
"nobody nows when *my time* will come to die" (8288)
"to assist me in *my last days*" (8094)
"he will serve *his time*" (8288)
"insted of *my correct date of birth*" (8070)
"he lied about *his age*" (8288)
"on account of *his minority*" (8173)

"you can get *his Birth date* from" (8280)
"Rite to me and Send me *your Pictuer*" (8181)
"*his pictures* show that he is very thin" (8250)
"I can not find *his Baptismal certificate*" (8000)

In respect to the form of the pronoun (whether genitive or dative-accusative) used before the verbal in *-ing,* the Vulgar English materials do not differ greatly from those of Standard English except for the fact that the construction as a whole appears much less frequently in Vulgar English. Only ten instances were found. Of these, three had the possessive form of the pronoun and seven the dative-accusative form.

The three instances are

"We knew of *his being* in the army" (8067)
"no doubt as to *his being* my son" (8067)
"and all work out soon for *his coming* to me" (8094)

The seven instances are

"I object to *him being* in millitery service" (8000)
"he went away without *me knowing*" (8040)
"without *us knowing* anything about it" (8018)
"he enlisted as a single man without *me knowing it*" (8012)
"if there is any grounds of *him getting* out" (8037)
"about *you not getting* our letters" (8087)
"refused to keep him any longer without *him paying* board" (8072)

In the facts concerning the genitive forms of nouns and pronouns as here displayed a few matters deserve especial notice by way of a summary.

1. Although the periphrastic genitive with the function word *of* has almost completely displaced the inflectional genitive form of *nouns* (95.7 per cent of the periphrastic genitive with *of* against 4.3 per cent of inflected genitive forms), in the *pronouns* the inflectional genitive form still predominates overwhelmingly (1.6 per cent of the periphrastic with *of,* against 98.4 per cent of inflected genitive forms). There is no essential difference between Standard English and Vulgar English in this respect.

2. The usual rule of the handbooks that the genitive case form of substantives must be used before verbals in *-ing* is certainly not a complete and accurate statement of the practice of the English language. In the case of nouns the usage of Standard English is overwhelmingly that of the uninflected form before this verbal. In the

case of pronouns the usage of Standard English as represented here is divided approximately half and half between the genitive form and the dative-accusative form. The letters of Vulgar English show much the same situation, although there is slightly less (not a significant difference) use of the genitive form.

3. Although the increasing use of the periphrastic genitive with *of* has had very little effect upon the use of pronouns with a genitive inflection, nevertheless there is very little difference between nouns and pronouns in the kinds of uses for which the genitive form is employed. In both nouns and pronouns about 40 per cent of the instances are genitives of possession, 20 per cent subjective genitives, 10 per cent objective genitives, 5 per cent genitives of origin, and 15 per cent a miscellaneous group in which the relation between the genitive and the noun it modifies is very hard to describe and classify. Again there seems to be no difference in this respect between Standard English and Vulgar English.

4. In view of the fact that less than half of all the instances in which the genitive form is used can be looked upon as *possessive,* even if the word *possessive* is interpreted very broadly, it seems not only inaccurate but very undesirable to call the genitive form "the possessive case."

5. There seems to be no point in the use of the genitive forms in which there is any clear difference in use between the practices of Standard English and those of Vulgar English sufficient to create the connotations of a class dialect, except in the matter of the *self* pronouns. Vulgar English uses *hisself* and *theirselves* along with *himself* and *themselves.*

II. THE DATIVE-ACCUSATIVE FORMS

The six case distinctive dative-accusative forms of pronouns (*me, us, him, them, her, whom*) are all that is left of the many distinctive dative *and* accusative forms that existed in Old English. In the nouns the dative was a distinctive form maintained clearly throughout the Old English period. Although the accusative of the nouns was most frequently like the nominative and therefore not a distinctive form in itself, both the adjectives and the definite articles used with these nouns had a clear accusative form so that in a great many situations inflectional evidence distinguished both datives and accusatives. With the loss of these inflectional forms during the Middle English period, however, the nouns in Modern English have no forms either in themselves or in the articles and adjectives used with them to indicate dative or accusative relationships. These relationships of the nouns are now expressed by the other two grammatical devices which Present-day English uses, namely, word order and function words.

The pronouns—the personal pronouns and the relative-interrogative *who*—had at least eight forms [29] for the dative and seven different forms for the accusative in Old English. Even in Old English times, however, the separate forms for the accusative of the pronouns of the first and second persons (*mec, þec, usic, eowic*) were almost completely displaced by the dative forms (*me, þe, us, eow*). By the end of the thirteenth century *hine,* the accusative masculine pronoun of the third person, was displaced by the dative *him* and in parallel fashion the accusative of the feminine pronoun, *hi* or *heo,* was largely displaced by the dative form *her*(*e*), and the accusative *hwone* by the dative *hwom* (*whom*). The neuter dative *him* as distinct from the nominative and accusative *it* continued to the end of the sixteenth century. In the seventeenth century the dative-accusative of the second person pronoun *you* displaced the nominative *ye*. As a result of these changes there remain in English only six forms (*me, us, him, them, her, whom*) to distinguish the dative or the accusative from the nominative, and in these there is no distinction between the dative and the accusative form. It is obvious that the grammatical ideas formerly expressed by the inflections for the dative and for the accusative must now be expressed by other means. The six case forms of these pronouns in their modern use do not function in the conveying of grammatical ideas; that is, where they are used, the expression of the dative or accusative relationship does not depend upon the form of the pronoun; they simply *accompany* the other grammatical devices that do function. In the sentence "The man gave the book to the boy" the relationship of *boy* is expressed by the function word *to,* and in the sentence "The man gave the boy the book" the relationship of *boy* is indicated by word order. In similar fashion in the sentences "The man gave the book to him" and "The man gave him the book" the relationship of *him* is expressed in the one sentence by the function word *to* and in the other by word order. It is not necessary that the pronoun have a distinct form to display its relationship. The dative-accusative form which it has in these situations is simply an accompaniment (a

[29] I have not included here the forms for the dual number.

remnant of an older method of showing this relationship) of the newer grammatical devices employed here. A sentence such as "Him and me hit the man" would normally be interpreted in accord with the word order rather than in accord with the case forms.

The growing importance of word order as a grammatical device to show the relationship between substantive and verb since the early fifteenth century has had an important effect upon the use of these six dative-accusative forms. Certain positions in the English sentence have come to be felt as "subject" territory, others as "object" territory and the forms of the words in each territory are *pressed to adjust themselves to the character of that territory.* The dative-accusative forms with no real function of their own but used only as an accompaniment of other devices offer very little resistance [30] to the pressures of word order.

Our Modern English "I was given a book" furnishes a good illustration of the pressure of word order. The Old English "Me waes gegiefen an boc," with the dative pronoun standing first, was a common construction. It was only after word order had become a vigorous device for the showing of grammatical relationships that the dative *me* standing in "subject" territory was changed to the nominative *I*. Ever since the sixteenth century this new construction has been normal English practice in spite of the protests of certain grammarians.[31] The dative with impersonal verbs which appeared frequently in Old and Middle English also shows the pressure of word order as these constructions were replaced by the nominative form of the pronoun and the personal verb.[32] *Him likode* became *He liked. Me greues* became *I grieve.* Altogether it is only in the few places where the pressures of word order conflict with the inertia of an older practice that problems arise concerning the use of these case forms of pronouns. In nearly all situations the older practice concerning the inflections (similar to that of Latin) agrees with the newer pressures of word order.[33]

[30] The only real resistance comes from the efforts of schools to make Modern English conform to the rules of a Latin grammar. For a more complete discussion of the rise of word order as a grammatical device see below, Chapter X.

[31] See the forty three quotations in Thomas R. Lounsbury, *The Standard of Usage in English* (New York, Harper & Bros., 1908), pp. 182–186.

[32] See the dissertation by Willem van der Gaaf, *The Transition from Impersonal to Personal in Middle English* (Hilversum, 1904).

[33] In those few situations in which it does not, the attempt of the schools to enforce a usage contrary to the pressures of word order seems to introduce considerable

The two situations in which the pressures of word order conflict with the older practice in the use of the pronoun inflections are (*a*) the personal pronouns as predicatives and (*b*) the interrogative and the relative *who* as object. The predicatives stand in "object" territory and personal pronouns so used tend therefore to take the dative-accusative form. As an interrogative, *who* usually stands in "subject" territory and tends therefore to discard the dative-accusative form even though the objective relationship remains.

The history of the first of these constructions reveals a series of changes connected with the pressures of word order.[34] In Old English the construction as it appears in Matthew 14:27 "Habbað geleafan, *ic hyt eom*" is normal. In this the *ic* (I) is the subject which determines the form of the verb *eom* (am), and *hyt* (it) also precedes the verb. In Middle English of the time of Chaucer the pronoun *I* (*thou, he, we,* etc.) normally appears after the verb and *it* before the verb as in "Wostow nought wel that *it am I*" (*Chaucer,* ed. Skeat, 214, 588). Here again the *I* still dominates the verb *am* as subject. By the latter part of the fifteenth century, however, the pressure of word order is such that the *it* which stands in "subject" territory is so much felt as the subject that the verb form is made to agree with it, as in "*It is I* that am here in your syth" (*Coventry Mysteries,* 291). By the time of Shakspere the pronoun that stands in "object" territory begins to show the pressure of word order in such examples as the following: "Sir Andrew. *That's me.* I warrant you." (*Twelfth Night,* II, 5, 87); "*'Tis thee,* myself, that for myself I praise." (Shakspere, Sonnet LXII.) From the sixteenth century to the present there has been considerable diversity of usage in the matter of the inflectional forms of these pronouns in predicative positions with unconscious colloquial practice yielding to the pressure of word order.[35]

---

confusion of practice. See Isabel Sears and Amelia Diebel, "A Study of the Common Mistakes in Pupils' Oral English," *Elementary School Journal,* Vol. 17, September, 1916, pp. 44–54. These authors found that the case forms of pronouns were used incorrectly more frequently in Grade VIII than in the lower grades and they raise the following question: "Is the present teaching of pronouns leading to a more confused state of mind in the eighth-grade child than existed when he was in the third grade and was entirely unconscious of the rules of grammar governing the use of such words?" (p. 51.)

[34] See the examples quoted by C. Alphonso Smith in *Studies in English Syntax,* pp. 77–86.

[35] It should be noted here that such an expression as "It is me" or "It is I" is primarily a matter of colloquial English. The situations which call for its use are

The actual facts of the use of the dative-accusative forms of the pronouns in the Standard English materials examined for this study are as follows:

a. After Prepositions—47.5%

These pronoun forms appeared after *to* and *for* most frequently (44 per cent of the instances). The figures for their use with other prepositions are as follows: *with*, 17.2%; *by*, 12.5%; *of*, 9.3%; *from*, 6.2%; *on*, 3.0%; *upon*, 2.4%; and *after*, *against*, *between*, *behind*, *without*, all together, 5.4%

b. After Verbs as Direct Object—26.6%

"Could assist *him*" (8240)
"he can support *her*" (8189)
"has called to see *me*" (9011)
"carelessly omitted *them*" (9040)
"to have *him* here" (8174)

c. After Verbs as Indirect Object (by position)—18.6%

"Nor does he send *her* any money" (8144)
"This error has caused *me* trouble" (8144)
"A letter from . . . informs *me* that there is no record of my service" (9055)
"have afforded *him* opportunities" (9023)
"we again wrote *her* a letter" (8299)

d. After Certain Verbs and Followed by Infinitives—7.3%

"They want *him* to come home" (8144)
"tried to get *him* to enlist" (8064)
"and found *them* to be suffering" (8266)
"so as to allow *me* to take leave" (9061)
"has asked *us* to write" (8189)

Altogether in the four groups just indicated, with a few miscellaneous cases of *whom* (to be discussed later), there appeared in the letters of Standard English 285 instances of the six dative-accusative forms. In the letters of Vulgar English there appeared two and one third times as many instances in approximately the same quantity of writing. There were in all 662 instances distributed as follows:

a. After Prepositions—26.3%

The prepositions appearing most frequently are *to* and *for;* together

conversation situations. Formal literary circumstances furnish practically no occasions for use of the construction; it is written only when there is an attempt to reproduce conversation.

they make 48.2% of the instances. The figures for the other prepositions are as follows: *from,* 18.2%; *with,* 6.8%; *on,* 3.2%; and *after, against, besides, by, near, over, upon, without,* all together, 6.3%.

b. After Verbs as Direct Object—47.7%
"he went to . . . and left *me*" (8048)
"I kneed *him* here" (8187) (8277)
"able to buy *him* out" (8187)
"we have to Doctor *her* all the time" (8028)
"towards supporting *us*" (8127)

c. After Verbs as Indirect Object (by position)—9.7%
"Please Write *Me* the amount" (8249)
"please tell *me* the right place" (8147)
"about getting *me* a discharge" (8030)
"bring *him* some clothes" (8290)
"work that will pay *him* a wage" (8251)

d. After Certain Verbs and Followed by Infinitives—15.2%
"begging *me* to let him stay" (8288)
"help *us* to get located" (8094)
"you would find *him* not to be very able bodied" (8117)
"and have *him* write to me" (8116)
"and perswaid *him* to join the army" (8045)

The figures here given show no significant difference between Standard English and Vulgar English with the possible exception of the fact that the Standard English materials have proportionally nearly twice as many instances of these pronouns used as indirect objects (by position) as do the materials of Vulgar English. In compensation the numbers of the dative-accusative forms with *to* and *for* are, in Vulgar English, distinctly higher. It would seem, therefore, that Vulgar English tends to use the function word method of indicating the indirect object relationship rather than the word order method.

The figures do show, however, that, in both Standard English and in Vulgar English, practically *all* the dative-accusative forms occur in positions that are normally "objective" territory. In the case of the interrogative *who* in nearly all situations and in the case of the relative *who* in some situations [36] the position of the word

[36] A relative immediately after a preposition in all cases had the dative-accusative form both in the Standard English and in the Vulgar English materials.
Examples are
"To all *with whom* he may come in contact" (9038)
"My wife *for whom* I am maintaining a place of abode" (9030)
"the concern *by whom* her son was employed" (8095)

must necessarily be in "subjective" territory. The pressure is generally, therefore, toward the use of the nominative rather than the dative-accusative form. This tendency reaches back to the Early Modern English period, as the following quotations from Shakspere demonstrate:

"O Lord, sir, *who* do you mean?" *1 Henry IV,* II, iv, 81.
"Here comes my servant Travers, *who* I sent on Tuesday last to listen after news." *2 Henry IV,* I, i, 28.
"you have oft inquired after the shepherd that complained of love, *Who* you saw sitting by me on the turf." *As You Like It,* III, iv, 50.

In the materials of Standard English *who* is the usual form of the interrogative. Examples are

"*Who* do you refer to as witness?" (7542)
"*Who* did you apply to for enlistment?" (7425)

No examples were found in which the *whom* was used as an interrogative.

In the case of the relative as "object" about one third of the instances appeared with *who* and two thirds with *whom.*

Examples of *who* are

"his brother and his brother's wife were coming with the girl *who* he was to marry" (7401)
"and others *who* I do not know the present address of" (9027)
"It has seldom been my pleasure to know a young man more efficient or *who* I felt to be better qualified for" (7403)

Examples of *whom* are

"will pay you or anyone *whom* you direct us to pay it to" (5113)
"leaving a wife behind *whom* he was deserting without support" (8076)
"I have one child *whom* I have not seen during that time" (7406)
"Were all the gentlemen *whom* you have mentioned engaged in the game?" (7405)

There appeared in the Standard English materials some uses of *whom* which should probably be looked upon as hyperurbanisms.[37]

"the young man *about whom* I spoke" (7420)
"this man *with whom* they went away" (7421)
"responsible for the security of all prisoners no matter *by whom* they are housed" (7417)

[37] See also discussions by Otto Jespersen in *Philosophy of Grammar* (New York, Henry Holt and Co., 1924) pp. 349–351.

"Would you kindly let me know *whom* should be notified in case of accident" (8075)
"There was one man's son in this country *whom* the majority believed would never be sent into service" (7404)
"A very nice woman *whom* we think is putting . . ." (8002)
"I desire to communicate with the following officers *whom* I understand are serving with . . ." (7402)

The Vulgar English materials contained a few uses of these dative-accusative forms which differed from any of those found in Standard English.

1. In clear "subjective" territory, a use which never seems to be found in Standard English

"After 13 days *him* and this man that was with him was found . . ." (8026)
"My son . . . *whom* is a soldier at that Post" (8029)

2. As "disjunctives," a use much more frequent in speech than in writing

"I am nearly 50 years old with 5 little ones to support and *me* with bothe knees all to Pieces with Rheumatism" (8187)
"He is so far away and *me* his mother cant see him" (8020)

The chief facts concerning the use of the six dative-accusative forms of the pronouns as shown in the materials examined here are as follows:

1. Practically all of the 947 instances of the dative-accusative forms of the pronouns occur *in positions that are normally "objective" territory.*

2. Only one instance appeared here of the personal pronouns as predicatives—a demonstration of the fact that only conversation situations provide the circumstances for the use of such expressions as *It is me* (*I*) where position would make a pressure for the dative-accusative form.

3. Every instance of the interrogative pronoun appeared with the form *who,* the nominative rather than the dative-accusative form. The "subjective" territory in which the interrogative stands seemed to have more force in determining the form than the *"objective" relationship* of the word. Expressions such as *"Who* do you refer to" are typical of Standard English.

4. In the case of the relative pronoun about one third of the cases in *"objective" relationship* appeared as *who* and two thirds as *whom.*

In addition, in the Standard English letters there were frequent instances of a "hyper-correct" *whom* in situations of a *"subjective" relationship*. Such expressions as "the girl *who* he was to marry" are not limited to Vulgar English.

5. The use of the dative-accusative forms in subjective relationship and in clear subjective territory was found in the materials of Vulgar English only.

6. The use of the dative-accusative forms as "disjunctives" appeared only in the writings of the Vulgar English group.

III. THE INFLECTION FOR COMPARISON

Most adjectives and adverbs which have meanings permitting comparison have some formal means (either inflection or function word) to indicate the comparative and the superlative degrees as distinct from the so-called "positive" degree. For this grammatical idea in the older stages of the language, inflection was the chief device. In Present-day English, inflection still persists but has given way to a very great extent to the use of function words—chiefly the particular words *more* and *most*.

The inflectional pattern for comparison in Present-day English consists of the endings *-er* for the comparative and *-est* for the superlative added to the simple or "positive" form of the adjective or adverb, as *high, high-er, high-est; cold, cold-er, cold-est; wide, wid-er, wid-est.*[38] There are, however, remnants of older forms that constitute exceptions to the inflectional pattern just indicated. Some of these exceptions are (*a*) forms preserving the umlauted vowel of the comparative and superlative, as *elder, eldest;* (*b*) forms from a different root to supply the lack of a regular comparative or superlative, as *good* or *well, better, best; bad(ly)* or *evil* or *ill, worse, worst; little, less* or *lesser, least; much* or *many, more, most; far, further* or *farther, furthest* or *farthest;* (*c*) defective or incomplete series, as *rather* and *next.*

One type of apparent inflection for comparison, differing from the pattern, needs especial comment. Words like *foremost, innermost, outermost, nethermost, eastermost, topmost* with such parallels as *innermore, outermore, nethermore* seem to furnish evidence for a suffix *-most* for the superlative degree and a suffix *-more* for the comparative degree, and for Present-day English these words

[38] In such words as *long* there is, of course, a phonetic adjustment in the inflected forms which does not show itself in the spelling, as, *long* [lɔŋ], *longer* [lɔŋgr̩].

have a limited use of this kind. Historically, however, this suffix *-most* is a popular etymologizing of the older *-mest* a double superlative with *-m-* and *-est*. The suffix *-more* was later used for the comparative in some similar situations on the analogy of *-most* for the superlative.

This development of a suffix *-most* and a parallel suffix *-more* in English had the support of the use of the adverbs of degree, *more* and *most* with such adjectives, notably participles, as did not admit of inflection for comparison. This use appeared in Early Middle English, and gradually these words *more* and *most* became function words of comparison that tended to displace the inflections. In Late Middle English and especially in Early Modern English the frequent use of *more* and *most* with inflected adjectives and adverbs in *-er* and *-est* seems to be evidence for the fact that these words were not felt as function words of comparison equivalent to the inflections and therefore not to be used with them, until the eighteenth century.

The first objection to using *more* and *most* with words having the *-er* and *-est* inflections as Shakspere rather frequently did [39] appeared in Robert Lowth's *Short Introduction to English Grammar* [40] (1762), and was repeated in Charles Coote's *Elements of English Grammar* [41] (1788), and in Lindley Murray's *English*

[39] The following uses by Shakspere of *more* and *most* together with words having the *-er* or *-est* inflections must not, therefore, be taken as instances of "double" comparison.

"*This* was the *most unkindest* cut of all" (*Julius Caesar,* III, ii, 187).
"A wall'd town is *more worthier* than a village" (*As You Like It,* III, iii, 59).
"I am *more better* than Prospero" (*Tempest,* I, ii, 19).
"*more corrupter* ends" (*Lear,* III, iii, 64).
"the most patient man in loss, the *most coldest* that ever turned up ace" (*Cymbeline,* II, iii, 3).
"My sister may receive it much *more worse*" (*Lear,* II, ii, 59).
"Am fallen out with my *more headier* will" (*Lear,* II, iv, 111).
"*More harder* than the stones" (*Lear,* III, iii, 64).

[40] Pages 27, 28, footnote 4, Section, *Adjective.*

"Double comparatives and superlatives are improper:
'The Duke of Milan, and his *more braver* daughter could controul thee' (Shakespear, *Tempest.*)
'After the *most straitest* sect of our religion I lived a Pharisee.'' (Acts xxvi. 5.)

. . . . .

"The double superlative *most highest* is a phrase peculiar to the old vulgar translation of the Psalms; where it acquires a singular propriety from the subject to which it is applied, the Supreme Being, who is *higher than the highest.*"

[41] Page 79, footnote (*e*).

" 'His *more braver* daughter.' Shakespeare's *Tempest.*
'Forasmuch as she saw the cardinal *more readier* to depart than the remnant;

Grammar [42] (1795). Since the eighteenth century the inflectional forms *-er* and *-est* have tended to give place to the use of the competing function words.[43] In the materials examined here for Standard English 56.4 per cent of the comparatives appeared with the inflectional *-er* as against 43.6 per cent with the function word. Of the superlatives, 47 per cent appeared with the inflectional *-est* as against 53 per cent with the function word.[44] In the Vulgar English materials the situation is very different, for the inflectional forms far outnumber the occurrences of the function word. There were 90 per cent of the comparatives with *-er* against 10 per cent with the function word *more.* Of the superlatives, 89 per cent appeared with the inflectional *-est* and 11 per cent with the function word *most.* Here again Vulgar English shows itself to be more conservative than Standard English and maintains the older inflections against the newer device of the function word.

The preponderance of the inflections in Vulgar English is probably due to the fact that the inflectional *-er* and *-est* are maintained on most words of one syllable, the popular words, and on a few words of two syllables and that the function word is used with all words of more than two syllables and with most words of two syllables—the less familiar or the more learned words. Some of the words appearing in Standard English (Group I) with the inflection are *greater* (9017), *higher* (9060), *larger* (9032), *lower* (9006), *shorter* (9012), *stronger* (9012), *younger* (8050), *older* (8279); *hardest* (9033), *highest* (9033), *nearest* (9043), *smallest* (9031), *strongest* (9037), *biggest* (8061), *greatest* (8086), *oldest* (8289),

---

for not only the high dignity of the civil magistrate, but the *most basest* handicrafts are holy, when they are directed to the honour of God.' Sir Thomas More.

'After the *most straitest* sect of our religion I lived a Pharisee.' (Acts xxvi. 5.)

"These comparatives and superlatives are ungrammatical, as they doubly express the degree of comparison; *more braver* being the same as *more more brave, most basest* as *most most base,* etc., a repetition which is absurd, and only justifiable when applied to the Creator, who is sometimes called the *most highest,* as His dignity is so infinitely superior to that of every other being."

[42] Page 137 (1800 ed.), *Syntax,* Rule viii, 4.

"Double comparatives and superlatives should be avoided: such as, 'A worser conduct'; 'On lesser hopes'; 'A more serener temper'; 'The most straitest sect'; 'A more superior work'; They should be, 'worse conduct'; 'less hopes'; 'a more serene temper'; 'the straitest sect'; 'a superior work.'"

[43] For the development of other function words of degree see below Chapter IX, pages 200–203, and Chapter X, page 259.

[44] I have omitted from these figures the sixty one cases of irregular comparison with such words as *last, best, next, worst,* and *further, former, better, worse, less, latter.*

surest (8061), *earliest* (9025), (8140), (9064). Typical examples of the words appearing with the function word are *more interesting* (9012), *more varied* (9028), *more interested* (9012), *more accurate* (9037), *more constrained* (8056), *more valuable* (8284), *more often* (8002), *more exact* (8144), *better satisfied* (9020), *better qualified* (9042); *most important* (8042), *most extensive* (8061), *most competent* (8061), *a most aged and needy grandmother* (8078), *most anxious* (8086), *most likely* (8102), *most earnestly* (8140), *most deserving* (8078), *most economical* (8061), *most interested* (9019), *most rigid* (9017), *most easy* (9032).

In the Vulgar English materials the words that use the *-er* and *-est* inflections duplicate in large measure those used in the Standard English letters. Typical examples are *older* (8244), *younger* (8080), *weaker* (8188), *stronger* (8038), *longer* (8005), *oldest* (8053), *youngest* (8067), *biggest* (8288), *earliest* (8224). Vulgar English does not frequently use the kind of words which are quoted above from the Standard English materials as used with the function words of comparison. In a few instances the function word is used in Vulgar English with one syllable popular words as in "I can not give you *more plane* proofs than I have" (8072).

Ever since the eighteenth century there has been considerable discussion [45] concerning the use of the inflections for the compara-

[45] For the earliest example of this discussion see George Campbell, *The Philosophy of Rhetoric* (Edinburgh and London, W. Strahan, 1776), Book II, Chapter III, Section ii.

"Sometimes indeed the comparative is rightly followed by a plural; as in these words, 'He is wiser than we.' But it cannot be construed with the preposition *of* before that to which the subject is compared. There is one case, and but one, wherein the aforesaid preposition is proper after the comparative, and that is when the words following the preposition comprehend both sides of the comparison; as 'He is the taller man of the two.' In these words, *the two,* are included he and the person to whom he is compared. It deserves our notice, also, that, in such cases, and only in such, the comparative has the definite article *the* prefixed to it, and is construed precisely as the superlative; nay, both degrees are in such cases used indiscriminately. We say rightly, either 'This is the weaker of the two,' or—'the weakest of the two.' If, however, we may form a judgment from the most general principles of analogy, the former is preferable, because there are only two things compared."

For more recent treatments of the problem with evidence in the form of quotations see the following:

J. Leslie Hall, *English Usage* (Chicago, Scott, Foresman and Co., 1917), pp. 279–280.

Otto Jespersen, *A Modern English Grammar* (Heidelberg, 1914), Vol. II, pp. 203–205 (7.771–7.775).

Russell Thomas, "The Use of the Superlative Degree for the Comparative," *The English Journal* (College Edition), Vol. 24, December, 1935, pp. 821–829.

tive and superlative degrees in accord with the number of the objects referred to. If the adjective modifies a noun naming a unit (object, person, group) of which only two units are mentioned or referred to in the context, the comparative has been insisted upon as the proper inflection; if the adjective modifies a noun naming a unit (object, person, group) of which more than two such units have been mentioned or referred to, the superlative has been urged as the proper inflection. This use of the comparative form where two are concerned and the superlative only where more than two are concerned seems to reflect the old distinction between a dual and a plural number which was set off by many clear forms in the older stages of Indo-European languages. In English the old dual forms disappeared early and our plural number means *more than one,* not *more than two*. Whenever the particular number is important it is specified by the numeral or some word such as *both,* which definitely indicates the number. We use, for example, *we two* or *both of us* instead of the old dual *wit* of the pronoun of the first person.

In the materials examined here the usage of the adjective is overwhelmingly against the distinction of the dual by means of the comparative. In the Standard English letters the comparative is used only once in such a situation.

> "My husband left me with two children; the younger is twelve years old" (8212)

Typical examples of the superlative form in this use are

> "the surest and most economical method" (8061)
> [two ways are indicated]
> "this is the best answer to give" (8298)
> [two answers are proposed]
> "I am asking that you grant my oldest son a discharge, both my boys are in . . ." (8222)

In the Vulgar English letters no example of the comparative degree inflection appeared as a dual distinct from a plural.

Typical examples of the superlative for two are

> "I have two children . . . my oldest boy is 17 years of age" (8053)
> "he is my youngest boy" [two sons indicated] (8067)

Concerning the adjective inflections for comparison the significant facts from the materials examined here are as follows:

1. The inflections *-er* and *-est* have been supplanted in Standard English by the function words *more* and *most* to such an extent that a trifle more than half of the comparatives and a trifle less than half of the superlatives still use the inflectional forms.

2. In Vulgar English approximately nine tenths of both the comparatives and the superlatives still use the inflectional forms.

3. The inflections are used with the simple (usually one syllable) and common words. These are chiefly old words in the language, many reaching back to the Old English period. The function words, on the other hand, occur sometimes with simple, one syllable words but most frequently with the longer, more learned words.

4. The use of the superlative rather than the comparative for two, thus ignoring a dual as distinct from a plural, is a fact of Standard English usage and not a characteristic limited to Vulgar English.

5. So-called "double" comparison did not appear in any of the letters either of Standard English or of Vulgar English.

IV. PERSON AND MOOD FORMS

A. Person

As used in discussions of grammar the term *person* refers to those distinctions which indicate whether the grammatical subject of a verb is the one speaking (the *first* person), or the one spoken to (the *second* person), or the one spoken of(the *third* person). *Person,* then, is an idea that attaches to the subject substantive. Those pronouns which make this distinction in their forms are, because of this fact, called "personal" pronouns, as *I, we,* those speaking (first person); *you,* those spoken to (second person); *he, she, it, they,* those spoken of (third person). Nouns as subjects are nearly always of the third person. As applied to verbs the word *person* refers to those distinctions of form which repeat whatever grammatical idea of person is expressed in the subject. In the older stages of the language, the verb, in a fairly large number of situations, had distinct forms to accompany or "agree" with the "person" of the subject. More than that, a verb form which was distinct in respect to person could stand alone without having the separate pronoun subject given and still be unmistakably clear. A good example is furnished by the well-known Latin message "Veni, vidi, vici." Modern English, however, has no such system of inflections for person in its verbs, for the personal endings, which even in Old English had been reduced to six distinct forms, have in Present-day

English been further reduced to one. Aside from the verb *to be* the -*s* of the third singular present indicative is the only form of the English verb that indicates person. In the verb *to be* only *am* of the first person and *is* of the third person remain to "agree" with the person of the subject. We must look to the subject itself to determine the person, and only in commands and requests can the verb stand without a subject expressed. The three verb forms of person are not a sufficient pattern to function grammatically; they simply *accompany* the appropriate subject forms whenever they happen to be used. As the following figures will show, they make up a comparatively small part of the verb forms used.

In the materials examined here there were a total of 4,918 finite verb forms used. These were almost evenly divided between the Standard English letters and those of Vulgar English. There were 2,421 in the Standard English materials and 2,497 in those of Vulgar English. The distribution of "persons" among these forms was as follows:

TABLE VIII

	Standard English	*Vulgar English*
1st person	773	1076 [46]
2nd person	36	187
3rd person	1612	1234

Only about one fourth of all these verb forms appeared with *distinctive person* forms. The figures are given in Table IX on the opposite page.

In these figures there seems to be no essential difference between the practice of Standard English and that of Vulgar English. There is indeed a remarkable correspondence in the relative number of person distinctive forms used by the two groups. There is, however, one difference between the two groups that shows itself in a very few examples. In Vulgar English there are some instances (thirteen in all) in which there is an elimination of the person distinct form in the first person of the verb *to be* and in the third person singular of other verbs.

[46] This difference in the distribution of the *persons* in Standard English and Vulgar English seems to me to show some difference in the formality of the material. The Vulgar English letters were somewhat more intimate and used a greater proportion of first and second person subjects.

Typical examples are

"*He want* to get out" (8107)
"*She want* him back home" (8288)
"*He write* me that he is to be" (8231)
"*He* just *be* seventeen years old" (8045)
"*I has* sum gud wite frens" (3005) [47]
"*I is* in lot of troble" (3006)
"*I has* a misery in my . . ." (3005)

TABLE IX

	Non-distinctive Forms	*Distinctive Forms*	*Per Cent Distinctive Forms*
Standard English			
1st person	671	102	13.2%
2nd person	36		
3rd person	1033	579	35.9
Totals	1740	681	28.1%
Vulgar English			
1st person	889	187	17.4%
2nd person	187		
3rd person	703	531	43.0
Totals	1779	718	28.7%

B. Mood

In the matter of person, the distinct verb forms have tended to disappear and no new device has taken their place; in the matter of mood, however, the passing of the inflections has been accompanied by a greatly increased use of the so-called modal auxiliaries—the function words used to express an emotional attitude toward the action or state.[48] In Old English there were distinctive verb forms for the subjunctive in both the present tense and the preterit. Within the subjunctive, singular and plural number forms were clearly separated, but there were no forms to distinguish person. These distinctive subjunctive forms, in the course of our language development, fell together with those of the indicative mode, until, in Present-day English, but one form remains, in all verbs except the verb *to be,* to separate subjunctive mood from indicative. In Present-day English, as in the past, the subjunctive has no distinct forms for the various persons, whereas the indicative still retains

[47] *I is* and *I has* appeared only in the writing of Negroes.
[48] See below Chapter VIII, pages 172–182.

the -*s* of the third person singular. As a matter of fact, however, this *s*-less subjunctive very rarely appears. In all the letters examined here only four instances occurred and these were all in Vulgar English. They are

"So *help* me god" (8005)
"God *bless* you and *speed* you on" (8005)
"insisted that he *join* the army" (8100)

In the verb *to be* there are more forms that are distinctly subjunctive and many more examples appear. Usually all *be* forms in the present and all *were* forms in the first and third persons singular of the preterit are called subjunctives.[49] The examples of these subjunctives in the Standard English letters were of two types.

a. Object clauses after such verbs as request, ask, recommend, suggest, order, direct, require, urge, demand, propose, insist,[50] *and after nouns or adjectives of similar meaning* [51]

"recommend that all references to A.W.O.L. *be* expunged from his records" (9007)
"I insist that I *be* given a new assignment" (5006)
"it is requested that the error *be* corrected if it is one, that my name *be* placed in its proper place on the promotion list and that I *be* informed of my new standing" (9022)
"I earnestly ask that it *be* granted" (8267)
"It is suggested that before he *be* classed for overseas that he *be* interviewed" (5003)
"I propose that adjustment for this overpayment *be* held in abeyance" (9032)
"it is urged that the transfer *be* expedited" (5007)
"This young man's wife is very anxious that he *be* discharged from Service" (5001)
"The request that the claim *be* paid" (9063)
"There was an order issued that my leave of absence *be* made effective upon . . ." (9043)

b. Conditional Clauses

"Even if the mother *were* well the father needs his son to help make a living for himself" (8064)

[49] Historically, of course, *be* forms in the present tense could be indicative as well as subjunctive.

[50] Thus in the formulas of parliamentary procedure the subjunctive is used in "that" clauses following the verb *move*.

[51] Other instances of subjunctives of this type are to be found in: 9016, 9001, 9029, 9028, 9027, 9026, 9025, 9042, 9024, 9039, 9036, 9050, 9053, 9052, 9054, 9055, 9056, 9058, 9059, 9060, 9061, 9062.

"If he *be* between 18 and 21 years of age he must have written consent of his parent or of his guardian if there *be* no parent" (8056)

"If I *were* transferred to . . . I would be able to get the practical experience that I need" (9050)

"I would be able to settle down to work, quicker than if I *were* at some institution not familiar to me" (9050)

"I feel certain that if I *were* detailed for duty at . . . I would not be handicapped by reason of a lack of knowledge of the French language" (9064)

"Request transportation for myself, wife, and infant daughter, . . . from . . . , or if it *be* possible by rail from . . . to . . ." (9043)

"They could file their claims for exemption, if there *be* any" (9012)

"*Were* I to advise Mr. W——, I would say to him . . ." (8296)

"And whether or not it *be* adopted, the fact that it is presented in open Conference should obtain for the idea much newspaper publicity" (9036)

In all, there were in the Standard English materials fifty nine instances of the use of the subjunctive—every one of the verb *to be*.

There were twelve cases of the subjunctive in "conditions" and forty seven of the subjunctive in *that* clauses following the kinds of words indicated above page 104 (*a*). On the other hand there were thirty three cases of the use of the indicative in "conditions" exactly paralleling those in (*b*) above for which the subjunctive was used. There were also sixty four cases of the use of the function word *should* rather than the subjunctive form in *that* clauses following such verbs as *ask, request, recommend,* etc., and sixty five cases of the infinitive rather than the *that* clause. On the whole, then, despite the nature of the material in the letters of Standard English which provides the conditions for an increased use of the subjunctive in *that* clauses following the words of request, the subjunctive forms are used in only 18.4 per cent of the situations in which we might expect them.

In the Vulgar English materials the situation in general is much the same as in the letters of Standard English except for the fact that there are by no means the number of instances of subjunctives in *that* clauses following such verbs as *ask, request, recommend, suggest, order,* etc. The situations in the Vulgar English letters were not such as lent themselves to the use of such formal requests. There were, however, the following types of subjunctives in the materials studied:

a. *Object clauses after* request, ask, recommend *and similar nouns and adjectives*

"I am asking that my Son *be* Discharged from . . ." (8225)
"I earnestly request that my husband *be* discharged" (8127)
"I request that he *be* sent home" (8098)
"he has already recommended to . . . that my transfer *be* disapproved" (8241)
"it is very necessary that he *be* discharged" (8130)

b. *Conditions*

"I would be better satisfied if I *were* allowed to transfer to a local post" (8082)
"If I *were* you I would keep away from . . ." (6101)
"and if he *were* back home he would do his best" (8152)
"if he *be* between 18 and 21" (8056)

c. *Wishes (especially formulas)*

"God *bless* you and *speed* you on" (8005)
"So *help* me god" (8005)
"Blessed *be* his name" (8005)

In all, there were in the Vulgar English materials nineteen instances of the use of the subjunctive. Six were in conditions, eight in *that* clauses following such words as *ask, request, recommend,* and five miscellaneous uses, chiefly wishes. On the other hand, there were twenty four instances of the indicative in "conditions" exactly paralleling those in (*b*) above, thirty seven cases of the function word *should* or *would* rather than the subjunctive form in *that* clauses following such words as *ask, recommend,* etc., and eighty five cases of the infinitive rather than the *that* clauses. Altogether the subjunctive forms were used in only 13 per cent of the situations in which we might expect them.

Three facts stand out from this survey of the uses of the subjunctive forms in our materials.

1. In general the subjunctive has tended to disappear from use. This statement does not mean that the ideas formerly expressed by the inflectionally distinct forms of the verb called the subjunctive are not now expressed but rather that these ideas are now expressed chiefly by other means, especially by function words.

2. In these materials taken all together not more than one fifth of the instances of *that* clauses after such words as *ask, request, com-*

mand, suggest, order, etc., used the subjunctive form, and only 22.6 per cent of the "non-fact conditions" used the subjunctive.

3. The failure to use the subjunctive form in non-fact conditions, and in *that* clauses after words of asking, requesting, suggesting, etc., is not a characteristic of Vulgar English only. The practices of Standard English and Vulgar English do not differ significantly in this respect.

VII

THE USES OF FUNCTION WORDS: WITH SUBSTANTIVES

The formal study of grammar in English and the other modern languages of western Europe was based upon the conventional study of Latin, for the grammatical apparatus that was available in the sixteenth century, when the first practical grammars of the vernaculars arose, was that which had been developed first in the study of Greek and later used for centuries for the Latin language. Latin was a highly inflected language and as a result the study of the grammar of that language necessarily centered attention upon the uses of the forms of words or inflections. The early grammars of English [1] imitated these grammars of Latin and attempted to find in English parallels to all the structures which were familiar in Latin. Despite the protests of a very few of the writers of English grammars,[2] who insisted that the apparatus of the Latin grammars was not suitable for the treatment of the English language, they all used it, fearing to introduce innovations and also desiring to lay a good foundation for the learning of Latin through the teaching of English grammar.[3] Therefore, in the common school grammars of English, inflections or the forms of words have received the major emphasis, and those matters of structure which did not parallel the

[1] See C. C. Fries, "The Rules of the Common School Grammars," *Publications of the Modern Language Association,* No. 42, 1927, pp. 221–237.

[2] See for example John Wallis, *Grammatica Linguae Anglicanae* (1653), and J. B. Priestly, *English Grammar* (1761).

[3] From an anonymous grammar entitled *A New English Accidence* (1736) are taken the following sentences: "It must be acknowledged that the *Plan of the Latin Grammar,* is not the best which might be contrived, especially for our English Youth, but as Custom and Authority have made it the Standard Rules of teaching them that Language, there seems therefore a necessity of making the Rules of an Introduction to an English grammar, as subservient thereunto as possible, (so far as the nature and Genius of our own Tongue will admit) that whilst we are teaching the one, we may at the same time be laying a good Foundation for the other. And this I think the only reason for keeping as close as we can to the Method and Rules there laid down; for otherwise, I should be the last to find fault with any Person for quitting the Old Track and setting out a better."

devices of Latin have received very little or no treatment. We have seen in the former chapters, however, that in English, inflections or the forms of words have tended to disappear as a grammatical device until in Present-day English the only really live uses of the forms of words to express grammatical ideas are (*a*) those to distinguish plural and singular number in substantives and (*b*) those to distinguish past and present tense in verbs. All the other inflections of which some remnants remain (case forms for the genitive and dative-accusative of substantives, comparison forms for adjectives, and person and mood forms for verbs) have in considerable measure been replaced [4] by other grammatical devices.

We come now to deal with these other means of expressing grammatical ideas—means which in the conventional grammars deriving from those modelled on Latin grammars receive very slight treatment. This chapter and the next two will contain a discussion of the grammatical ideas expressed by function words and Chapter X a discussion of the grammatical ideas expressed by word order.

By a *function word* I mean a word that has little or no meaning apart from the grammatical idea it expresses. In such an expression as "The mother of the boy will arrive tomorrow," it is quite clear that the words *mother, boy, arrive,* and *tomorrow* have meaning in themselves apart from their grammatical relation in the sentence. They are *full words* and have an independent meaning. But the words *of* and *will* express primarily grammatical ideas and have little or no meaning apart from the grammatical function they indicate. *Of* makes the word *boy* a modifier of the word *mother;* it is equivalent to a genitive inflection and the same idea would have been expressed by *the boy's mother*. *Will* here indicates primarily that the "arriving" will occur in the future and it is equivalent to a future tense inflection; it has no independent meaning. These words *of* and *will* are therefore called *function words.*[5] They are typical of a fairly large class of words that in similar fashion express primarily grammatical ideas and relationships rather than

[4] "Person" forms as shown above (pages 102–103) have almost disappeared completely with no other device to take their place.

[5] Henry Sweet calls these words *form words.* See his explanation in *New English Grammar* (Oxford, Clarendon Press, 1892), Part I, pp. 22–24, 58, 59, 60, 61. I prefer the term *function word* because *form words* sounds so much like the expression *the forms of words,* which I use for *inflections,* that students are often confused.

full word meanings. Some of the words that we shall deal with in this treatment of function words are (*a*) the so-called "prepositions"—the function words that are used with substantives, (*b*) the so-called "auxiliaries"—the function words that are used with verbs, (*c*) the words modifying adjectives that become function words of degree, (*d*) the so-called "conjunctions"—the words expressing the relationships of such word groups as we call clauses.

These function words have tended to supplant certain inflections in Modern English and therefore have become one of the important methods by which Present-day English expresses its grammatical ideas and relationships. Whether or not the function word is a more precise definition of a grammatical relation than an inflection is, as the following quotation indicates, may be open to question, but all will agree that this change in the grammar of our language is a matter of fundamental importance.

"The general movement by which single words have in part taken the place of inflection is the most sweeping and radical change in the history of the Indo-European languages. It is at once the indication and the result of a clearer feeling of concept-relation. Inflection in the main rather suggests than expresses relations; it is certainly not correct to say that in every case the expression of relation by a single word, e. g., a preposition, is clearer than the suggestion of the same relation by a case-form, but it is correct to say that the relation can become associated with a single word only when it is felt with a considerable degree of clearness. The relation between concepts must itself become a concept. To this extent the movement toward the expression of relation by single words is a movement toward precision. . . . The adverb-preposition is the expression in more distinct form of some element of meaning which was latent in the case-form. It serves therefore as a definition of the meaning of the case-form." [6]

FUNCTION WORDS USED WITH SUBSTANTIVES

Table X on the opposite page gives the actual number of the occurrences of each of the function words used with substantives in the letters of Group I (Standard English) and in those of Group III (Vulgar English).

Some facts in the figures of Table X that seem significant follow on page 112.

[6] Edward P. Morris, *On Principles and Methods in Latin Syntax* (New York, Charles Scribner's Sons, 1901), pp. 102, 103, 104.

TABLE X

FUNCTION WORDS WITH SUBSTANTIVES

In the Standard English Materials

	With Nouns	With Pronouns	Total
about	30	4	34
after	17	2	19
against	2	1	3
at	229	0	229
before	12	1	13
between	4	1	5
by	99	29	128
during	31	0	31
for	288	45	333
from	192	24	216
in	561	12	573
into	15	0	15
near	3	0	3
of	897	9	906
on	224	4	228
over	7	0	7
since	7	0	7
through	5	0	5
to	337	91	482
toward(s)	2	0	2
under	33	0	33
until	18	0	18
up	2	0	2
upon	27	4	31
with	133	31	164
without	14	1	15
	3189 92.4%	259 7.6%	3448
among	2	0	2
onto	1	0	1
within	10	0	10
	13	0	13
Total	3202 92.5%	259 7.5%	3461

In the Vulgar English Materials

	With Nouns	With Pronouns	Total	Numbered Senses in OD
about	28	24	52	11
after	7	1	8	16
against	3	1	4	18
at	179	1	180	39
before	2	0	2	12
between	1	0	1	20
by	40	4	44	39
during	7	0	7	1
for	142	92	234	31
from	85	58	143	15
in	324	2	326	40
into	6	0	6	22
near	2	1	3	
of	352	33	385	63
on	94	7	101	29
over	14	1	15	19
since	8	0	8	2
through	8	0	8	8
to	184	104	292	33 {+ 22 with vb.
toward(s)	4	0	4	8
under	26	0	26	25
until	4	0	4	6
up	9	0	9	7
upon	1	1	2	26
with	45	20	65	40
without	43	7	50	15
	1618 81.9%	357 18.1%	1975	
around	1	0	1	4
as	6	1	7	(34) [not prep.]
beneath	1	0	1	7
besides	2	1	3	{5 besides 5 beside
but	3	0	3	3
concerning	1	0	1	4
except	3	0	3	2
like	2	1	3	
off	1	0	1	4 as prep.
till	4	0	1	6
	24	3	27	
Total	1624 82%	360 18%	2002	

1. These particular function words, those commonly called "prepositions," are used primarily with nouns but comparatively little with pronouns. In the Standard English materials 92.4 per cent of the instances occur with nouns and but 7.6 per cent with pronouns.

2. In the Vulgar English materials, however, 82 per cent of the instances occur with nouns and 18 per cent with pronouns; that is, a distinctly larger proportion of the instances occur with pronouns in the Vulgar English letters than in those of Standard English.

3. Nine of these function words with substantives occur very frequently; in fact, 92.6 per cent of the instances in the Standard English materials have the following nine words:

at	229	instances	
by	128	"	
for	333	"	
from	216	"	
in	573	"	
of	906	"	
on	228	"	
to	428	"	
with	164	"	
Total	3,205	"	out of 3,448 or 92.6%

4. These same words occur most frequently also in the Vulgar English materials.

at	180	instances	
by	44	"	
for	234	"	
from	143	"	
in	326	"	
of	385	"	
on	101	"	
to	292	"	
with	65	"	
Total	1,770	"	out of 2,002 or 88.4%

5. These nine words that are used most frequently as function words with substantives have many meanings. The *Oxford English Dictionary* lists an exceedingly large number of separate senses and uses for each one.

Word	*Separately numbered senses given in the* Oxford Dictionary
at	39
by	39
for	31

from	15
in	40
of	63
on	29
to	33
with	40

The average number of separately numbered senses recorded and illustrated by the *Oxford Dictionary* for each of these nine words is thirty six and a half. With this great variety of meanings carried by each of these words it is difficult to agree with the assertion in the quotation given above, that, unlike inflection which "rather suggests than expresses relations, . . . the adverb-preposition . . . serves . . . as a definition of the meaning of the case-form." As a matter of fact I should like to urge that perhaps the meanings displayed by the *Oxford Dictionary* are not in each of these words in themselves but lie rather in the whole context in which the words are used and *depend upon the meanings of the words that are brought into relationship* by these function words. This does not mean that these function words are interchangeable, but each one serves to connect nouns that are related to each other in a great variety of ways, and in many cases there are therefore such areas of overlapping that any one of several different function words might be used to connect the nouns. In such cases it is very hard to see and describe any difference in meaning that lies in the function word itself. We feel a difference between the expressions with the various function words, but we define it in terms of the context, and I am inclined to believe that this difference in feeling arises out of the fact that, although these words overlap in certain segments of their uses, their total areas of use diverge. We feel the words as different because of the suggestions coming from those portions of their uses that do not overlap.

In reading the following examples one must, if he would illustrate the view just stated, put the stress on the two nouns, not upon the function words. The function words italicized are *without* stress:

A

The house *at* the corner
The house *by* the corner
The house *on* the corner
The house *in* the corner
The house *of* the corner [7]

B

The man *of* the street
The man *in* the street
The man *on* the street
The man *from* the street [7]

C

To arrive *at* the stroke of twelve
To arrive *on* the stroke of twelve
To arrive *by* the stroke of twelve
To arrive *with* the stroke of twelve

[7] These last examples seem to me less natural English.

It will be our task, therefore, not to analyze the *meanings* which it is alleged that these words express but rather to indicate the grammatical relationships into which the substantive is brought by the use of the function word. This matter will be discussed below (pages 118–127).

6. There are some differences in the particular words that appeared in the two lists. There is not much that seems significant, but the following items should be noted:

a. within—appeared only in the Standard English materials.[8]

b. until—appeared more frequently in Standard English; on the other hand *till,* the older form, appeared in the Vulgar English materials only.[9]

c. off, but, like, as—used as function words with substantives appeared only in the Vulgar English materials.[10]

d. Both *beside* and *besides,* in the sense of "in addition to," are used in Vulgar English as function words with substantives. In the particular examples found, there seemed to be no difference in the use of the two forms.

"has 2 small children *besides* him" (8035)
"*besides* my discharge I can show to the Court my Army Service Record" (8157)
"*Beside* the above named reasons why I wish . . . theres these to think of" (8284)

In addition to the "single" function words with substantives as shown in Table X above there are a fairly large number of what may be called "compound" function words that operate as units. It is difficult to draw a definite line between the two groups, and I have

[8] Typical examples are
"receive a reply *within* ten days" (8299)
"parents lived *within* a few miles" (8060)
"acting *within* my rights" (9032)
"her condition *within* the last month and a half had grown much worse" (8240)
Other examples are in 9021, 9064, 9065, 9033, 9053, 8296.

[9] Typical examples of the uses of *till* are
"her grandmother cared for her *till* her death" (8028)
"from July 1924 *till* September 1925" (8157)

[10] Typical examples of *off, like, but, as* are
"he hasnt been *off* the island" (8005)
"in a case *like* this" (8026)
"i hafent got any thing *But* a Job" (8097)
"nothing *but* bad health and expense" (8052)
"he enlisted *as* a single man" (8012)
"all kind of letters the same *as* this" (8005)
"At a time when a soldier was classed *as* a bum" (8057)
"he enlisted *as* twenty one years of age" (8084) (8136)

included in Table X above as "single" function words such combinations as *into, onto, without, within,* etc. It is even more difficult to draw a satisfactory line to separate "compound" function words from completely free expressions in the same pattern. We may all agree that the combinations *on account of, for the sake of,* and *in view of* do operate as single units because they occur frequently enough to be felt as bound forms, but it is not so easy to procure agreement upon the less frequently occurring combinations in the same pattern, as *on completion of, for the support of,* and *in event of*. In this matter, however, a precise classification is of little or no use and I shall, therefore, use the term *compound function words* loosely to stand for the various kinds of word groups I shall now try to describe and discuss. In many cases the range of examples will include some that appear frequently enough to be felt as formulas, and some that are clearly free expressions. This looseness of definition, however, will permit a more adequate representation of the facts involved.

There are three important varieties of these compound function words that appeared frequently in the materials examined.

1. There is, first, the expansion of the function word which amounts to an analysis and emphasis of the precise meaning relationship involved. Thus *at,* which by itself may refer to position or time, becomes expanded to "*at the place of* his abode" (9030), "*at the time of* the occurrence" (9007), "*at the rate of* $25 per week" (8283). In similar fashion *for,* which alone may denote purpose or advantage, becomes expanded to "*for the sake of* his mother" (8267), "*for the purpose of* visiting Canada" (9024).

Likewise *during* becomes expanded to "*during the time of* his illness" (8139), "*during the time of* his service" (9013). The simple *by* is expanded to *by reason of,* as in "several men were overpaid *by reason of* the non-reduction of allotments" (9032); or to *by the use of,* as in "a spark is introduced in the cylinder *by the use of* a spark plug" (9027); or *by way of,* as in "return to the United States *by way of* Europe" (9021).

The pattern of this expansion consists of three elements—(*a*) the function word (in nearly all cases one of the nine indicated above as used most frequently and as having many meanings), (*b*) a noun which names somewhat precisely the meaning relationship involved, and (*c*) the function word *of.* (In a much less number of cases this second function word may be *to* or sometimes *with,* as in "*with a view to* his remaining" (8296), "*in regard to* the examination" (9027), or "*in company with* this officer" (8296).) This particular pattern of compound function words, although it appears in both the Standard English and the Vulgar English materials, seems to be much more a characteristic of Standard English, for approximately three times as many instances appeared in the Standard English letters as in the Vulgar English letters, that is, 156 instances in the former and fifty seven in the latter.[11] This pattern, especially common in the Stand-

[11] Of the fifty seven instances in the Vulgar English letters twenty nine were the expression "*in regard(s) to.*" Examples are in 8029, 8035, 8038, 8113, 8126, 8152, 8153, 8165, 8190, 8193, 8293, 8259, 8270.

Other examples of this pattern in Vulgar English are

"*at the time of* his birth" (8280)
"*at the time of* his enlistment" (8036)
"*for reason of* his mother who cannot . . ." (8115)
"*in behalf of* the chaplin" (8218)
"*in case of* war" (8063)
"*in need of* his support" (8270) (8237)
"writing you *in regards of* my husband" (8229) (8230)
"*in view of* this calling" (8251)
"*on account of* his minority" (8173) (8233) (8288) (8005) (8028) (8036)
"*with the exception of* one little boy" (8253)

Typical examples of this pattern in the Standard English materials other than those given in the discussion above are

"*after the close of* the schools" (8060)
"*at the time of* our interview" (8240) (8142) (9014) (8183)
"*by direction of* the president" (9050)
"*by reason of* the solidity" (9041)
"*by way of* protection" (8139)
"*during the time of* his service" (9013)
"*for purposes of* recreation" (9058)
"*for the sake of* convenience" (9053)
"*in case of* accident" (8075) (9053) (9040)
"*in line of* duty" (9002)
"Infantry *in place of* cavalry" (9058)
"*in the event of* my promotion" (9022) (9043)
"*in the interest of* more varied service" (9028)
"*in the way of* helping to make a living" (8180)
"*in view of* the fact" (9033) (9000) (8240) (9053) (9062) (9042) (9027) (9030) (9026)
"*in behalf of* Mrs. . . . " (8023)
"*on behalf of* the boy" (8095) (8204)
"*on account of* this accident" (8095) (9030) (8064) (8294) (8711) (8137) (8144) (9000) (9001) (9006)
"*on the part of* headquarters" (9007) (9022)
"*since the date of* his enlistment" (8081)
"promoted *to the grade of* Captain" (9016)
"contributed *to the support of* the family" (8081) (8142)
"*under date of* May 11th" (8299) (9065)
"*upon completion of* his duty" (9023) (9002) (9061) (9042)
"*with the exception of* the stop-over" (9016) (8240) (8239)
"*in regard to* the examination" (9027) (8002) (9030) (8262) (8283) (8260)
"*with a view to* remaining" (8206)

ard English practice, seems to come from an effort to fix more precisely the point of the meaning relationship between the following substantive and whatever it modifies.

2. There is, second, the use of two function words (it makes little difference whether they are called two prepositions or an adverb and a preposition) side by side, so joined in use as to operate as a unit. In respect to these "compound" function words it is also difficult to set precise boundaries because they extend over a wide range of possible combinations from such clear cases as *into, unto, until, upon, throughout, within, without,* to such doubtful and free expressions as *in at,* as in "put my petition *in at* the Prothonotary Office" (8157); *off from,* as in "he ran *off from* home last January" (8277) (8190); *over in,* as in "he was stationed *over in* Panama" (8123); *up till,* as in "where he made his home *up till* the time of his absence" (8257); and *ever since,* as in "I have had the care of the boy *ever since* the death of his mother" (8077). Unlike the "expansion" pattern above, which was especially characteristic of Standard English, this "addition" of function words seems to be especially frequent in the Vulgar English materials. In the Standard English letters there were but twenty four instances all told; in the Vulgar English letters there were ninety seven instances [12]—four times as many in the same amount of material.

"*with reference to* your son" (8143) (8163) (8183) (9029) (9000) (8163)
"*without regard to* personal quarters" (9030)
"*with respect to* the General Staff" (9000)
"*in accord with* those" (9000)
"*in company with* this officer" (8296)
"*in connection with* my duties" (9033) (8076) (9023)
"*in contact with* the distressed people" (8073)

[12] Typical examples of this pattern of compound function words, in the Vulgar English Materials are

"stay *away from* home" (8190) (8165) (8005) (8202) (8201) (8211) (8261) (8291)
"information *as to* the where bouts of my son" (8175) (8074) (8067) (8032) (8235)
"we are *back in* are rent" (8178)
"he was sent *back to* Honolulu" (8193) (8138) (8030) (8033) (8038) (8039) (8218) (8106) (8229) (8028) (8250) (8045)
"I have tried *ever since* May 2nd to locate him" (8149)
"ben sick *for over* a year" (8055) (8052)
"put my petition for naturalization *in at* the Prothonotary office" (8157)
"They found him *out by* Catalina Island" (8026)
"I could pick him *out from* a million" (8067)
"as we are *up against* it" (8033)
"a man that is getting *up in* years" (8173)
"we have raised him ever since *up until* the time he . . ." (8084)
"*up to* that time I was . . ." (8060) (8193) (8072)
"take me *up to* Fort Slocum" (8005)

3. There is, third, the combining of such adjectives as *according, owing, relating,* and *due* with the function word *to* so that the two words operate as a single word.[13] This pattern seems to be more characteristic of Standard English, for there were approximately three times as many instances of its use in those letters as in the letters of Vulgar English.

Of these three important varieties of compound function words the first (the expansion pattern) and the third (the combination of an adjective, especially a participial adjective with the word *to*) appeared much more frequently in the Standard English materials; the second (the addition of two simple function words) appeared much more frequently in the Vulgar English materials.

As indicated above (page 114), the particular function words that we are discussing serve to bring each of the substantives that follow them into some type of grammatical relationship with a word that precedes. In respect to the materials examined here Table XI (pages 120 and 121), will show the number of instances in which each of these function words is used to bring the following

---

In the Standard English materials typical examples are
"three days *ahead of* time" (9034)
"information *as to* the possibility of getting the . . ." (9061) (9010) (9004) (9052) (9042) (9040) (8296)
"to get the boy *out of* the army" (8189) (8017) (8068) (9033) (9024) (9027) (9040)
"he has been *out of* employment" (8283)
"as much as he could spare *out of* his pay" (8303) (9052)
"brought the allies *down on* her" (9017)
"turned *over to* the new hospital" (9002)
"the aforementioned $5.59 *together with* the enclosed sum" (9016)
"I have just gone *through with* the hardest blow of my life" (9033)
"who is well *up in* the seventies" (8095)
"has been in . . . *up to* the date of my examination" (9022)

[13] Typical examples in Standard English are
"*according to* the Congressional Record I was promoted" (9016) (8240) (8144) (9007)
"The need of . . . at home *owing to* the condition of his father's health" (8207) (8240) (9036)
"transactions *pertaining to* property" (9040)
"his death was *due to* foul play" (8095) (8283) (9020) (9024) (9027) (9054) (9036) (9053) (9007) (9003) (9001) (9057) (9058) (9066) (9059) (9030)

Typical examples in Vulgar English are
"*according to* her friends it is doubted . . ." (8017)
"grant him clemency *owing to* his services" (8153)
"*owing to* his physical condition" (8153) (8089) (8251)
"their appeal *relating to* various difficulties" (8073)
"I am writing you *relative to* my son" (8079)
"*Due to* my financial condition I am more . . ." (8056) (8137) (8002)

substantive into the various grammatical relationships. The figures for the nine most frequently used of these function words are given in Table XII, pages 120 and 121.

The tables there given indicate the types of grammatical relationships into which substantives (primarily nouns) are brought by the use of function words and something of their relative frequency. Each of the groups there counted needs some comment and illustration. In the Standard English materials there are the following matters to be noted:

a. The most common grammatical relationship is that in which a noun is made a modifier of another noun. Nearly half of all the instances of the function word with a substantive (43.4 per cent of all; 45.8 per cent of the most used nine) are of this type. Typical examples are [14]

"any news *about my son*" (8075)
"vaccinations *against typhoid*" (9055)
"the other men *at this place*" (9031)
"employment *at $45.00 per week*" (8086)
"The business *before the court* was" (9028)
"a widow *without means*" (8023)
"the plan *under consideration*" (8137)
"granted leave *until December*" (9050)
"I can afford leave *at half pay*" (9001)
"the temple *on the right side*" (9042)

[14] A more complete representation of the various function words in this particular grammatical relationship appears in the following examples:

"his arrival *at Camp Knox*" (9043)
"the information *at hand*" (8260)
"the competition *between companies*" (9040)
"a reconciliation *between him and his wife*" (8296)
"a toolmaker *by occupation*" (8081)
"a journey *by transport* within . . ." (9053)
"the clothing *for the children*" (8260) (8296)
"his application *for discharge*" (8240)
"the mother's request *for his discharge*" (8234)
"the taxes *for this year*" (8283)
"a varied and wholesome diet *for Mrs.* ——" (8266)
"one's prospects *for the future*" (9033)
"a discharge *from the service*" (8234)
"a divorce *from bed and board*" (8296)
"the statement *from Dr.* ——" (8294)
"extracts *from my military record*" (9027)
"instruction *in flying*" (9029)
"a course *in trigonometry*" (9027)
"absence *in France*" (9053)
"duty *in the Air Service*" (9027)
"all officers *on duty* at the training camps" (9060)

(*Continued on p. 122*)

TABLE XI

Standard English

	Mod. of Noun	Mod. of Verb	Mod. Verb or Noun	Type of Obj.	Pred. Adj.	Mod. of Adj.	Obj. Compl.	Mod. of Adv.
about	6	17	0	5	2	0	0	0
after	0	16	0	3	0	0	0	0
against	1	0	0	2	0	0	0	0
at	63	140	8	2	2	6	0	0
before	1	10	1	0	1	6	0	0
between	5	0	0	0	0	0	0	0
by	5	104	0	0	1	6	0	0
during	2	26	1	0	0	0	0	0
for	114	74	28	75	3	25	0	0
from	70	81	3	30	0	12	0	1
in	115	210	17	12	28	9	2	0
into	3	11	0	1	0	0	0	0
near	1	2	0	0	0	0	0	0
of	697	0	0	33	20	13	0	0
on	38	126	0	5	25	8	0	0
over	0	3	0	1	0	0	0	0
since	0	6	0	0	0	0	0	0
through	0	5	0	0	0	0	0	0
to	85	176	7	6	0	48	0	0
toward(s)	1	1	0	0	0	0	0	0
under	4	19	0	0	4	1	0	0
until	1	14	0	0	0	0	0	0
up	0	0	0	1	0	0	0	0
upon	0	14	0	0	0	3	0	1
with	45	63	2	18	9	11	3	0
without	1	10	0	0	2	3	0	0
among	0	2	0	0	0	0	0	0
onto	0	1	0	0	0	0	0	0
within	0	10	0	0	0	0	0	0
Totals	1258 43.4%	1141 39.7%	67 2.3%	184 6.3%	97 3.3%	145 5%	5 0.1%	2
Totals for nine most frequently used.	1232 45.8%	974 36.2%	65 2.4%	181 6.7%	88 3.2%	142 5.2%	5 0.1%	

TABLE XII

For Standard English

	Mod. of Noun	Mod. of Verb	Mod. Verb or Noun	Type of Obj.	Pred. Adj.	Mod. of Adj.	Obj. Compl.
at	63	140	8	2	2	6	0
by	5	104	0	0	1	6	0
for	114	74	28	75	3	25	0
from	70	81	3	30	0	16	0
in	115	210	17	12	28	9	2
of	697	0	0	33	20	13	0
on	38	126	0	5	25	8	0
to	85	176	7	6	0	48	0
with	45	63	2	18	9	11	3
Totals	1232	974	65	181	88	142	5

TABLE XI (*Continued*)

Vulgar English

	Mod. of Noun	Mod. of Verb	Mod. Verb or Noun	Type of Obj.	Pred. Adj.	Mod. of Adj.	Obj. Compl.
about	8	2	7	32	0	4	0
after	0	4	0	3	1	0	0
against	1	2	1	0	0	0	0
at	30	143	0	1	3	0	0
before	0	1	0	0	0	0	0
between	0	1	0	0	0	0	0
by	5	31	2	0	0	3	0
during	1	6	0	0	0	0	0
for	27	113	12	44	1	24	1
from	15	53	13	40	0	5	0
in	32	170	4	49	17	8	1
into	0	1	0	3	0	0	2
near	0	1	0	0	0	1	1
of	312	4	3	29	10	1	0
on	13	42	6	16	1	5	1
over	0	5	0	2	2	0	0
since	0	6	0	0	0	0	0
through	0	5	0	2	0	1	0
to	23	159	10	6	0	17	0
toward(s)	1	1	2	0	0	0	0
under	2	8	0	1	14	0	0
until	0	3	0	0	0	0	0
up	0	1	0	4	0	0	0
upon	0	1	0	0	0	1	0
with	9	45	3	5	0	3	0
without	3	45	3	0	0	0	0
around	0	1	0	0	0	0	1
as	3	2	0	0	0	0	0
beneath	0	1	0	0	0	0	0
besides	0	3	0	0	0	0	0
but	2	0	0	0	1	0	0
concerning	0	1	0	0	0	0	0
except	2	0	0	0	0	0	0
like	1	1	0	0	1	0	0
off	0	1	0	0	0	0	0
till	0	1	0	0	0	0	0
Totals	490 27.4%	864 48.6%	66 3.7%	235 13.1%	49 2.7%	73 4.1%	6 0.3%
Totals for nine most frequently used.	466 29.6%	760 48.4%	53 3.3%	190 12.1%	32 2%	66 4.2%	3 0.1%

TABLE XII (*Continued*)

For Vulgar English

	Mod. of Noun	Mod. of Verb	Mod. Verb or Noun	Type of Obj.	Pred. Adj.	Mod. of Adj.	Obj. Compl.
at	30	143	0	1	3	0	0
by	5	31	2	0	0	3	0
for	27	113	12	44	1	24	1
from	15	53	13	40	0	5	0
in	32	170	4	49	17	8	1
of	312	4	3	29	10	1	0
on	13	42	6	16	1	5	1
to	23	159	10	6	0	17	0
with	9	45	3	5	0	3	0
Totals	466	760	53	190	32	66	3

b. The next most common grammatical relationship is that in which a noun is made a modifier of a verb. A little over one third of the instances of the function word with a substantive (39.7 per cent of all; 36.2 per cent of the most used nine) are of this type. Typical examples are [15]

"he enlisted *about May 8*" (8303)
"he will preside *at the coming conference*" (9036)
"her husband was *at one time* in the company's employ" (8034)
"I actually arrived *at Baltimore*" (9034)
"it was received *by me*" (9050)
"he took *with him* $500.00" (9032)
"Dr. —— served *with the American Red Cross*" (9005)
"I will return *to my home*" (9053)

"dependency *on him*" (8081)
"personal business *on the pacific coast*" (9066)
"the troops *on the Mexican border*" (9041)
"carelessness *on my part*" (9040)
"the affidavit *of the parents*" (8183)
"the personal care *of this son*" (8023)
"part *of a larger amount*" (9032)
"January *of this year*" (9014)
"letters *of recommendation*" (9010)
"a great benefit *to me*" (9052) (9030)
"in your letter *to her*" (8234)
"my visits *to headquarters*" (9052)
"his service *with the government*" (9013)
"men *with a general knowledge*" (9012)
"experience *with horses*" (9015)

[15] The following examples will furnish a more complete representation of the various function words used in connection with this particular grammatical relationship:

"*About that time* she slipped on the sleety street" (8095)
"having resigned his reserve commission *about December*" (9022)
"Examination was made *about March 1st*" (8266)
"*After thorough investigation* . . . I believe that" (9061)
"leave this Department *after June 24*" (9028)
"I am *at present* holding a commission" (9005)
"*at my request* he resigned" (9013) (9026)
"She lives *by herself*" (8294)
"reasonable precautions were taken *by me*" (9032)
"he was sentenced *by the federal court*" (8296)
"she has had *for the past seven or eight years* the care of" (8114)
"She pays $7.00 per week *for board*" (8081)
"they were depending *on him* for their bread and butter" (8004)
"I have paid the . . . *from time to time*" (9033)
"notification is just coming *to me from the Adjutant General's Office*" (9010)
"I could get the exact dates *from the records*" (7022)
"I graduated *from that university*" (7064)
"there is a great deal to be learned *in the infantry*" (7027)
"she resides *in San Antonio*" (7000)
"it originated *in line of duty*" (9002)
"he failed *in everything*" (9029)

(*Continued on next page*)

c. In a certain number of instances (approximately 2.5 per cent) it is difficult to determine whether the noun is really a modifier of the verb or of a preceding noun. In these instances the preceding noun is usually the object of the verb in question. This fact is especially true of nouns with the function words *for, in, at,* and *to.* Typical examples are

> "I am maintaining a place of abode *at Ashville*" (9030)
> "a company which made satisfactory records *at target practice*" (9014)
> "competent to make a living *for herself and her daughter*" (8139)
> "There is no hope *for her*" (8064)
> "I received a letter *from the Adjutant General*" (8160)
> "I have no interest *in the matter*" (8260) (8139)
> "I prepared affidavits *in connection with the dependency application*" (8240)
> "to obtain employment *in the above corporation*" (8174)
> "the training received . . . would be a great help *to me*" (9015) (9032) (9144)

d. Although the two uses given in *a* and *b* above (those in which the function word makes the noun a modifier of either another noun or a verb) make up 80 per cent of the total number of instances, there are three other important relationships which these function words serve. In the first of these the noun by means of the function word is made into some type of object of the verb. Frequently the verb is one that does not normally take an object. In many of these instances the function word could be considered part of the verb itself. At any rate the instances in this whole group, which comprises 6.5 per cent of the total instances, differ distinctly from those included in *b* above. Typical examples are

> "I don't *remember of any instructions* in regard to that" (7037)
> "I *remember of going* to a picture show with ——" (7401)
> "that I be *informed of my new standing*" (9022)
> "he was *relieved of the responsibility*" (9032)
> "he had been *robbed of his last pay*" (8095)

"the officer of the day would frequently come down *of an evening*" (5024)
"considerable time was spent *on other duties*" (9019)
"he landed *on the coast* of America" (9012)
"received a commission *on April the 21st*" (9022)
"They are *on a small farm*" (8183)
"he contributed *to the support* of the family" (8260)
"he gave his wages *to his mother*" (8283)
"he returned *with the request* that . . ." (9063)
"the papers are filed *with my application*" (9027)
"he served *with the Machine Gun Company*" (9015)

"to *notify you of my change* of address" (9027)
"will hardly *pay for the groceries*" (8260)
"my folks *fought for the nation*" (9036)
"*arrange for the rental*" (9054)
"to *care for his children*" (8286)
"circumstances *call for a varied diet*" (8266)
"his duties *differ from other . . . men*" (9031)
"he *engaged in cutting lumber*" (8180)
"I *believe in God*" (7032)
"*believe in this case*" (9032)
"This letter . . . *elaborates upon the Western Union night letter* which I . . ." (9005)
"*look into this matter*" (8004)
"N —— *took after his father*" (8002)
"they *talked over the things*" (9040)
"I *spoke about the fixing up*" (9040)
". . . to *furnish us with the desired report*" (8299)
"to *fool with liquor*" (8296)
"I started to *comply with this order*" (9022)
"She could not *look after him*" (8114)

e. In the second of these groups that lie outside the two that make up 80 per cent of the instances, the noun is made into a modifier of an adjective. About 5 per cent of the instances are of this kind. Typical examples are

"The driver, *sober at this time,* called for his papers" (7042)
"Major —— appears very much *excited at the idea*" (9000)
"These men *available at this time* were not considered" (7025)
"A task *impossible under my present assignment*" (9062)
"A position *consistent with my abilities*" (9028)
"a mother *dependent on him*" (8114)
"a condition *impossible for the family*" (8303)
"a contribution not *necessary for their support*" (8027)
"*sufficient for the needs*" (9019)
"*available for* such temporary *duty*" (9031)
"*suitable for a . . .*" (9028)
"*eligible for promotion*" (9027) (9042)
"*ripe for conquest*" (9017)
"*ready for duty* the next morning" (9007)
"*unfitted for military service*" (9002)
"*difficult for me*" (9030)
"*inconsistent with the exigencies*" (9028)
"*satisfied with my work*" (9020)
"a position *similar to that* of other officers" (9030)
"an offer *acceptable to the State authorities*" (9029)

"for some time *previous to* ——*'s enlistment*" (8240) (8303)
"an officer *friendly to me*" (9000)
"a line *parallel to that line*" (9003)
"*familiar to me*" (9050)

f. In the third of these groups that lie outside the two that comprise 80 per cent of the instances, the noun is made into a modifier of the subject although it stands after the verb *to be* as a predicate adjective. About 3 per cent of the instances are of this kind. Typical examples are

"he was as yet unmarried and *without dependents*" (9021)
"they were *without these forms*" (9039)
"who is *under 21 years*" (8294)
"the playground is *for boys*" (7012)
"my war experience has been *with Machine Guns*" (9014) (9015)
"this is *for his mother*" (8308)
"half of the instructional work . . . is *on the subject of gas engines*" (9052)
"I am at present *on leave*" (9054)

g. There are a few cases of uses (less than one tenth of 1 per cent) that do not fit into any of the categories named above. Some examples are

"will find these papers *in proper form*" (8267)
"they want him *with her*" (8064)
"more good than having him here *with her*" (8174)
"to have my wife *with me*" (9030)
"I feel myself *in need of the instruction*" (9021)
"he took F—— *for his confirmation name*" (8101)
"he took John *for a name*" (8201)
"give me back my soldier boy *for a present*" (8038)
"the city *of Atlanta*" (9013)

If the figures here are to be trusted, Vulgar English seems to differ from Standard English in the frequency of the use of the function word to make a substantive a modifier of another substantive. In the Standard English materials this use accounts for approximately 45 per cent (nearly half) of the instances; in the Vulgar English materials it accounts for considerably less than a third (27.4 per cent of all; 29.6 per cent of the most used nine) of the instances. In the other categories there is no significant difference between the uses recorded here of Standard English and those of Vulgar English with the possible exception of those listed above in *d,* in which the noun by means of the function word is made into some type of object of the verb. These uses in the Vulgar English materials make a larger proportion of the total instances than they do in the Standard English materials (13.1 per cent as against 6.3 per cent).

In brief summary, the most significant facts concerning the use of function words with substantives are as follows:

1. Function words with substantives are of very great importance in the grammar of Present-day English. Both simple and compound forms are used freely to indicate relationships for which earlier stages of English and other Indo-European languages used word forms or case inflections. These function words, however, are used primarily with nouns rather than with pronouns. Approximately 90 per cent of the instances in these materials occurred with nouns and but 10 per cent with pronouns.

2. Nine of these function words are especially frequent in Modern English: *at, by, for, from, in, of, on, to, with.* In fact, these nine words occur in about 92 per cent of the instances.

3. These function words not only occur very frequently, they also are the means of expressing a great variety of relationships. If one attributes to these words "meaning," then, according to the *Oxford Dictionary,* there are at least a total of 329 different "meanings" for the nine most frequently used of these function words. If one insists that these meanings are not in the words themselves but in the context, or in the meanings of the words brought into relationship by means of these words, there is still a considerable variety of relationships in which these words function. They serve to make substantives (chiefly nouns) into (*a*) modifiers of other nouns, verbs, or adjectives; (*b*) various types of objects; (*c*) predicate adjectives; (*d*) appositives; (*e*) "object complements."

4. Present-day English shows a very definite tendency to the use of compound function words with substantives. The three most frequent types of compounding used are (*a*) the expansion which amounts to an analysis of and the precise indication of the particular meaning relationship involved (one of the many that can be carried by the particular function word which begins the compound); (*b*) the adding together of two or more function words which operate as a unit; (*c*) the combining of such adjectives as *according, owing, relating,* and *due,* with the word *to.* Those described in (*a*) and (*c*) occur most frequently in the materials of Standard English; those in (*b*) occur more frequently in Vulgar English.

5. There are only a few points upon which Standard English and Vulgar English seem to differ.

a. Some of the particular function words used with substantives occur only in the Standard English matter—*within,* for example. Others occur only in the Vulgar English letters—*till, off.* Some, like *until,* although they occur in both, appear less frequently in one type of English than in the other.

b. As indicated above (pages 111 and 112), although it is true that in both the Standard English materials and in the Vulgar English matter these function words are used primarily with nouns rather than with pronouns, it is also true that in the Vulgar English letters a distinctly larger proportion of the instances occur with pronouns. (In Standard English 92.4 per cent with nouns as against 7.6 per cent with pronouns; in Vulgar English 82 per cent with nouns as against 18 per cent with pronouns.)

c. The use of compound function words is common in both Standard English and in Vulgar English, but there is a distinct difference in the relative frequency of the three most important types of such compounds. The expansion pattern which amounts to an analysis and emphasis of the precise meaning relationship involved occurs much more frequently in Standard English, as does also the type which consists of an adjective (especially a participial adjective) with the function word *to* following. On the other hand, the adding together of two or more function words, as *off from, up till,* occurs about four times as frequently in Vulgar English as it does in Standard English.

d. For some reason that is not evident, the Vulgar English materials here examined use much less frequently than the Standard English materials the function word to make a substantive a modifier of a noun. In seeming compensation they use the function word to make the substantive a modifier of a verb much more frequently. (In the Standard English letters the function word is used to make a substantive a "modifier of a noun" in 45.4 per cent of the instances; in the Vulgar English letters only 27.4 per cent of the instances. In the Standard English letters the function word is used to make a substantive a "modifier of a verb" in 39.7 per cent of the instances; in the Vulgar English materials in 48.6 per cent of the instances.) In all the other relationships the two sets of material show remarkably close frequencies except that Vulgar English uses a greater number of the "types of object" variety than does Standard English.

VIII

THE USES OF FUNCTION WORDS: WITH VERBS

Some doubt arises concerning the appropriateness of the word "verbs" in connection with the uses of function words, for the function words that we shall be concerned with here—most of them commonly called "auxiliaries"—are not used with the so-called finite verbs (those verb forms that had personal endings) but almost solely [1] with certain derived forms called "infinitives" and "participles." This is not the place to discuss the nature of the infinitive and of the participle. It will be sufficient to say here that the infinitive is a verbal *substantive* [2] and the participles (both

[1] It is hardly sound, however, to assert, as our common school grammars usually do, that the "auxiliary" *have,* for example, is used *only* with the past participle and *never* with the simple past tense form of the verb, when at least 10 per cent of the strong verbs that have not gone over to the regular pattern in Modern English use the *simple past tense form* with this auxiliary. Such verbs are *abide, shine, stride, sit, stand, hold,* in which the past participle forms *abidden, shinnen, stridden, setten, standen,* and *holden,* have disappeared. All the weak verbs, of course, have, by regular historical sound change, lost all distinction of form between the simple past tense and the participle. See also above pages 61–62.

[2] "The infinitive was originally a *nomen actionis,* formed by means of various suffixes in the different Indo-European languages."—Joseph Wright and E. M. Wright, *Old English Grammar* (London, H. Frowde, 1908), p. 480.

The following quotations from Karl Brugmann's *Comparative Grammar of the Indo-Germanic Languages* touch briefly the usual views concerning infinitives and participles:

"Since the *nomina actionis* denote not merely a continuous activity but also one which may be defined in point of time, they sometimes come to be used in verbal constructions. Here, . . . the connective with the verb may include the power of governing a case, and of distinguishing differences in time, different kinds of action (such as momentary, continuous, inceptive) and Voice (*diathesis, genus verbi*).

"This kind of assimilation to the character and construction of the verb appears e. g. in Gr. *τὴν τοῦ θεοῦ δόσιν ὑμῖν* (Plat.) 'the gift of God to you' . . . But a still more complete identification is seen in what are called infinitives (and supines), which are crystallised cases (generally acc., dat., loc.) of *nomina actionis.* An infinitive may be said to be completely formed when the noun is no longer regarded as a case-form belonging to its own system, and its construction no longer follows the analogy of its original use as a noun; . . . Before, however, such forms were completely isolated from the nominal system, they passed through a number of intermediate stages, and hence it is often hard to say whether any particular form should be called an infinitive in the strict sense of the word. . . . The infinitive reached its

"present" and "past") are verbal *adjectives.* All but one of the function words to be treated here (i. e., *keep*) are used with the infinitives; three of these function words, however—*be, keep,* and *have*—are also used with the participles—*keep* with the present participle, *be* with both the present and the past participles, and *have* with the past participle.

These function words will be discussed in the following order:

I. Function Words Used with the Infinitive
  A. *To,* frequently called the "sign" of the infinitive
  B. *Do,* "emphatic" form, substitute verb, but especially in questions and with negatives
  C. *Shall, will,* the so-called "auxiliaries of the future tense"
  D. *Be,* in its various forms, with *to* and the infinitive
     Be, in its various forms, with *about* and *to* and infinitive
     Be, in its various forms, with *going* and *to* and infinitive; all three expressions also dealing with the "future"
  E. *Have,* with *to* and infinitive, as an expression of obligation or duty
  F. *Get,* often together with *have,* and with *to* and infinitive; also as an expression of obligation or duty
  G. *Used,* with *to* and infinitive, for customary action
  H. *May, can, must, might, could, would, should,* and *ought,* with the infinitive, the so-called modal "auxiliaries"

II. Function Words Used with the Participles
  I. *Be,* in its various forms, with the present participle, the so-called "progressive form," sometimes called the "definite tenses"
  J. *Get,* in its various forms, with the present participle, expressing inchoative action
  K. *Keep,* in its various forms, with the present participle, expressing continuous or repetitive action

---

most characteristic development in Greek and Latin, the only languages in which we find a special expression for differences in voice."—Vol. II, Part I, § 156, pp. 470–471.

"An adjective can be used to denote not only a quality inherent in the nature of the thing, but a transitory attribute, defined in regard to time according to the standpoint of the speaker; thus it comes to have somewhat of a verbal character, in other words it becomes a participle (μετοχή). Its verbal nature may include the power of governing a case, and of distinguishing different epochs of time, different kinds of action (momentary, continuous, inceptive), and Voice (*diathesis, genus verbi*)."—Vol. II, Part I, § 144, p. 456.

". . . no clear line can be drawn between Verbal Adjectives (Participle, Gerundive) and other Adjectives."—Vol. IV, Part III, § 1099, p. 605.

L. *Be,* in its various forms, with the past participle, the so-called "passive" form
M. *Get,* in its various forms, with the past participle
N. *Have,* in its various forms, with the past participle, forming the so-called "perfect tenses"

I. FUNCTION WORDS USED WITH THE INFINITIVE

A. To, *the "sign" of the infinitive*

In Old English there were two infinitive forms. First, there was what is sometimes called the "simple" infinitive. It always had the ending *-an* and in origin seems to have been the petrified nominative-accusative case of a neuter verbal noun ("se abbot ongan *singan*" = the abbot began [to] *sing*). Second, there was what is frequently called the "prepositional" infinitive (sometimes called the "gerundial" infinitive or "gerund"). The prepositional infinitive was made up of the preposition or function word *to* and the dative case of a verbal noun, ending in *-enne* (or *-anne*) ("sele us flæsc *to etanne*" = give us flesh *to eat*).[3] This infinitive with *to* had a much narrower range of use in Old English than the simple infinitive. The *to* with the inflected dative infinitive seems to have had originally the same meaning and use it had before ordinary substantives—motion, inclination, and thus purpose. This narrower range of use in Old English shows itself in the relative frequency of the *to* infinitive and the simple infinitive. Out of 9,495 instances of the infinitive in Old English only 2,402 or 25.3 per cent are the infinitive with *to,* while 7,094 or 74.7 per cent are the simple infinitive without *to.*[4]

From Old English to Present-day English there has been a spread of the word *to* into nearly all the uses of the infinitive so that there has been a complete reversal in the relative frequency of the *to* in-

[3] For a complete treatment of the infinitive in Old English see the monograph by Morgan Callaway, Jr., *The Infinitive in Anglo-Saxon* (Carnegie Institution of Washington, 1913). This study "is based upon a statistical reading of the whole of Anglo-Saxon literature with the exception of the glosses and a few out-of-prints." To it I am indebted for the statistics concerning the forms and uses of the infinitive in Old English. The display of examples and the exact references to all the occurrences of the infinitive in the materials covered are invaluable. For early Middle English see the monograph by Hermann Sanders, *Der syntaktische Gebrauch des Infinitivs im Frühmittelenglischen* (Heidelberg, 1915).

[4] In both the figures for Old English and those for Present-day English the number of instances used with the future auxiliaries and the modal auxiliaries have been omitted, for there has been no shift here in the infinitive form used.

finitive and the simple infinitive in Present-day English. In the materials examined here, there are, in all, 1,085 instances of the infinitive, of which only 196 or 18 per cent are the simple infinitive, and 889 or 82 per cent the infinitive with *to*.

The significance of this extension of *to* to nearly all the infinitives used in Present-day English [5] seems to be that the word *to* has lost practically all meaning in this connection except that of a function word operating as a marker for the infinitive, parallel to a distinguishing inflectional form.

Perhaps this fact is the basis for the pressure to place the func-

[5] As will be seen below, the simple infinitive without *to* is still used with the function words *shall, will, may, can, must, might, could, would, should,* and *do,* although the instances of these uses do not bulk large in the materials examined. Certain verbs of full word meaning were also found with the simple infinitive in our materials. These are, in the Standard English letters, *let, please, help, make, see.*

"the hospital authorities *let* me *get* up" (9006)
"if you would *let* me *know*" (8075)
"*let* the boy *come* home" (8064)
"*Please pardon* the delay" (8144)
"I will ask you to *please look*" (8004)
"*Please forgive* me" (9033)
"He has *helped pay* for his father's funeral expenses" (8303)
"an attendant *helped support* the left side" (9006)
"I cannot *help* but *feel* that this boy should be discharged" (8073)
"I *have seen* him *mount* a truck any time of night" (9009)
"impossible for the family to *make* ends *meet*" (8303)

[*Make,* however, is also used with the *to* infinitive, as in "which I voluntarily had cancelled to *make* me *to attend* this school" (9015).]

In the Vulgar English letters these same words and, in addition, *leave* and *have* appear with the simple infinitive without *to*. The number of instances in the Vulgar English materials, however, greatly exceeds that of the instances in the Standard English letters; in fact, there are eight times as many.

Examples are

"Please *leave* my son *come* home" (8178)
"*leave* me *know*" (8310)
"I hate to *let* it *go* so bad" (8080)
"kindly *let* me *hear* from you" (8136)
"to please *lett* my Boy *come* home" (8179)
"to *please discharge* him at once" (8126)
"will you *please give* him his ticket" (8118)

[Though rarely, the verb *please* also appears with the *to* infinitive, as in "*Please to look* in this affair" (8288).]

"to *help support* the family" (8129)
"*help save* our crops" (8258)
"and *help rase* the twoo little boys" (8220)
"*help* me *get* him out or transferred back" (8018)
"that I can not *help* but *make* one more effort" (8080)
"*have* him *write* to me" (8116)

Have in this use also appears with the *to* infinitive as in the following instances:

"So want you to *have* his Captain *to discharge* him" (8190)
". . . *had* the Red Cross *to write* to Captain ——" (8028)

tion word *to,* the infinitive "sign," immediately before the infinitive itself and to avoid an intervening adverb—the so-called "split" infinitive. The "split infinitive" construction does occur, however, in the materials examined here, although it is by no means frequent. It is certainly not limited to Vulgar English, for of the twenty instances found, eighteen were in the Standard English letters and only two in those of Vulgar English.

"I desire *to so arrange* my affairs . . ." (9033)
"that —— did conspire with other men *to not enter* their allotments" (9032)
"his ability *to effectually carry* on any project" (9020)
"that he may help me *to properly support* my family" (8056)
"would incur such delay as *to almost defeat* the purpose of . . ." (9001)
"in such manner as to enable him *to properly perform* his work" (9011)
"appreciate anything it may be possible to do *to favorably consider* his request" (9061)
"training is desired in order *to better acquaint* myself with the problems of . . ." (9061)
"and will be able *to successfully fill* any ordinary business position" (9039)
"*to adequately prepare* myself for this examination" (9027)
"His pay is not sufficient *to properly care* for me" (8127)
"he does not make enough . . . *to properly support* [6] me and his mother" (8270)

The instances of the function word *to* with the infinitive that appeared in the materials here examined can be grouped as follows:

1. To + *infinitive as a verb (or sentence) modifier, expressing "purpose."*

In Old English *to* with the inflected infinitive very frequently expressed purpose. In the history of the language, as the word *to* was increasingly attached to other uses of the infinitive, there arose the expanded function word expression *for to* [7] to indicate purpose as in Chaucer's lines

[6] Parallel with the insertion of an adverb between the function word *to* and the infinitive is the frequent use of an adverb between the other function words and the infinitive used with them, as in "so that he *can properly support* his parents and myself" (8270)

[7] Compare other expanded function word expressions discussed above, pp. 115–117, (1), (2), and (3).

"For he was late y-come from his viage
And wente *for to doon* his pilgrymage" [8]

In our materials two other compound function word expressions for purpose appeared, *in order to* and *so as to.*

The number of occurrences is indicated in the following table:

TABLE XIII

"TO" + INFINITIVE, EXPRESSING "PURPOSE"

	Standard English	*Vulgar English*
Simple form:		
a. to + inf.	63	123
Expanded or compound forms:		
b. for to + inf.	0	1
c. in order to + inf.	7	0
d. so as to + inf.	4	0
Total	74	124

STANDARD ENGLISH

a. "he ran off and joined the army *to keep* out of trouble" (8017)
"if any thing can be done *to secure* this boy" (8189)
"and had to drink *to keep* from going crazy" (8296)
"suits are now being tried *to obtain* the land" (9060)
"I am writing *to assure* you" (9061)
"I shall do my best *to have* this account settled" (9033)

b. No instances

c. "the practical experience I should have *in order to pass* these tests" (9050)
"if her son —— could be discharged *in order to return* home" (8163)
"a person must be 21 years of age *in order to enlist*" (8056)
"I am needed at home *in order to accomplish* . . ." (9040)
"*In order to enable* me to comply with the above, I request that . . ." (9055)

d. "I request that the attached order be modified *so as to allow* me to. . ." (9061)
"Can the examination be given . . . *so as to give* ample time for him to be prepared" (9043)
"Had my orders read *so as to take* effect after July 1 . . . I would have been able to . . ." (9052)

[8] Geoffrey Chaucer, *Canterbury Tales,* Prologue, lines 77–78. Some other examples from the Prologue are lines 17, 73.

VULGAR ENGLISH

a. "i am righting *to see* if you could . . ." (8313)
"So he lied *to enlist* . . ." (8238)
"I had to borrow *to get* him home" (8288)
"I worked *to bring* him where he is" (8005)
"I wish I was there *to do* for her what I could" (8039)
"after a Mother & Father suffer *to raise* a Boy" (8074)

b. "I am asking for your help *for to locate* my son" (8106)

c. No instances

d. No instances

In these uses, Vulgar English again shows itself more conservative than Standard English. Nearly twice as many of the old simple infinitive of purpose appeared in the Vulgar English letters; and in these letters, too, appeared the only example of the Middle English expanded form, *for to*. Only in the Standard English letters appeared the newer compound forms *in order to* and *so as to*.[9]

2. To + *infinitive as object of such verbs as* attempt, begin, continue, decide, desire, endeavor, expect, fail, hate, help, intend, like, promise, refuse, start, threaten, try,[10] undertake, want, wish.

These are the verbs that occurred in the Standard English letters. In the Vulgar English materials many of the same verbs appeared, as *begin, decide, desire, endeavor, fail, hate, like, promise, refuse, try,*[10] *want,* and *wish*. Some verbs, however, appeared only in the Vulgar English materials, as *afford, ask, beg, consent, hope, mean, need,* and *say*. In all, there were in the Standard English materials seventy one instances; in the Vulgar English letters, 121. Examples are

STANDARD ENGLISH

"I . . . did not *attempt to advocate* . . ." (9057)
"and was just *beginning to be* a good officer" (9018)

[9] The first quotation in the *Oxford Dictionary* for *in order to* is dated 1655, and that for *so as to* is dated 1680.

[10] The construction *try and* rather than *try to* appeared much more frequently in the Vulgar English letters. Examples are

"please *try an let* him come back" (8288)
"please *try and find* out . . ." (8088)
". . . please *try and get* my son" (8079)
"i want your department to *try and locate* ——" (8154)
"I want you to *try and send* —— home" (8311)

Four examples, however, occurred in the Standard English materials. They are

"B—— went there to *try and apprehend* him" (9567)
"if you will *try and locate* this man" (7530)

(*Continued on next page*)

"the same influence will *continue to make* his life . . ." (8296)
"—— has *decided to take* the examination" (9027)
"I *desire to visit* my parents" (9065)
"we will still *endeavor to secure* same" (8299)
"I *expect to be located* near ——" (9050)
"I *failed to pay* the assessment" (9059)
"but *hate to be kicked* out in this manner" (9033)
"The boy . . . *helped to support* the family" (8260)
"I *intended to put* in the request" (9040)
"I would *like to report* for . . ." (9027)
"I can only *promise to do* my best" (9033)
"He *refused to return* . . ." (8144)
"I *started to comply* . . ." (9022)
"he *threatened to enlist*" (8002)
"His father *tried to get* him not to . . ." (8064)
"I *tried to avoid* . . ." (9057)
"in any undertaking that he might *undertake to do*" (8060)
"where no true wife and mother *would want to stay*" (8296)
"I hereby *wish to make* application" (8056)

VULGAR ENGLISH

"his health *began to fail*" (8072)
"My little son —— *decided to join* . . ." (8244)
"the only reason he *desires to stay* . . ." (8057)
"I *endeavored to go* to ——" (8039)
". . . and *failed to tell* . . ." (8274)
"I *Hate to seem* impatient" (8135)
"we would *like to have* him home" (8154)
"I *promised not to do* . . ." (8265)
"his wife *refuses to live* with me" (8199)
"He *tried to work*" [10] (8233)
"I *want to get* him out" (8165)
"I *wish to ask* for a discharge" (8152)

Examples of the *to*-infinitive as object with verbs that do not appear in the Standard English letters are

"we cannot *afford to send* her" (8233)
"he *is asking* in a letter *to get* hime out of" (8005)
"I also *beg to release* him" (8251)
"if you will *consent to have* him come home" (8075)
"I *hope to find* him" (8151)
"I do not *mean to insinuate*" (8251)
"they *need to be* fed" (8288)
"He *says to tell* you . . ." (8219)

"she will *try and get* a statement" (8283)
"*to try and find* the missing articles" (5112)

3. To + *infinitive with a substantive subject (pronouns in accusative form), the whole expression serving as object of such verbs as* allow, ask, compel, direct, enable, estimate, find, get, know, lead, order, permit, want, write.

These are the verbs that appeared in the Standard English letters and are "active" in form. To be considered with the *to*-infinitives of this group are also those rather frequent instances in which the substantive that might have been the subject of the *to*-infinitive appears as subject of the main verb, and this main verb has the so-called "passive" form.[11] The list of verbs so used is as follows: *advise, authorize, compel, destine, direct, force, inspire, make, oblige, order, prepare, recommend, require, select, sentence.*

In the Vulgar English materials instances of both constructions appeared but with some differences especially in the frequency of their use. Of the first construction (the *to*-infinitive with a substantive subject, the whole expression as object of a verb, as "They directed *me to return*") more than twice as many instances occurred as in the Standard English letters; but in more than half of these instances the *to*-infinitive with substantive subject was object of one of the three verbs *ask, want, tell.* Other verbs which appeared were *advise, beg, expect, forbid, get, help, lead, persuade, request, wish.*

Of the second construction (the *to*-infinitive depending upon a main verb in "passive" form, as "I was directed to return") very few instances occurred in the Vulgar English letters—in fact, only one third as many as in the Standard English materials. The particular verbs so used were *allow, beg, entice, suppose, tell, warn.*

The exact number of instances that appeared in our materials is as follows:

	Standard English	*Vulgar English*
Of the first construction	21	53
Of the second construction	24	7

Examples from Standard English of the first construction are

"to *allow me to take* leave" (9061)
"—— has *asked us to write*" (8189)

[11] Compare, for example, "*I* was directed *to return*" with "They directed *me to return.*"

"The conditions which *compel the parents* of this boy *to request* . . ." (8183)
"—— *directed me to return*" (9050)
"*enable me to comply*" (9055)
"I *estimate it to be* well over 500" (9031)
"I *have . . . found them to be suffering* from . . ." (8266)
"His father tried to *get him not to enlist*" (8164)
"I *know him to be* an honorable and truthful man" (8064)
"this *has led me to make* a further investigation" (9063)
"I *have ordered him to report*" (9023)
". . . *will permit me to leave* this" (9028)
"they do *want him to come home*" (8144)
"we *wrote the Red Cross Representative* of —— *to furnish* us . . ." (8299)

Examples from Standard English of the second construction are

"*I was* also *advised to give*" (9054)
"that *I be authorized to remain* on active duty" (9027)
"the *father is compelled to work*" (8183)
"*I have been compelled to establish* a place of abode" (9030)
"the *airplane is destined to play* a very great part" (9028)
"*I was directed to look* . . ." (9050)
"*I was forced to leave* college" (9036)
"*they will not be inspired to become* leaders" (8296)
"*he cannot be made* to send . . ." (8174)
"*She was obliged to discontinue* . . ." (8260)
"*I . . . was ordered to report* at ——" (9022)
"*I would be recommended to attend* this school" (9033)
"*I am required to submit* . . ." (9055)
"*the undersigned was not required to take* . . ." (9054)
"*I had been selected to attend* the school" (9025)
"*he was sentenced . . . to pay* only a nominal fine" (8296)

Examples from Vulgar English of the first construction are

"—— *advise me to write* to you" (8251)
"I ernestly *ask you to do* all you can" (8020)
"We *are Beging you to lett* him come Home" (8179)
". . . as they *expect a man to do* these days" (8018)
"the doctor *forbids me to do* . . ." (8235)
"a couple of his boy chums *got him to go* with them" (8018)
"if you would please *help me to get* him out" (8074)
"that my letter to you *lead you to think* . . ." (8251)
". . . *perswaid him to join* . . ." (8045)
"She *requested me to write* . . ." (8035)
"as one of the commanders *told us to do*" (8242)

"... to *tell you to write* ..." (8219)
"I *want you to get* this verry plain" (8005)
"I *want you all to send* him back to me" (8045)
"I *wish you to Discharge* him" (8236)

Examples from Vulgar English of the second construction are

"*he will never be allowed to vote*" (8038)
"if *I were allowed to transfer* to a local post" (8082)
"*he was beged to join* the ..." (8025)
"My *Son was inticed to Join* the ..." (8100)
"*he is supposed to be posted* in ..." (8288)
"*I was told to write* you" (8074)
"*She was also warned not to go* to work" (8005)

4. To + *infinitive as the predicate of an indirect question after such verbs as* ask, know, tell, write.

Very few instances of this construction appeared in the materials examined here and most of them (eleven out of twelve) occurred in the Vulgar English letters.

STANDARD ENGLISH

"This information is desired so that I may know *where to report*" (9042)

VULGAR ENGLISH

"let me know *what to do* about it" (8084)
"you can tell me *who to write* to" (8038)
"Please write me the amount and *who to send* it to" (8249)
"let me know *how to proced* in getting his release" (8257)
"Please write me ... *whether to send* money order or check" (8249)

5. To + *infinitive as modifier of a noun.*

The *to*-infinitive is fairly often used in Modern English as an adjunct modifier of a noun. In the Standard English letters forty instances occurred; in those of Vulgar English there were twenty seven instances.

STANDARD ENGLISH

"accentuates my *desire to be returned* at any early date" (9019)
"a *tendency to equalize* each other" (9024)
"a definite *call to preach*" (9036)
"for many *years to come*" (9061)
"the *right to visit* them" (8296)

"in a *position to assist*" (8283)
"*funds to buy* the son out" (8073)
"the additional *opportunity to develop*" (9061)
"only one *subject to be examined in*" (9027)

VULGAR ENGLISH

"5 yr's is his *limit to live*" (8153)
"I never had *Occasion to use* Geometry" (8057)
". . . *inibility to take* this examination" (8057)
"this was his second *time to leave* home" (8218)
"the *party to write* to" (8249)
"have *cause to know*" (8072)
"no fit *Place to go*" (8187)

Belonging with the construction illustrated here perhaps, but also partly fitting in with the use of the *to*-infinitive as a modifier of an adjective (see group 6 below), are the following examples:

STANDARD ENGLISH

"neither was the *proper person to have* such custody" (8296)
"I do not have *sufficient funds to meet* the required expenses" (9036)
"to raise *sufficient funds to buy* the son out" (8073)
"the *necessary arrangements to take* this course" (9024)
"I had *sufficient funds to cover* . . ." (9057)
"One gave *sufficient evidence to cause* the closing of the —— Hotel" (9036)

VULGAR ENGLISH

"We didn't have *anoff money to pay* our way" (8005)
"to do *enough work to bring* them up" (8187)

6. To + *infinitive as a modifier of an adjective.*

The *to*-infinitive is frequently used in Modern English as a modifier of an adjective. In the Standard English letters sixty five instances occurred; in those of Vulgar English there were seventy nine instances. In about a third of the instances from Standard English the infinitive was a modifier of the adjectives *able* or *unable;* and nearly half of those from Vulgar English were modifiers of these same two adjectives.[12]

[12] Here also should be considered those examples in which the *to*-infinitive introduced by *as* modifies an adjective (or an adverb) and expresses "result."
From Standard English
"My work . . . has been such *as to make* me . . ." (9042)
". . . be so kind *as not to send* this boy away" (8160)

(*Continued on next page*)

STANDARD ENGLISH

"her husband has become helpless and *unable to work*" (8189)
"—— may in all probability be *able to obtain* employment" (8174)
"I am not financially *capable to return*" (9036)
"who is *anxious to have* her son" (8023)
"I am *anxious to help* these people out" (8004)
"I am *tickled* to death *to get* out of . . ." (9033)
"we shall be *pleased to obtain* . . ." (8239)

VULGAR ENGLISH

"I am sickly and not *able to do* any work" (8127)
"his father . . . is *disable to work* . . ." (8255)
"We hant *able to work* much" (8246)
"he is verry *young to be* in . . ." (8167)
"he was making money *enough to support* me" (8230)
"work is *hard to get*" (8293)

In these Vulgar English materials also appeared six examples of the *to*-infinitive as a modifier of an adjective qualified by *enough* as an adverb of degree.

"until they are *old enough to understand*" (8067)
"he is not *old enough to be* . . ." (8280)
"if you will be *kind enough to help* me" (8018)
"he is all the boy I have that is *big enough to work*" (8025)
". . . you would be *kind enough to send* him . . ." (8211)
". . . only other *old enough to help*" (8176)

7. To + *infinitive as a noun—subject, appositive, or predicate nominative.*

The *to*-infinitive is fairly frequently used in the functions of the simple noun other than that of object, as indicated above in group 2, although these subject, appositive, and predicate nominative uses are by no means as common as the object construction.

First, there are those cases in which the *to*-infinitive is frequently called the "logical" subject, but the actual position of subject is occupied by the function word *it* [13] and the *to*-infinitive stands next to an adjective as it does in the instances just listed in group 6.

From Vulgar English
"I have gotten in such circumstances *as to have* to sell our little home" (8152)

[13] See below pages 240–244 in Chapter IX for a discussion of *it* as a function word.

STANDARD ENGLISH

"It was *impracticable to leave* my dependent wife" (9052)
"It is *impossible to go* at any other period" (9036)
"If it would be *necessary to procure* leave of absence" (9065)
"it is *right to send* him . . ." (9018)
"Was it *correct to have drawn* pay . . ." (9035)
"if it is *possible to do* so" (8267)

VULGAR ENGLISH

"if it is at all *possible to get* him out" (8270)

Second, there are those cases in which the *to*-infinitive is the "logical" subject with the function word *it* in the subject position, but no adjective is present. Only six instances were found.

STANDARD ENGLISH

"It will be appreciated *to have* you devote your . . ." (9029)
"it would be of no more expense *to send* me there" (9042)

VULGAR ENGLISH

"it hurts me *to see* him in this condition" (8251)
"it bothers her quite a bit *to work"* (8129)
"He dont know what *it* is *to stay* away from Home" (8190)
"I[t] makes me worry very much *to lose* my son" (8048)

Here probably belong also such instances as the following, in the first of which the *to*-infinitive is the "logical" subject of the subordinate clause as well as modifier of the noun *duty*. In the second, the *to*-infinitive is the "logical" subject but also the "object" modifier of the noun *desire*. Both these instances are from the Standard English letters.

"I think *it* is my *duty* as a citizen *to help* them out" (8004)
"it is my *desire to spend* my leave of absence . . ." (9043)

Of rare occurrence in our materials was the *to*-infinitive as subject without the *it* function word, as in the following example from the Standard English letters:

"to detail me to another station is an unnecessary expense" (9042)

Third, there are those cases in which the *to*-infinitive is an appositive. In the first example from Standard English it is only formally an appositive of the function word *it* which occupies the "object" position. The second example is from the Vulgar English letters.

"I took *it* upon myself *to talk* with him" (8296)
"I would ask a *favor* of you *to let* him come" (8155)

Fourth, there are those cases in which the *to*-infinitive appears as a predicate nominative.

STANDARD ENGLISH

"My object in seeking this detail is *to better* myself" (9032)
"The purpose of this request is *to enable* me to acquire instruction" (9019)

VULGAR ENGLISH

"all I can do is *to plead* . . ." (8052)

8. To + *infinitive preceded by the function word* for *and a substantive, the whole expression being a modifier of a noun or an adjective, or the "logical" subject with* it *in the subject position.*

These uses parallel those without *for* and a substantive given above in groups 5, 6, and 7.

STANDARD ENGLISH

"so as to give ample time *for him to be prepared*" (9043)
"A most easy matter *for him to accomplish*" (9032)
"The resulting situation will be a difficult one *for me to meet*" (9056)
"The fact that . . . is going to make it difficult . . . *for me to get settled*" (9033)
"it is impossible *for me to settle* this account" (9033)
"It seems impossible *for the family to make* ends meet" (8303)
"it would be impossible *for them to raise* sufficient funds . . ." (8073)
"it was well nigh impossible *for an error or other irregularity to escape* notice" (9032)

VULGAR ENGLISH

"i didn't sign the papers *for him to go*" (8246)
"I havent sined any papers up *for him to get* in the . . ." (8045)
"my daughter gave concent *for her 18 year old son to enlist*" (8274)
"Is there any way *for him to be restored*" (8038)
"it takes 6 days *for a letter to get* to New York" (8096)
"it is a proper thing and a good thing *for a young man to belong* to any . . ." (8018)
"it would be better *for him to be* at home" (8113)
"it is really necessary *for me to get* this boy" (8152)

"I would be very glad *for you to advise* me" (8028)
"it is impossible *for him to support* me" (8127)

Some examples of uses of this construction (*for* + substantive + *to* + infinitive) that did not appear in the Standard English materials are the following. In most of these examples the whole expression depends upon the verb as modifier or as object.

"the Mother signed *for him to go*" (8005)
"I cant hardly stand *for him to be away*" (8204)
"I dident sign up *for him to join*" (8261)
"I . . . would also like *for him to finish* his education" (8022)
"I sigen up *for this boy to go* to work" (8025)
"I mean *for him to be sent* Back at once" (8045)
"The Dr. said . . . *for him not to take* any long walks" (8190)

In addition to the eight groups of uses of the *to*-infinitive here described, there are those in which the *to*-infinitive is used with certain function words to make up a so-called verb "phrase." As listed above (pages 129 and 130) they are

a. be, in its various forms, with *to* and the infinitive, as in
"Mrs. —— *is to accompany* me . . ." (9055)
"this land *is to be presented* to the government" (9062)

b. be, in its various forms, with *about* and *to* and infinitive, as in
"I *was about to have* —— released in the proper way" (8281)

c. be, in its various forms, with *going,* and *to* and infinitive, as in
"he *was going to do away* with himself" (8076)
"The fact that my pay will soon be reduced . . . *is going to make* it difficult to . . ." (9033)
"if they *are going to discharge* him" (8072)

d. have, with *to* and the infinitive, as an expression of obligation or duty, as in
"she frequently *had to support* the entire family" (8144)
"My children *have to have* books and clothes to go to school" (8235)

e. get, often together with *have,* with *to* and the infinitive; also an expression of obligation or duty, as in
"he is my only surporte and I *have* just *got to have* him" (8059)

f. ought, with *to* and the infinitive, an expression of (moral) obligation, as in
"that *ought to be* enough" (8157)
"anyone *ought to know* as much" (8067)

g. used, with *to* and the infinitive, an expression of customary action, as in
"I *used to wash* for a living" (8235)

These seven, simply listed and illustrated here, will be discussed below in connection with each of the function words by which they are introduced.

The following table gives the precise figures of all the occurrences in each group of the function word *to* with the infinitive.

TABLE XIV

	Standard English	*Vulgar English*
1. As a verb or sentence modifier, expressing "purpose":		
Simple form, *to* + inf.	63	123
Compound form, *for to* + inf.	0	1
Compound form, *in order to* + inf.	7	0
Compound form, *so as to* + inf.	4	0
2. As object of such verbs as *attempt, begin, decide, expect, help, intend, try, want, wish,* etc.	71	121
3. With subject substantive (pronouns in acc. form), whole expressions object of such verbs as *ask, compel, enable, get, permit, want,* etc.:		
"Active" construction	21	53
"Passive" construction	24	7
4. As predicate of indirect question after such verbs as *ask, know, tell,* etc.	1	11
5. As a modifier of a noun	40	27
6. As a modifier of an adjective	65	79
7. As a noun—subject, appositive, or predicate nominative	18	8
8. With *for* + sb. + *to* + inf., the whole expression as modifier or as "logical" subject	11	25
9. Uses with other function words	33	56
be + *to* + inf.		
be + *about* + *to* + inf.		
be + *going* + *to* + inf.		
have + *to* + inf.		
get + *to* + inf.		
ought + *to* + inf.		
used + *to* + inf.		
10. The so-called "split" infinitive not included in classes indicated above	18	2
Total	376	513

This survey of the function word *to* with the infinitive shows a number of facts that seem somewhat significant.

1. The spread of the use of the word *to* from a somewhat narrow range of use in only 25 per cent of the instances of the infinitive in Old English to a much wider range of use in 82 per cent of the instances in Present-day English justifies its designation as the "sign" of the infinitive, for it has become in most respects a pure function word operating as a marker for the infinitive, parallel to a distinguishing inflectional form.

2. The so-called "split" infinitive—the separation of the function word *to* from the infinitive by means of an intervening adverb—is not a matter of Vulgar English. Of the twenty instances appearing in our materials eighteen were found in the letters of Standard English.

3. In the use of the *to* + infinitive for the expression of "purpose" the Vulgar English materials contain twice as many instances as do the Standard English letters, but there seems to be little or no significance in this fact. On the other hand, there does seem to be significance in the fact that, of the three "compound" forms to express purpose, *for to* appears in the Vulgar English only, and *in order to* and *so as to* appear only in the Standard English letters.

4. In the use of the *to* + infinitive as object of such verbs as *attempt, begin, continue, decide, desire, help, intend, like, promise, try, want, wish,* etc., two matters of difference between Standard English and Vulgar English appeared. First, the verb *say* in such a construction as "He *says to tell* you . . ." (8219) occurs in the Vulgar English letters only. Second, with the verb *try*, the construction *try and* rather than *try to,* although four instances appeared in the Standard English letters, occurred much more frequently in the Vulgar English materials.

5. Although the use of the *to*-infinitive with a substantive subject (pronouns in accusative form), the whole expression being object of such verbs as *allow, ask, get, permit, want,* etc., as in "—— *has asked us to write*" (8189) occurred frequently in both groups of materials, especially in Vulgar English, the construction with the *to*-infinitive depending upon a verb in "passive" form, as in "We *were asked to write,*" occurred rarely in Vulgar English (seven instances in all).

6. In the use of the *to*-infinitive as the modifier of a noun, certain constructions appeared in Vulgar English only. These were the cases in which the noun modified by the *to*-infinitive was also modified by a genitive case substantive. Examples are

> "this was *his* second time *to leave* home" (8218)
> "5 yr's is *his* limit *to live*" (8153)

In place of such a genitive modifier the more usual Standard English construction is

"this was *the* second time *for him* to leave home"
"five years is *the* limit *for him* to live"

7. In connection with the *to*-infinitive preceded by the function word *for* and a substantive, one type of construction occurs in the Vulgar English materials only. In this construction the whole expression, instead of being a modifier of a noun or an adjective, or the "logical" subject with *it* in the subject position, depends upon the verb as a modifier or as an object. Examples are

"the Mother signed *for him to go*" (8005)
"I cant hardly stand *for him to be away*" (8204)
"I . . . would also like *for him to finish* his education" (8022)
"I mean *for him to be sent* back at once" (8045)
"The Dr. said . . . *for him not to take* any long walks" (8190)

B. Do, *especially in questions and with negatives*

The verb *do,* in its various forms, has, in Modern English, a variety of uses. It still retains, for example, its full word meaning of *perform, accomplish, make, bring about, produce,* as in the following examples:

"he seemed remorseful for what he *had done*" (8076)
"Mrs. —— *did* housework for Mrs. ——" (8240)
"he never *did* a stroke of work" (8144)
"she is unable to work or *do* anything" (8142)
"get work and *do* the right thing" (8139)
"anything that you can *do* for them" (8004)

But more frequently *do* operates as a function word followed by the simple infinitive. As a function word it has four important uses.

First, but least frequently, it is used to make an "emphatic" form—a form that receives strong stress in speech and one that usually stands in a statement offered as an answer to a preceding question or a contradiction of a preceding assertion. The following instance is the only one that appeared in the Standard English letters:

"In answer to a direct question . . . as to whether or not they would like him home, they agreed that . . . they *do want* him to come home . . ." (8144)

Second, it is used as a substitute verb, a word that serves to repeat or refer to the meaning of any verb that has been used before it in the immediate context. Thirteen instances of this use appeared in the Standard English letters.

> "it is doubted whether her son would return to his home, and in case he *did* it is . . ." (8017)
> "knowing these conditions as I *do,* I am sure . . ." (8180)
> "she has been asked to give her entire pay to her mother which she *does* at the present time" (8081)
> ". . . he promised to let it alone, and for a number of months he *did* so" (8296)
> "I am informed that the mother who is illiterate and has a minor female to support needs this young man to provide the financial means *to do* so" (8234)
> "The government does not especially need his services while from all indications his family *does*" (8073)

Third, and of especial importance for Modern English, the function word *do* is used with the negative verb. In this situation the word *do* seems to be a pure function word with no content of meaning; it serves as the formal element of the verb, bearing the inflectional signs of tense and number. The simple infinitive which follows the negative particle carries the full word meaning of the verb. Thus with *do* the "verb" is divided, and the negative particle retains its usual place immediately before the full word meaning element of the verb, and the subject can immediately precede the element bearing the formal characteristics. This use of the function word appeared in the fifteenth century [14] and seems to have some relation to the development of the use of word order as a grammatical device.[15] Thirty seven instances of this use of *do* as a function word with a negative verb were found in the Standard English letters. Examples are

> "people who know the father *do not think* a great deal of him" (8002)
> "I *do not believe* he is on that transport" (8075)
> "She *does not expect* to receive any damages" (8095)
> "The government *does not especially need* his services" (8073)
> "Her son B—— *did not support* her before he went . . ." (8144)
> "she stated that she *did not know* . . ." (8139)

[14] The earliest example given in the *Oxford Dictionary* is from Caxton, dated c. 1489, "It is to late to repente me that I *dyde not doo.*"
[15] See below Chapter X.

Fourth, and of equally great importance for Modern English, the function word *do* is used in questions. This use of *do* even more clearly than the use of *do* with negative verbs seems also to be related to the development of the use of word order as a grammatical device and arises at the end of the Middle English period.[16] Reversal of the subject-verb word order has been the normal order for questions throughout the history of the English language. With the "dividing" of the verb by means of the function word *do*, the element of the verb that carries the formal characteristics of tense can precede the subject and the full word meaning element of the verb can follow the subject. In questions, in the present or past tense, therefore, the pattern in Present-day English is

> *do* (carrying the formal verbal characteristics) + subject + verb (carrying full-word verbal meaning)

This arrangement is especially necessary in Modern English whenever a transitive verb with an object is used. To make a question out of "The man killed the bear" one cannot simply shift the subject and the verb as in "Killed the man the bear?" With the use of the function word as in "Did the man kill the bear?" the subject is still distinguished from the object by means of the word order, and the interrogative reversal of subject and verb is also accomplished. Although this is a frequent use of *do* in Modern English,[17] the materials examined here were not such as to make possible its frequent use. In fact only one example was found.

> "*Do you think* any mother would . . ." (8005)

In the Vulgar English letters the same uses of *do*, both as full word and as function word, appeared in about the same proportions.

Examples of the full word *do* are

> "have been *doing* business since . . ." (8094)
> "I wish I was there *to do* for her what I could" (8039)
> "If I had this *to do* over again" (8039)
> "I would of never let him *do* such a thing" (8074)
> "Not able *to do* any work . . ." (8127)

[16] The earliest example given in the *Oxford Dictionary* is from Chaucer, dated c. 1386, "Fader why *do* ye *wepe?*"

[17] Note, for example, the 1,424 instances counted by Thorndike *et al.* and its rank of 6 on his scale of 1 to 9 (9 being most frequent). "Inventory of English Constructions," *Teachers College Record,* Vol. 28, February, 1927, pp. 580–610.

"he would *do* his best" (8152)
"it will *do* him good" (8218)
"I was glad to get out of *doing* 7 years" (8039)

Examples from Vulgar English of *do* as the function word to make a so-called emphatic form—often an answer to a preceding question or a contradiction of a preceding assertion—are

"I sure *do* worry over him" (8190)
"I *do* believe you know a fathers circumstances" (8079)
"We *do* need his support and need it bad and *did* need it when he went away" (8218)
"Please *do* give him a discharge" (8121)
"I *do* hope you will do one or the other" (8122)
"for my sake *do* let him out" (8204)

Examples from Vulgar English of *do* as a function word with negative verbs are

"he *does not give* much money" (8233)
"If we *dont get* this Boy out" (8005)
"if you *don't think* I am is lawful Gardine" (8025)
"he *did not come* home from there" (8038)
"I guess my clouds *dont have* those bright lineings" (8038)
"Some *do not need* there boy" (8187)
"I *dont know* what I am going to do" (8053)

The exact number of occurrences of *do* in our materials is as follows:

TABLE XV

	Standard English	*Vulgar English*
Do as a full word	19	61
Function word *do*—		
"Emphatic"	1	9
Substitute verb	13	8
With negative	37	40
In questions	0	1

C. Shall *and* will, *the so-called "auxiliaries of the future tense"* [18]

The school grammars of Modern English usually give as the one means of indicating future time the combination of *shall* and *will* with the infinitive, and name it the "future tense." Some give two forms for the future tense: one for "simple futurity" and another for the "emphatic future" or the "future of determination." As a matter of fact, however, the use of the function words *shall* and *will* with the infinitive is but one of several important methods of expressing future time. The present tense form of the verb, for example, frequently refers to future time both in subordinate clauses and in independent sentences when some other word than the verb, or the context in general, indicates the time notion. "He *returns* from his trip tomorrow." "If he *comes,* I must question him."

Some other combinations which should also be included as devices for an English "future tense" are those to be considered in section D, below. Examples of them are

"The man *is to accompany* me."
"He *is about to dive* from the bridge."
"They *are going to discharge* him."

On the other hand, the use of *shall* and *will* to express "determination"—the so-called "emphatic future" or "modal future"—is no more entitled to be included in the name "future tense" than many other combinations of function words, and even full word verbs, with infinitives, which, because of their meaning, look to the future for fulfilment. This is especially true of the two function words to be treated below in sections E and F and of those so-called "modal auxiliaries" to be discussed in section H. Some examples of these expressions are

"The men *have to go* to the city."
"He is my only support and *I've got to have* him."

[18] For the discussion of *shall* and *will* here, I have drawn freely upon my two earlier articles: "The Periphrastic Future with *Shall* and *Will* in Modern English," *Publications of the Modern Language Association,* Vol. 40, 1925, pp. 963–1024; and "The Expression of the Future," *Language,* Vol. 3, 1927, pp. 87–95. For permission to use this material I am grateful to the editors of these periodicals

"We {*ought to build* / *must build* / *may build* / *intend to build*} a new house."

Concerning the use of *shall* and *will* there have been many vigorous discussions through more than a hundred years. One cannot read through the mass of these discussions without being impressed by the wide diversity of the points of view and the definite conflict of the opinions and conclusions thus brought together. Even among the articles that can be grouped as expressing the conventional rules there is considerable variety and contradiction,[19] not in the general rule for independent-declarative statements (that a *shall* with the first person corresponds with a *will* with the second and third) but in the other rules concerning questions, reported discourse, and subordinate clauses. The conclusions expressed in the more scientific studies are not only in opposition to the conventional rules but they also conflict sharply with one another.[20] In all this mass of material there is hardly a general statement concerning *shall* and *will* for which a direct contradiction cannot be found coming from a source that merits careful consideration. Thus, after more than a century of discussion of the use of *shall* and *will*, there are no accepted views of what the actual usage of these two words is, of the meaning and trend of the development of that usage, and of the causes that gave rise to it.

[19] Compare, for example, the rules for *shall* and *will* as given in the three following books:

Alma Blount and C. S. Northup, *English Grammar* (New York, Holt and Co., 1914).

Edwin C. Woolley, *Handbook of Composition* (New York, D. C. Heath and Co., 1907).

H. W. Fowler and F. G. Fowler, *The King's English* (Oxford, Clarendon Press, 1906).

[20] See, for example, the conflict of statements and conclusions in the following treatments of *shall* and *will:*

Henry Sweet, *New English Grammar,* Vol. 2, "Syntax," 1898, pp. 92–96.

Krüger, *Syntax der Englischen Sprache,* Vol. 4, "Zeitwort," 1914, pp. 1425–1500.

Oxford Dictionary, articles on *shall, will.*

C. B. Bradley, "Shall and Will—An Historical Study," *Transactions of American Philological Association,* Vol. 42, 1911, pp. 5–31.

G. O. Curme, "Has English a Future Tense?" *Journal of English and Germanic Philology,* Vol. 12, 1913, pp. 515–539.

Philip Aronstein, "Shall und Will zum Ausdrucke der Idealität im Englischen," *Anglia,* Vol. 41, 1917, pp. 10–93, 301–392.

For a listing of some of the outstanding conflicts in the statements appearing in

That there is a considerable body of literary usage which conflicts with the conventional rules is clearly proved by the many pages, in the books setting forth these rules, which are devoted to pointing out the "violations" and "blunders" which even "the best of our authors" have made. Thus in Fowler and Fowler, *The King's English,* pages 141 to 153 contain examples of such "blunders" taken from the following: *Daily Telegraph, London Times,* Richardson, Jowett, F. M. Crawford, *Westminster Gazette,* Burke, S. Ferrier, Wilde, Stevenson, Crockett, Conan Doyle, *Spectator,* H. Sweet, Gladstone.

Richard Grant White, in *Every Day English,* gives "a long series of plain unmistakable examples of its misuse" by Cowley, Richard Burthogge, Samuel Shaw, Steele, Addison, Swift, Samuel Palmer, Shenstone, Burke, Landor, Robert Blakey, and Sydney Smith. The Society for Pure English, Tract VI, in the article "*Shall* and *Will, Should* and *Would* in the Newspapers of Today," devotes five pages to examples, "all from newspapers of the better sort" [21] in which one or another of the "rules" has been violated.

The conventional rules for *shall* and *will* with something of the fullness they have in the school grammars of today first appeared in William Ward's *Grammar of the English Language* (1765), pages 121–123. This grammarian frankly makes a thoroughgoing attempt to form the rules on the basis of the "fundamental meanings" of the two words.[22]

Before Ward's grammar, George Mason, in his *Grammaire Angloise* of 1622, had made the first statement of a distinction of use between *shall* and *will;* [23] John Wallis, in his *Grammatica Linguae*

---

these six treatments of *shall* and *will* see C. C. Fries, "The Periphrastic Future with *Shall* and *Will* in Modern English," pp. 965–966, Note 6.

[21] These are British papers.

[22] He says "Of the difference between the Future by *shall* and that by *Will*":

"The Verb by *shall,* States of fixed Order shows: Or States which Chance directs, as we suppose. And *shall* those verbal Future States declares Which *for itself,* an Object hopes or Fears, Thinks *of itself,* surmises, or foresees; But which for other Objects it decrees. . . . The Verb by *will* those Future States declares For others, which an Object hopes or fears, Of others thinks, surmises or foresees; But *for itself,* States which itself decrees."

[23] George Mason, *Grammaire Angloise* (1622), pp. 25–26:

"Le signe du futur est, *shall* ou *will,* mais il n'en faut pas user indifferement: car si vous usez de ce signe, *shall,* quand il faut dire, *will* il a mauvaise grace, oultre qu'il semblera que vous parliez d'audace: example; vous pouvez dire elegamment, *If I doe eate that, I shall be sicke, si je mange cela, je sera malade:* au lieu que se vous disiez, *I will be sick,* il sembleroit que volontairement vous volussiez estre malade:

Anglicanae (1653), had given the first rules for the use of *shall* and *will* in independent-declarative sentences; [24] and Bishop Robert Lowth, in *A Short Introduction to English Grammar* (1762) had added a brief statement, concerning questions.[25] But William Ward first developed the complete set of rules, adding to Lowth's statement concerning questions and setting forth the uses in the subordinate clauses of what he calls "Compound Sentences" and "Suppositions."

In many of the grammars before 1765 and in a number that followed there is no indication of any discrimination between the uses of *shall* and *will* in the formation of the future. The first grammar following Ward's of 1765 to accept his explanation of the meanings of *shall* and *will* and incorporate the rules he thus derives is that of Lindley Murray of 1795. Only after the first quarter of the nineteenth century did the complete discussion of the rules for *shall* and *will* in independent-declarative statements, in interrogative sentences, and in subordinate clauses become a common feature of text books of English grammar.

The conventional rules for *shall* and *will* did not arise from any attempt to describe the practice of the language as it actually was either before the eighteenth century or at the time the grammar was written in which these rules first appeared. The authors of these

---

ains vous pouvez dire: *I hope you will be my friend, j'espere que vous me serez amy: If you doe that you shall bee beaten or chidden. Si vous faites cela, vous serez batu ou tancé: But I shall not, mais non seray: but you shall not chuse, mais vous ne choisirez pas,* c'est a sçauoir, *ce ne sera pas á vostre chois:* pour le fair court, il est malaisé d'en bailler reigle certaine, parquoy je vous r'envoye a l'usage, auquel, á fin de mieux y parvenir, nous vous proposerons la variation de certains verbes."

[24] John Wallis, *Grammatica Linguae Anglicanae* (1653), pp. 94–95:

"*Shall* and *will* indicant Futurum. . . . Quoniam autem extraneis satis est cognitu difficile, quando vel hoc vel illud dicendum est; (non enim promiscue dicimus *shall* & *will*) ; neq; tamen alii quos vidi ullas tradidere regulas quibus dirigantur; has ego tradere necessarium duxi, quas qui observaverit hac in re non aberrabit.

"In primis personis *shall* simpliciter praedicentis est; *will*, quasi promittentis aut minantis.

"In secundus & tertiis personis, *shall* promittentis est aut minantis, *will* simpliciter praedicentis."

[25] Robert Lowth, *A Short Introduction to English Grammar* (1762), pp. 64–65:

"*Will*, in the first Person singular and plural, promises or threatens; in the second and third Persons, only foretells; *shall* on the contrary, in the first Person simply foretells; in the second and third Persons, promises, commands, or threatens. But this must be understood of Explicative Sentences; for when the Sentence is Interrogative, just the reverse for the most part takes place: Thus, *I shall go; you will go;* expresses the event only; but *will you go?* imports intention; and *Shall I go?* refers to the will of another. But again, *He shall go,* and *shall he go?* both imply will, expressing or referring to a command."

grammars (Lowth and Ward) definitely repudiated usage, even that of "our most approved authors," as the basis of correctness in language.[26] Ward frankly insisted that his grammar is an attempt to discover "the Reason of every Part of Construction" and to correct that construction "where Custom is erroneous," so that "Reason will go Hand in Hand with Practice." These rules, then, are part of the eighteenth century search for a "rational grammar" and cannot safely be assumed to represent usage in any respect.

That the general usage of *shall* and *will* did not at any time during the history of Modern English agree with the conventional rules is a conclusion that can be reasonably drawn from the facts revealed in the following charts. These charts are based upon a recording and examination of some twenty thousand instances of *shall* and *will* occurring in (*a*) fifty British dramas produced during the last three hundred and fifty years, (*b*) eighteen British dramas produced from 1902 to 1918, and (*c*) eighteen American dramas produced from 1906 to 1918.[27]

The facts set forth in these three charts seem to justify the following conclusions concerning the history of the use of *shall* and *will* in independent-declarative statements throughout the Modern English period:

A. With the first person

1. The approximate stability of the relation of *shall* and *will* indicates that there has been no great change of use in the first person from the middle of the sixteenth century to the present time.

2. *Will* with the first person has, during all this time, always been more frequently used than *shall* (*I* [*we*] *will* from 70 per cent to 93 per cent and *I* [*we*] *shall* from 7 per cent to 30 per cent).

B. With the second person

3. In contrast with the approximate stability of the relation of *will* to *shall* in the first person for the past three hundred and fifty years, in the second person there has been practically a complete reversing of the situation existing in the sixteenth century. In the sixteenth century *shall* predominated, being used in more than 80 per

[26] See Lowth, *op. cit.*, Preface, iv, v; and W. Ward, *Grammar* (1765), Preface, v, xvii, xxi.

[27] For a more complete analysis of the materials here briefly set forth see the articles referred to in Note 18 above. For corroborating figures from English novels see W. F. Luebke, "The Analytic Future in Contemporary American Fiction," *Modern Philology*, Vol. 26, 1929, pp. 451 ff.

CHART I

Independent-Declarative Statements

First Person

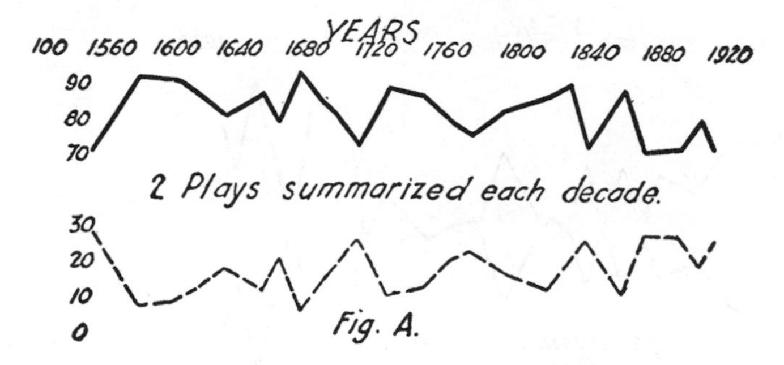

Fig. A.

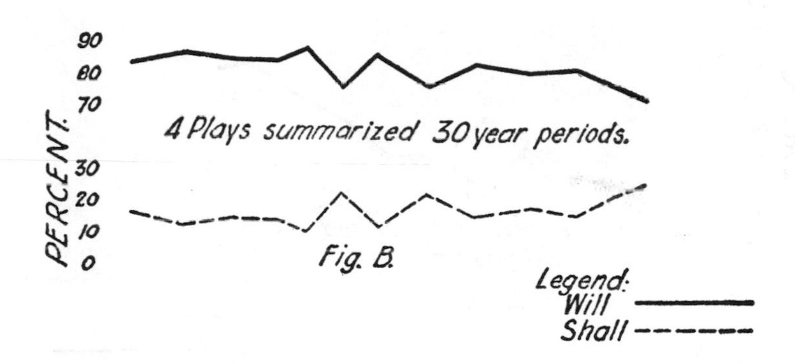

Fig. B.

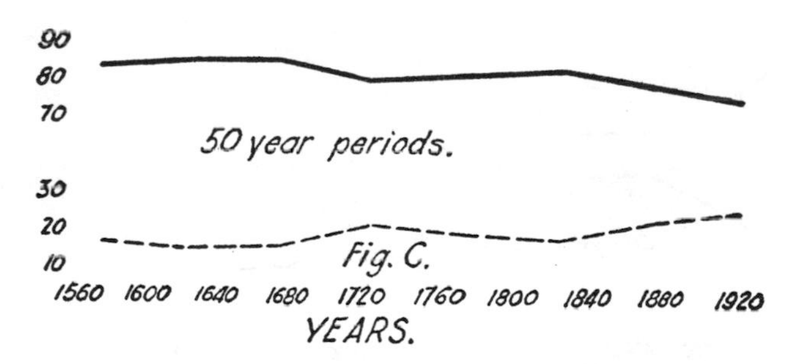

Fig. C.

Note.
From 30 to 70% is omitted in each graph.

CHART II

INDEPENDENT-DECLARATIVE STATEMENTS

SECOND PERSON

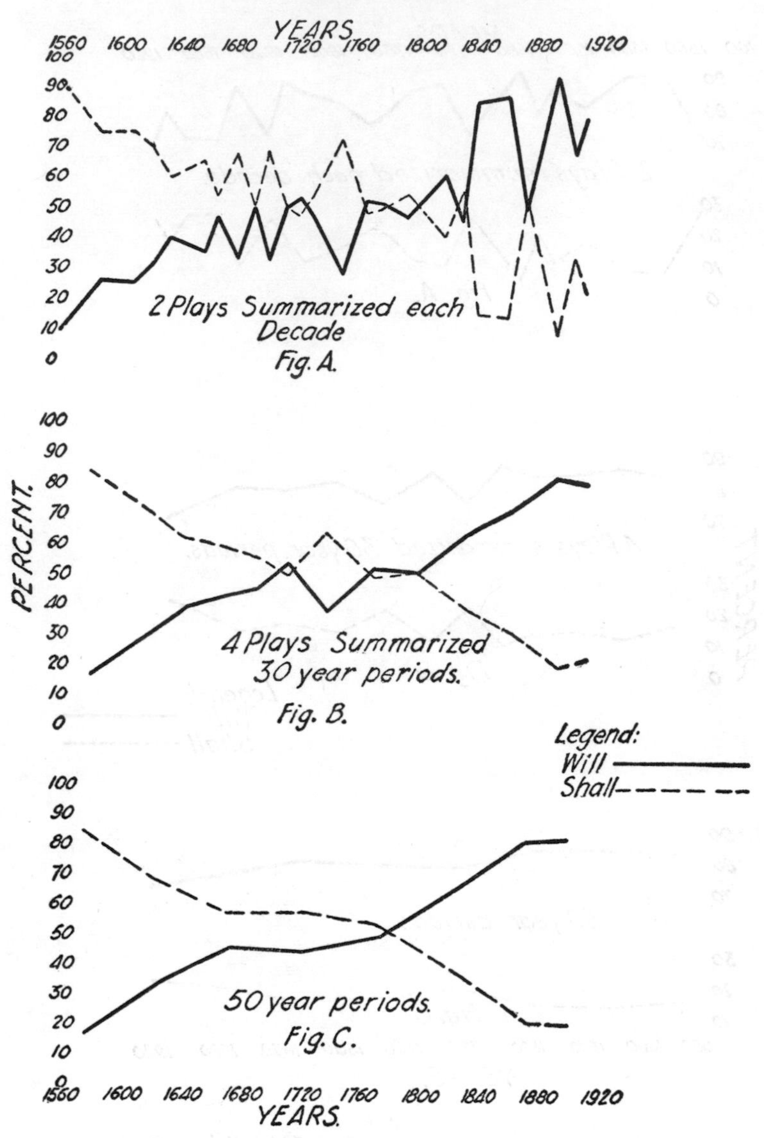

CHART III

Independent-Declarative Statements

Third Person

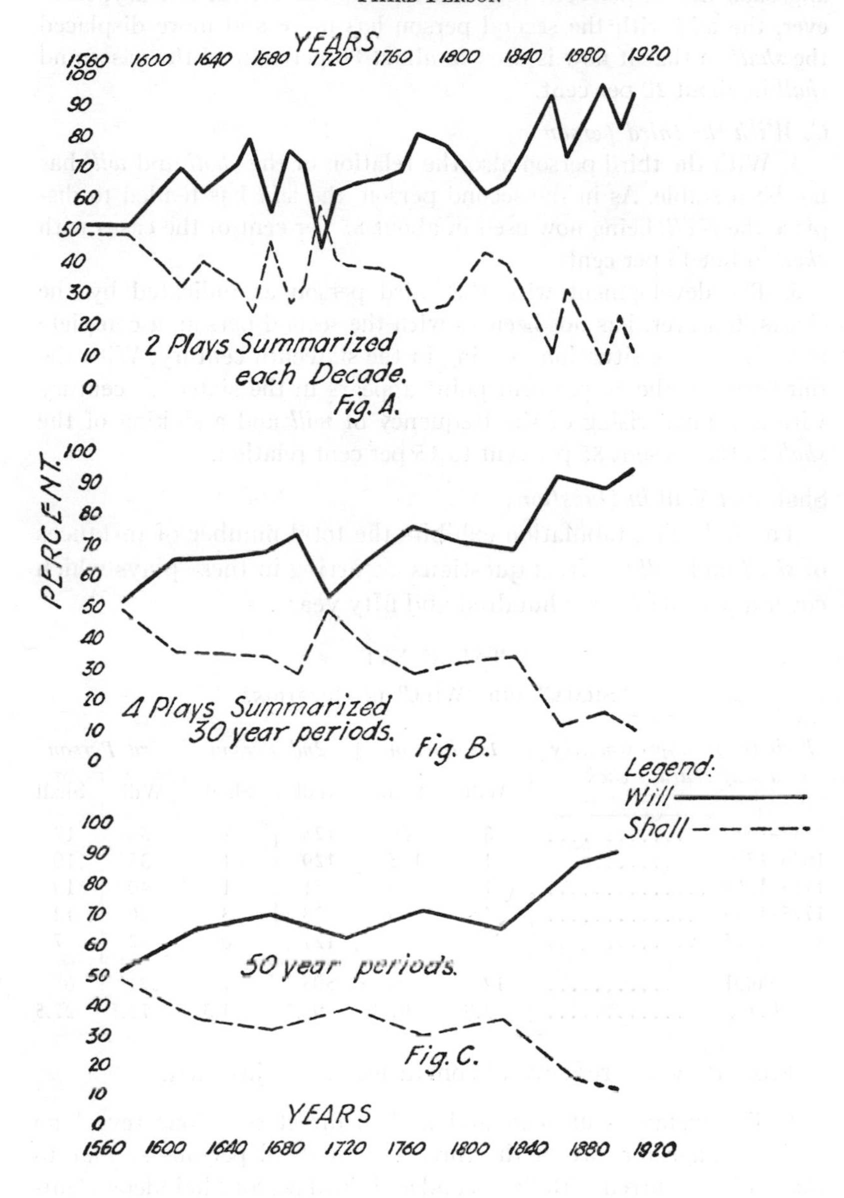

cent of the instances; *will* correspondingly being used in less than 20 per cent. Throughout the eighteenth century the two words seem to have been used with the second person about equally—the curves approach the 50 per cent line. During the nineteenth century, however, the *will* with the second person has more and more displaced the *shall* so that it now is used in about 80 per cent of the cases and *shall* in about 20 per cent.

C. With the third person

4. With the third person also the relation of the *shall* and *will* has not been stable. As in the second person, the *will* has tended to displace the *shall,* being now used in about 85 per cent of the cases with *shall* in but 15 per cent.

5. The development with the third person as indicated by the charts, however, has not been as with the second person, a complete reversing of the situation existing in the sixteenth century. With the third person, the 50 per cent point appears in the sixteenth century with a gradual rising of the frequency of *will* and a sinking of the *shall* to the present 85 per cent to 15 per cent relation.

Shall *and* Will *in Questions*

The following tabulation exhibits the total number of instances of *shall* and *will* in direct questions occurring in these plays which cover a period of three hundred and fifty years.

TABLE XVI

"SHALL" AND "WILL" IN QUESTIONS

Periods of approximately a half century each	*1st Person*		*2nd Person*		*3rd Person*	
	Will	Shall	Will	Shall	Will	Shall
1557–1637	3	69	125	2	38	17
1656–1703	1	105	129	1	35	10
1713–1768	1	80	51	1	40	19
1775–1843	4	63	73	3	36	12
1860–1915	3	78	127	0	22	7
Total	12	395	505	7	171	65
Percent	2.9	97.1	98.7	1.3	72.5	27.5

From these figures several conclusions seem justified.

1. The instances of *shall* and *will* in direct questions reveal no shift in usage for any of the three grammatical persons similar to that which occurred with the second and third persons in independent-declarative sentences.

2. With the first person *shall* has overwhelmingly predominated in questions although *will* has always been more frequently used in independent-declarative statements.

3. The frequent statement, however, that *will* is impossible in questions with the first person is inaccurate. *Shall* could hardly be used with the first person in such a question as appears in the following example: [28]

VIOLA. Haven't you seen the house, Mrs. Whipple?
HELEN. Not above this floor.
ALICE. Would it interest you?
HELEN. Very much.
ALICE [*to Helen*]. *Will I do* as your guide?

4. In second person questions *shall* has never been common, even during the sixteenth and early seventeenth centuries when in independent-declarative sentences more than 80 per cent of the instances with the second person appeared with *shall*. Of the 512 questions in the second person only seven or 1.3 per cent use *shall;* the rest (98.7 per cent) use *will*.

The facts set forth in Chart IV seem to justify the following statements concerning contemporary English and American usage of *shall* and *will:*

A. Independent-declarative statements

1. In independent-declarative statements, the *shall* forms have been almost eliminated from American usage with all three grammatical persons. In contemporary English usage the *shall* forms are somewhat more frequent, although the figures do not support the rule that a *shall* in the first person corresponds to a *will* in the second and third persons.

TABLE XVII

"SHALL" AND "WILL" IN INDEPENDENT-DECLARATIVE STATEMENTS: CONTEMPORARY USAGE

	American *		*English* *	
	Will	Shall	Will	Shall
1st person	87	13	70	30
2nd person	94	6	78	22
3rd person	96	4	90	10

* Expressed in terms of percentage.

[28] Augustus Thomas, *The Witching Hour,* edited by Quinn, 771, b.

CHART IV

Independent-Declarative Statements

English and American Contemporary Usage

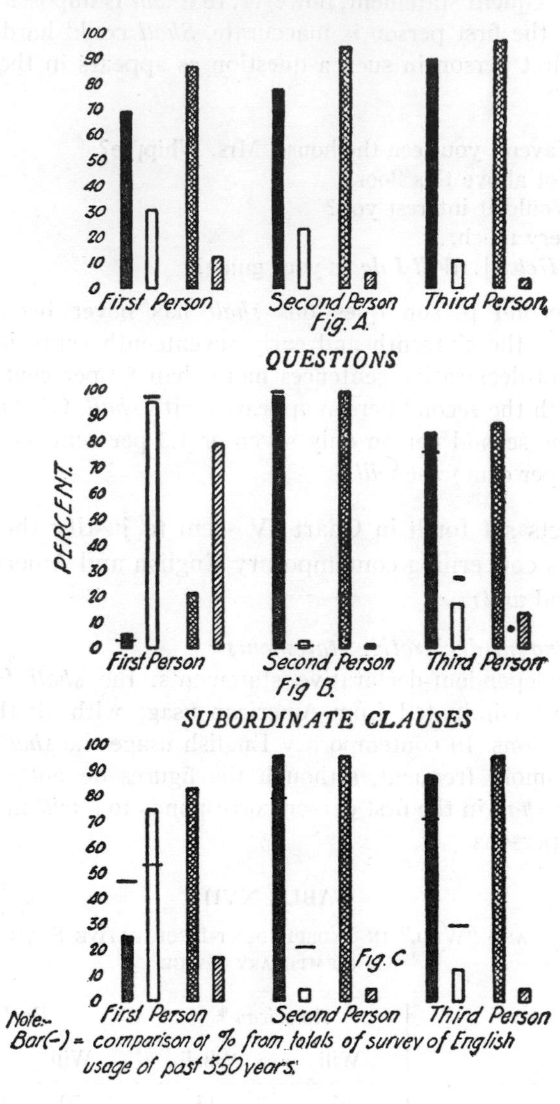

Legend.

English		American.	
will	shall	will	shall.

2. This difference between American and English usage *is not confined to the first person,* as has frequently been asserted. The degree of difference between American and English usage is practically the same with the second person as with the first.

3. In independent-declarative statements there seems to be no marked difference in usage between Americans and Englishmen except in the fact that with all three grammatical persons American usage shows a greater elimination of *shall* forms and a corresponding increase of *will* forms.

B. Questions

4. In questions there is a close agreement between American and English use. Especially is this noteworthy in respect to the second person where there is the same overwhelming use of *will* to the practical exclusion of *shall.*

5. English and American usage also agree in the fact that *shall* is overwhelmingly the word used in questions with the first person. This is the one situation in which American usage has *shall* rather than *will.*

C. Subordinate Clauses

6. In subordinate clauses of all types there is the same great preponderance of *will* in both American and English usage with the second and third persons.

TABLE XVIII

"SHALL" AND "WILL" IN SUBORDINATE CLAUSES: CONTEMPORARY USAGE

	American *		*English* *	
	Will	Shall	Will	Shall
2nd person	96.4	3.6	95.6	4.4
3rd person	95.3	4.7	88.6	11.4

* Expressed in terms of percentage.

7. In the case of the first person, a striking conflict appears between English and American usage. Here the American usage is predominately *will,* that of England predominantly *shall* (see Table XIX).

If, then, these figures force us to conclude that the conventional rules do not now represent and never have represented the practice of Standard English, either in England or in America, concerning *shall* and *will* what can be offered in a positive way concerning the use of these two function words? There seems to be agreement among the grammarians that those words or inflectional forms have

TABLE XIX

"SHALL" AND "WILL" IN SUBORDINATE CLAUSES: CONTEMPORARY USAGE

	American *		*English* *	
	Will	Shall	Will	Shall
1st person .... (esp. reported speech clauses)	86	14	29	71

* Expressed in terms of percentage.

been used for future tense devices which were expressions naturally looking to the future for fulfilment. Such words were those of "volition," "purpose," "obligation," "necessity," "compulsion," "motion," and such inflectional forms were those modal inflections like the present subjunctive expressing "possibility." It is noteworthy that a considerable number of diverse languages tried out the same set of devices for the future, although with differing results. The Germanic languages thus used *haban, munan, skulan, wiljan, wairþan.* Late Latin and the Romance languages tried out *velle, posse, debere, vadere, ire, venire,* as well as *habeo.* Late Greek used not only the subjunctive but also ἔχω and θέλω. Coptic used *NA,* the primitive word meaning "to go" and also the preposition *E* meaning "toward" as devices for the future.

The course of development of such expressions, as these are used with stress upon the future, seems to be in the direction of their losing their original full word meanings and becoming more and more function words for the future—future tense signs. Thus, *shall,* which in Old English meant "to owe" as in "agief þæt þu me *scealt*" ("repay that which thou *shalt* [i. e., owest] me") gradually loses its original meaning of "obligation" and becomes an "empty" word indicative of the future. It is often assumed that this loss of full word meaning to become a function word is the end of the process and that whatever connotations there may be other than its function use are the "glimmerings through" of previous full word meanings. This assumption, however, seems inadequate to account for the facts. It would account for suggestions of "compulsion" or "necessity" that might attach to a future phrase with *shall* as in "You *shall* answer this at full," but it would not account for the suggestions of "intention" or "volition" on the part of the subject in such a sentence with an emphasized *shall* as "Damme! Sir, have a care! Don't give me the Lye, ***I shan't*** take it, Sir." [29] Nor would it account for the connotations of "compulsion" in the following sentence with *will:* [30]

KURANO. Kira taught you the wrong ritual?
ASANO. Yes.
KURANO. You *will* not go unavenged.

And this assumption of the "glimmering through" of earlier meanings would not account for the suggestions of "intention" or "determination" in the following: [31]

KURANO. Are they *going to kill* me?
4TH RONIN. They said they were *going to make* sure of you.

Even in Old English one finds such a passage as the following, in which all four expressions seem to suggest with the future the "purpose of the speaker"—a meaning which is in no way related to the full word meanings of two of the three expressions used: [32]

> "Eac *ic wille geswigian* Tontolis & Philopes þara scondlicestena spella; hu manega bismerlica gewin Tontolus gefremede syððan he cyning wæs; . . . ."
> "*Ic sceall eac ealle forlætan* þa þe of Perseo & of Cathma gesæde syndon, ..."
> "Eac *ic wille geswigian* þara mandæda þara Lemniaðum & Ponthionis þæs cyninges. . . ."
> ". . . *ic hit eall forlæte.* Eac *ic hit forlæte,* Adipsus hu he ægþer ofsloh ge his agenne fæder . . ."

In order to account for such facts as these the process of development of these function words with the future could in general be summarized as follows: a certain limited range of meanings furnish the grounds upon which the future is predicted. Any word or form with meanings within this range may be taken up and used as a device for the expression of the future. As it becomes such a device, the emphasis gradually shifts from the full word meaning to the function word use as a future tense marker. But now as a device for the expression of the future it may suggest (depending on the circumstances and without limitation of its original meanings) any of that range of meanings which are the bases of future pre-

[29] Colley Cibber, *Love's Last Shift* (1696), IV, 66.
[30] John Masefield, *The Faithful* (New York, The Macmillan Co., 1915), I, ii, 11.
[31] *Ibid.*, II, i, 62.
[32] Alfred, *Orosius*, E.E.T.S., I, 42

dictions. Of course, in a rapid impression with an entirely unemphasized phrase, the general future prediction may be all that registers, but with more attention put upon the statement, directed by greater emphasis upon some part of the word group or by the reader's attempted analysis, there often stand out prominently some of the connotations of the grounds upon which the future is predicted—"intention," "resolve," "determination," "compulsion," "necessity." In respect to both *shall* and *will,* the lighter colorings shade into the unmistakable modal uses so inseparably as to make a dividing line impossible and no *rules* seem adequate to distinguish them satisfactorily.

In the letters examined for this study, the situations dealt with were so overwhelmingly matters of the past and of the present that comparatively few references to the future appeared. In all, there were only 139 instances of *shall* and *will* in the Standard English letters and 189 in those of Vulgar English.

The distribution of these instances appears in Tables XX and XXI.

Even with these few instances, however, it is possible in the light of the discussion above to make some statements.

1. In American English *shall* has been almost completely eliminated in all situations except as shown above in questions with the first person, where it is used in at least 80 per cent of the instances. *Shall* and *will,* therefore, are certainly not interchangeable.

2. There is in American English some use of *shall* with the first person in independent-declarative sentences, but these uses of *shall* cannot all be taken as expressing simple futurity. The "intention," even the "determination" of the speaker seems to be clearly indicated in some of the instances.

Examples from the Standard English letters of *shall* with the first person in independent-declarative sentences are

"I *shall take up* the matter with my wife at once" (9057)

". . . she will . . . get a statement to this effect . . . and we *shall forward* it to you" (8283)

"I dare say you have forgotten, but I *shall* not, nor the magic that you worked" (9018)

"If anything is needed in addition to the affidavit of —— we *shall be pleased* to obtain and forward this additional evidence" (8239)

"I *shall finish* the course of instruction . . . on or about June 15 . . ." (9066)

TABLE XX

STANDARD ENGLISH

	Independent-Declarative Sentences		*Questions*		*Subordinate Clauses*			
					Indirect Discourse		Conditions, Result, etc.	
	Shall	Will	Shall	Will	Shall	Will	Shall	Will
1st person ...	9 26.4%	25 73.5%	0	0	0	6	0	1
2nd person ...	0	5	0	4	0	5	0	2
3rd person ...	0	54	0	1	0	14	0	13

TABLE XXI

VULGAR ENGLISH

	Independent-Declarative Sentences		*Questions*		*Subordinate Clauses*			
					Indirect Discourse		Conditions, Result, etc.	
	Shall	Will	Shall	Will	Shall	Will	Shall	Will
1st person ...	3 6%	48 94%	0	0	0	3	0	1
2nd person ...	0	8	0	19	0	24	0	17
3rd person ...	0	35	0	4	0	15	0	14

"I *shall have* approximately three months of leave accrued on July 1 . . ." (9064)
"I *shall settle* this account as rapidly as possible" (9033)

Similar examples from the Vulgar English letters are

"I *shall depend* on you that you will release ——" (8274)
"but if —— dont come back I *shall not be* able to stand it" (8274)

3. The use of *will* with the first person in independent-declarative sentences to express simple futurity is not a matter peculiar to Vulgar English. The Standard English letters and those from Vulgar English both furnish a good number of instances of *will* with the first person, some of which do express "intention" or "determination" but others simple futurity.

Examples from Standard English are

"I *will have,* on May 1 . . . , seventy-four days leave due me" (9050)
"On the above date I *will complete* the course . . . at . . ." (9058)
"I have two months accrued leave and *will have* another month due on July first" (9058)
"I *will receive* some compensation for . . ." (9040)
"After April 11 . . . , my duties as . . . will have terminated . . . and I *will be* available for such temporary duty as . . ." (9031)
". . . and being instructor in . . . I *will be called upon* to take charge of . . ." (9031)
"I *will ask* you to please look into this matter . . ." (8004)
"If you will kindly pass on this and give me your opinion, I *will appreciate* it very much" (8183)
"we *will take* up the case thru . . ." (8299)
"as I *will try* to set forth later" (9032)

Examples from Vulgar English are

"we *will have to go* to the County farm" (8155)
"I am a man that is getting up in years and *will soon have to give up* hard work" (8173)
"Kindly consider my case and I *will be* very grateful" (8265)
"By doing so I *will be sent* to Pittsburg with a guardian" (8219)
"If you can do eny theng for us we *will be* very thankful to you" (8200)
"I *wont be* any better until I undergo an operation" (8052)
"Please do this for me and I *will come* home to stay" (8219)
"I *will tell* you about everything" (8087)
"I *will pay* you for it" (8096)

4. In these particular materials all the questions with the second person used *will,* but there seems to be no significance in that fact, for in all cases the situation was such that the *will you* was a petition. No cases appeared of what could be called a simple future in a question with the second person.

5. The use of *will* with all persons in subordinate clauses of all kinds is not limited to Vulgar English. In this respect there was no difference between the instances from Standard English and those from Vulgar English.

Standard English examples of the first person with *will* are

". . . it seems probable that I *will draw* foreign service within a year or two" (9021)
"I do not know what number I *will be assigned to*" (9027)

"... and I believe that given a chance to ... I *will make* myself of more value to the service" (9050)
"... I am writing to assure you that I *will* very much *appreciate* anything it may be possible to do to ..." (9061)

Some examples from Vulgar English are

"... if he cannot come home I don't know what I *will do*" (8274)
"I hope I *will See* yo at Judment day" (8181)
"Henry I hope I *will See* you again" (8181)

D. Be (*in its various forms*) + to + *infinitive*
Be (*in its various forms*) + about + to + *infinitive*
Be (*in its various forms*) + going + to + *infinitive*

As indicated above (page 150) the combinations of *be* + *to* + infinitive, *be* + *about* + *to* + infinitive, and *be* + *going* + *to* + infinitive, which are to be discussed here are expressions for the "future" and deserve a place with *shall* and *will* as function words of an analytic or periphrastic "tense." The development of these words into such function words seems to me to have been along the path marked out above (pages 161–164) especially for *shall* and *will* and applicable to any words that express meanings which look to the future for fulfilment. The meanings underlying these three expressions—"purpose" in the first, "proximity" in the second, and "motion" in the third—are all such as would lend themselves to the same sort of development as that of the words *shall* and *will*. So far as our present records go, the first is the oldest, arising in Middle English; [33] the other two appear first in Early Modern English.[34] The first tends to stress "necessity," "obligation," "duty," and constitutes a future of "appointment" or "plan." The second and third tend to express a "near" or "immediate" future.

In as much as the *be* may be used in its past tense form as well as in its present tense form, each of these three combinations can express a future either with reference to the present time or with reference to the past time.

The instances appearing in the materials examined here show

[33] The first quotation given in the *Oxford Dictionary* for this use is c. 1200.

[34] The first quotation given by the *Oxford Dictionary* for the second is from Coverdale, dated 1535 and for the third is 1482, but the *going to* future certainly is not used with any frequency until the second half of the seventeenth century. See also J. F. Royster and J. M. Steadman, "The *going-to* Future," *The Manly Anniversary Studies* (Chicago, University of Chicago Press, 1923), pp. 394 ff.

no difference in the use of these expressions in Standard English and in Vulgar English.

Some examples from these letters are

be + *to* + infinitive

"Mrs. —— *is to accompany* me" (9055)
"I *am to be placed* on the retired list" (9033)
". . . the officers *are to be given* an opportunity . . ." (9027)
". . . he *is to be discharged*" (8075)
"this land *is to be presented* to the government" (9062)

. . . . .

"i would like to know when he *is to reach* ——" (8290)
"he *is to be transferred* . . ." (8231)
"They *are to send* him back to —— April 10" (8193)
"I *am to be sent* to —— the 19th of this month" (8198)

. . . . .

"letter from —— said that by direction of —— I *was to be retained* in the service" (9050)
"What would have been the proper interpretation then is the proper interpretation now. Quarters *were to be assigned* where quarters were available." (9030)
"Upon receiving notice that I *was to be discharged* . . . I asked for and . . ." (9050)

be + *about* + *to* + infinitive

"I *was about to have* —— released in the proper way" (8281)

be + *going* + *to* + infinitive

"that fact that I have . . . *is going to make* it difficult . . ." (9033)
"I *am going to prove* it to you" (8038)
"they *are going to discharge* him" (8072)
"he *is going to be turned* loose" (8205)
"I dont know what I *am going to do*" (8053)

. . . . .

"he *was going to do* away with himself" (8076)
"I had heard that . . . *was going to be* one of the questions" (9227)
"when —— saw that his absence *was going to exceed* 30 days he should have . . ." (9217)
"I *was going to write* you . . ." (8038)

E. Have + to + *infinitive*

For some reason, words with the meaning "possess" seem to tend naturally to take on the meanings of "obligation" and "necessity" and develop function word uses. Thus *owe* which most frequently meant "possess" in Old English soon took on the meaning of material obligation, and with its preterit *ought* also expressed moral obligation. In similar fashion, *have* meaning "possess" became in Early Modern English [35] a function word used with the *to*-infinitive to express "obligation" and "necessity." [36] In the development of this use there seems to have been an intermediate stage in which an object substantive immediately followed the *have* and the infinitive came after the substantive. Examples of this use from our materials are

"I *have* a family *to support*" (9033)
"he *has* a big board bill *to pay*" (8088)
"he *had* $6.00 *to pay*" (8218)
"he *has* a wife and one child *to support*" (8258)
"if I *had* this *to do* over again . . ." (8039)

In all these examples, except possibly the last, the full word meaning of "possession" is clear in the word *have*.[37] Only when the word order is shifted and the infinitive immediately follows the *have*, does the *have* become a function word in an expression of "obligation" or "necessity." [38] That in such combinations the function word has lost its full word meaning of "possession" is clear from such instances as the following in which the function word *have* is used with the full word *have:*

"My children *have to have* books and clothes to go to school" (8235)

In this use of *have* with the *to*-infinitive as a function word of "obligation" or "necessity," all tense forms of the verb *have* can be

[35] The earliest quotation of this use given in the *Oxford Dictionary* is dated 1579.

[36] The use of *have* as a function word with the past participle will be discussed below in section N.

[37] Compare also such expressions as the following in which the meaning "possess" is carried by the function word *with:*

"I am nearly 50 years old *with* 5 little ones *to support*" (8187)
"I am unable to go out to work *with* a 8 months old baby and sick husband *to care for*" (8211)

[38] The contrast of the meanings expressed by this difference in word order is shown in the following sentences:

"I have from the first felt sure that the writer, when he sits down to commence his novel, should do so, not because *he has to tell a story*, but because *he has a story to tell*."—*An Autobiography by Anthony Trollope*, XII.

"Speeches may be broadly divided into two kinds. There is the speech a man makes when *he has something to say*, and the speech he endeavours to make when he *has to say something*."—*Literary World*, May 10, 1901.

used and thus in so far as the "obligation" or "necessity" looks to the future for its fulfilment, it can be a "future" with reference to a time point in the present, in the past, or itself in the future.

Examples are

"he *has to be operated* on" (8193)
"In the case of small articles that *had to be obtained* to finish . . ." (9040)
"she *will have to go* to work" (8003)
"Enclosed you will find . . . birth certificate which you said you *would have to have* before you would . . ." (8218)

In the instances of this construction found in the materials examined for this study there are no differences in the usage of Standard English and that of Vulgar English. Some further examples from these letters are

". . . just what *has to be done*" (8189)
"he *had to come* by water" (8078)
"she *had to stay* in bed" (8002)
"he was living in hell all the time and *had to drink* . . ." (8296)
"I *have to carry* her" (8291)
"We *have to deny* ourselves . . ." (8251)
"My mother *has to take in* washing" (8129)
"we *have to Doctor* her all the time" (8028)
"and *we haft to pay* rent" (8246)

F. Get, *often together with* have, + to + *infinitive*

The word *get,* another word of "possession," has developed a wide variety of uses in addition to the sense of "obtain possession of (property, etc.) as the result of effort or contrivance." In the *Oxford Dictionary* there are given thirty four numbered senses in addition to the thirty eight uses of *get* with prepositions in specialized meanings, such as *get at, get off, get over, get ahead, get away, get back, get out, get up.* Within the thirty four numbered senses there are seventy two separately indicated divisions of meaning. Of these, only twenty three were in use in Middle English, so that the great expansion of the use of this word *get* has occurred in Modern English, chiefly in Early Modern English, before the end of the seventeenth century. If the materials examined for this study can be taken as typical, there is a distinct difference between Standard English and Vulgar English in the use of this word *get.* Of the thirty four numbered senses listed in the *Oxford*

Dictionary, twenty six were found in our materials. All but one of these twenty six senses were found in the Standard English letters as well as in the Vulgar English materials. The differences between the two sets of material lay not primarily in the kinds of uses employed by each group but in the amount of use. In all, there were 316 instances of *get* in its various forms, but only thirty one of these came from the Standard English matter. One can probably conclude, then, that although Standard English as well as Vulgar English does at times employ all the uses of *get,*[39] nevertheless the very frequent use of this word seems to be a characteristic of Vulgar English.

The one use of *get* that did not appear in the Standard English letters was *get,* meaning "to receive, suffer by way of punishment."

> "a fellow who was going away 8 day and *got* 15 years and another was gon three months and got three month in the guard hous" (8039)
>
> "If he *gets* a right good scaring it will do him good" (8218)

As a function word, the use of *get* was rare in the materials examined here. With the infinitive[40] the following instances appeared:

STANDARD ENGLISH

> "he *has got to serve* his sentence" (9531)

VULGAR ENGLISH

> "he is my only support and I *have just got to have* him" (8059)
>
> "I *have got to take* care of three little children" (8593)
>
> "the poor people *haven't got to pay* anything" (8504)

The following instances of *get* with the infinitive differ from the above:

> "his chums *didn't get to go* with him" (8518)
>
> "after that he *got to be* a friend of . . ." (6645)

[39] The use of *got,* the past participle, with the function word *have* "in senses equivalent to those of the present tense of *have* or *possess"* is not a matter peculiar to Vulgar English.

> "but now we *haven't got* the money to hire any more. . ." (8244)
>
> "As for having money to buy him out I *haven't got* it" (8235)

[40] The use of *get* with the participles will be commented on below.

G. Used + to + *the infinitive, for customary action*

The verb *use* in its various forms followed by *to* and the infinitive as in "His modir *usith* euery day gretly to sorowe" [41] appeared in Middle English in the sense of "to be accustomed or wont to do something." In Late Modern English, however, the past tense form *used* is the one employed with the *to*-infinitive and seldom do other words separate this word *used* from the *to*-infinitive that follows. It seems justified to call this *used* a function word to express "customary action" as an aspect of the verb. Only one example appeared in our materials.

"I *used to wash* for a living" (8235)

H. May, might, can, could, would, should, must, ought + *the infinitive, the so-called "modal auxiliaries"*

All of the words listed here except *would* belong to a small group of verbs which are frequently called "preteritive-present" verbs. For some unknown reason, the preterit or past tense forms of these verbs seem always to take on "present" meanings. In Old English the forms which were used with present tense meanings had previously been preterit or past tense forms fitting into the patterns of the "strong" verb.[42] In order to express the past tense meanings of these verbs in Old English there were used preterit forms of newer formation which had been made in accord with the pattern of the "weak" verb by the addition of a "dental" suffix.

TABLE XXII

Old preterit forms which in OE had present tense meanings	*New preterit forms created by the use of the weak verb dental suffix, which had past tense meanings*
may	*might*
can	*could*
[*shall*]	*should*
[*mot*]	*must*
[*owe*]	*ought*

[41] *Gesta Romanorum*, v. 12.

[42] It is for this reason that such forms as *may* and *can* do not have the inflectional *s* [z] in the third person singular.

But even these "double" preterits, *might, could, should, must, ought,* do not, in Present-day English, carry past tense meanings; all of them, when joined with the infinitive form of the verb, express a present or even look toward the future.[43] In other words, the semantic drift of whatever preterits have been formed for these verbs seems to have been toward present meanings.

In older stages of the English language these words had full word meanings and were frequently used without following infinitives; throughout their history they have experienced various shifts of meaning and now can be used only as "auxiliaries" (function words) in connection with other verbs which do carry a full word meaning. As function words, whatever meanings these old verbs now express seem to have to do with various attitudes toward the "action" or "state" expressed by the verb to which they are attached. These function words can, therefore, with some justification be called "modal auxiliaries."

The chief shifts of meaning which these words have undergone [44] are roughly indicated in the diagram on page 174.

Examples from the materials of Old English to illustrate the full word meanings of these verbs are the following:

> "Twegan gafolgydon wæron sumum lænende; an *sceolde* fif hund penega [one *should* (= *owed*) five hundred pennies], and oðer fiftig."—*Gospels,* Luke 7:41.

> "Þær wearð ofslægen Harold cyng, ... and fela godra manna, and þa Frenciscan *ahton* wælstowe geweald" [and the French *ought* (= *possessed*) control of the slaughter-place (= battle-field)].—*Anglo-Saxon Chronicle,* A. D. 1066.

> "and þær bædon Scottas þæt hi þær *mosten* wunian [and there they begged the Scots that they *must* (= *permit*) them to dwell there]; ac hi noldon him lyfan, for þon þe hi cwædon þæt hi ne *mihton* ealle ætgædere gewunian þær [because they said that they *might* not (= *were not able to*) all live there together]."—*Anglo-Saxon Chronicle, Description of Britain.*

> "þa cwædon hi þæt hi naðer ne scincræftas *cuðon* [Then said they that they *could* (= *knew*) neither magic arts], ne hi mid nængum

[43] To refer to the past these words are joined with the past participle form of the verb used with the function word *have.* Compare, for instance, "He *might go*" with "He *might have gone.*"

[44] See articles in the *Oxford Dictionary* for each of these words and also the discussion by C. B. Bradley, "*Shall* and *Will*—An Historical Study," *Transactions of the American Philological Association,* Vol. 42, pp. 5–31.

TABLE XXIII

	OE Meaning as Full Word	*Later Developments of Meaning*				
[*shall*] *should*	indebtedness; material obligation	moral obligation	fitness; propriety	coercion	necessity	future prediction
[*owe*] *ought*	ownership	possession	indebtedness; material obligation	moral obligation	fitness; propriety	
[*mot*] *must*	permission	possibility	obligation	coercion	necessity	prediction (with certainty)
may, might	physical ability; power	objective possibility; opportunity	permission; sanction	supposition; subjective possibility		
can, could	knowledge; know how	general ability	possibility	permission; sanction		
[*will*] *would* *	desire; wish	determination; resolve	intention; willingness	accustomed or habitual activity	past future prediction	

* [*will*] *would* did not belong to the group of "preterit-present" verbs.

godum weorcum þæt noht swiðe to Gode geearnod hæfdon" —*Anglo-Saxon Chronicle,* A. D. 565.

MAGISTER: *Canst* þu ænig þing? [MASTER: *Canst* (= *knowest*) thou any thing?]

VENATOR: Ænne cræft ic *cann.* [HUNTER: One craft I *can* (= know).]

—Aelfric, *Colloquy*

"And he *wolde* geseon [and he *would* (= *wished*) to see] hwylc se Hæland wære; þa ne *mihte* he [when he *might* (= *could*) not] for ðære menegu, for þam þe he wæs lytel on wæstmum."—*Gospels,* Luke 19:3.

In respect to the later developments of meaning carried by these words, the situation is exceedingly complex and no rules yet formed seem adequate to mark out precisely their areas of use. Something of their overlapping can be indicated by the following arrangement.

TABLE XXIV

Meanings	*Words by Which They* {may, can, could, might} *Be Indicated*
a. Ability or power	*may, can, could, might*
b. Possibility or doubt	*may, might, can, could*
c. Permission	*may, might, can, could, must (not)*
d. Duty or obligation	*should, ought, must*
e. Customary activity	*would*
f. Fitness, propriety	*should, ought*
g. Futurity, prediction	*should, must, would*
h. Wish, willingness	*may, would*

The table on pages 176 and 177 shows the actual number of occurrences of each of these words in the letters examined for this study.

Examples of the uses of each of these words are the following: [45]

should

STANDARD ENGLISH

(*f*) "We *should have* a military training . . ." (9012)

(*f*) "The Act of Congress *should* not *receive* a different interpretation now" (9030)

[45] The small letter attached to each example indicates the particular meaning in Table XXIV which it probably illustrates. It will be understood that this assignment of a particular area of meaning to each of these words in the examples given is highly

TABLE XXV

Standard English							Vulgar English						
	Person	Independent-Declarative	Questions	Subordinate Clauses	Sub-totals	Totals		Person	Independent-Declarative	Questions	Subordinate Clauses	Sub-totals	Totals
should	1	2	1	0	3		*should*	1	0	0	0	0	
	2	0	0	0	0			2	0	0	0	0	
	3	9	1	10	20			3	2	0	3	5	
Total		11	2	10		23	Total		2	0	3		5
would	1	14	0	8	22		*would*	1	44	0	13	57	
	2	0	2	2	4			2	4	2	17	23	
	3	19	0	16	35			3	8	1	17	26	
Total		33	2	26		61	Total		56	3	47		106
							(*maybe*)					9	
may	1	1	0	8	9		*may*	1	0	2	0	2	
	2	0	0	0	0			2	0	0	2	2	
	3	8	0	10	18			3	2	0	1	3	
Total		9	0	18		27	Total		2	2	3		16
might	1	0	0	2	2		*might*	1	0	0	0	0	
	2	0	0	1	1			2	0	0	0	0	
	3	2	0	6	8			3	0	0	1	1	
Total		2	0	9		11	Total		0	0	1		1

(*d*) "Was it correct . . . or *should* the amount over and above the pay for that period *be returned?*" (9035)

(*d*) "he feels he *should be* with her" (8095)

(*g*) "the order provides that the father *should have* the right to visit them at all seasonable hours upon his compliance with the order of the court" (8296)

(*g*) "If I *should succeed* in having this resolution passed it would be placed before the general body of . . ." (9036)

(*g*) "I *should* greatly *appreciate* having this information as I wish to . . ." (8075)

(*g*) "The physical benefits alone *should be* worth the time spent" (9012)

---

subjective and depends solely upon the context in which the expression stands. It is impracticable to give in each instance all the features of context that determined the classification assigned.

TABLE XXV (*Continued*)

	Standard English							*Vulgar English*					
	Person	Independent-Declarative	Questions	Subordinate Clauses	Sub-totals	Totals		Person	Independent-Declarative	Questions	Subordinate Clauses	Sub-totals	Totals
can	1	3	0	2	5		*can*	1	31	0	26	57	
	2	1	1	1	3			2	9	3	29	41	
	3	6	0	11	17			3	20	0	23	43	
Total		10	1	14		25	Total		60	3	78		141
could	1	4	0	2	6		*could*	1	10	0	9	19	
	2	1	1	0	2			2	1	1	13	15	
	3	13	0	13	26			3	7	1	12	20	
Total		18	1	15		34	Total		18	2	34		54
must	1	0	0	0	0		*must*	1	1	0	0	1	
	2	0	0	0	0			2	0	0	0	0	
	3	0	0	3	0			3	0	0	0	0	
Total		0	0	3		3	Total		1	0	0		1
ought	1	1	0	0	1		*ought*	1	0	0	2	2	
	2	0	0	0	0			2	0	0	0	0	
	3	0	0	1	1			3	2	0	0	2	
Total		1	0	1		2	Total		2	0	2		4
TOTAL		84	6	96		186			141	10	168	9*	328

* maybe

VULGAR ENGLISH

(*f*) "I think after a Mother & Father suffer to raise a Boy to become the age of 17 they *should be* some help to their parents" (8074)

(*g*) "it is becoming necessary that he *should come* home as soon as he can . . ." (8072)

(*d*) "but as he has the chance now we thought he *should take* it" (8251)

(*g*) "We would like to know if he *should come* up on a Transport to —— or by rail to Newark and when he would arrive" (8290)

would

STANDARD ENGLISH

(*g*) "I *would appreciate* it very much if . . ." (9016)

(*g*) "It *would kill* her" (8139)

(*g*) "I *would like* to locate a white canvas bedding roll marked as follows . . ." (9053)

(*g*) "I *would be pleased* if you will kindly forward to me any information or . . ." (8294)

(*g*) "I will be assigned in the . . . and *would appreciate* this information" (9027)

(*g*) "It is quite possible that I *would* not *receive* a reply" (9005)

(*e*) "In speaking about . . . he *would* always *bring* up something immoral" (7040)

(*h*) "I *would request* assignment to ——" (9022)

(*h*) "We *would request* that . . . " (6303)

(*e*) "and this reward *would be charged* against the pay of the men" (7125)

(*e*) "After this for a while . . . he *would call* us in for a conference with him, and things went on pretty well" (5129)

VULGAR ENGLISH

(*g*) "I did not think for one minute that I *would be* where I am now" (8265)

(*g*) "I *would like* to hear something" (8029)

(*h*) "*Would* you please *find* out if . . ." (8310)

(*g*) "If T—— *would* only *come* back home everything *would straighten* out right again" (8033)

(*e*) "In the days when the public *would* not *Associate* with Soilders" (8057)

may

STANDARD ENGLISH

(*b*) "This income of $60.00 *may be withdrawn* at any time" (8260)

(*a*) "I desire this duty at —— in order that I *may* again *become* an active pilot" (9031)

(*c*) "This request is being made at the request of the athletic authorities at —— in order that I *may assist* in the coaching of . . ." (9026)

(*b*) "There *may be* some obstacles in the way" (8267)

(*c*) "I trust I *may entertain* your consideration" (9000)

(*a*) "I sincerely trust that the data I have submitted in this matter is sufficient and that we *may have* early action" (8203)

(*b*) "any news you can give me about my son and when he *may arrive* in New York" (8075)

VULGAR ENGLISH

(*c*) "*May* I *ask* you to hold me here?" (8198)

(*c*) "I also beg of you to release him owing to his condition, also that he *may take* up his life work of being a Minister" (8251)

(*b*) "I can git eny kind of Papers signed you *may send* me" (8171)

maybe

VULGAR ENGLISH

"*Maybe* I hadn't ought to write" (8038)
"Well *maybe* I will be there" (8039)
"could he be released or *may be* brought closer home" (8038)

might

STANDARD ENGLISH

(*a*) "and began to work so that she *might assist* in the support of her mother's family" (8081)
(*b*) "I want to speak for him any favor that you *might have* that you could . . ." (8060)
(*b*) "suspected that he *might join* the ——" (8076)
(*a*) "The officer . . . had not notified the guard at any time that he *might be found* in the quarters of the Chaplain" (5230)
(*c*) "They all join in the request that he *might come* home before Christmas" (6403)

VULGAR ENGLISH

(*a*) "—— advise me to write to you for a dismissal blank, that he *might be released* immediately" (8251)

can

STANDARD ENGLISH

(*a*) "I feel that I *can pass* the examination" (9027)
(*c*) "and now *can* I *tell* you how he happened to be there?" (5229)
(*b*) "whether or not his eyes *can be treated*" (9011)

VULGAR ENGLISH

(*a*) "We *cant* hardely *get* a Long With out him" (8293)
(*a*) "I hear I *can get* him out by him not being of age" (8170)
(*a*) "*Can* you please *help* us out on this matter" (8193)
(*c*) "and we need the boy to care for him [his father] then when he is a little older he *can Join* the —— again if he wants to" (8121)

could

STANDARD ENGLISH

(*a*) "He *couldn't find* any visible evidence of rupture" (9006)
(*b*) "From the information contained in our letter . . . it would seem that this boy *could* hardly *be expected* to take care of his grandmother in the event he is discharged from service" (8095)
(*a*) "I *couldn't bend* over very far" (9006)
(*a*) "*Could* you please *let* me know what steamer he is coming in on" (8075)

VULGAR ENGLISH

(*a*) "I'd never *could earn* the money" (8187)
(*a*) "I *cood* not *change* his mind" (8285)
(*c*) "I would appreciate it very much if I *could have* my Son home to take care of me" (8225)
(*a, c*) "and if he *could* only *be released* he *could go* back to his old job" (8080)
(*b*) "both of his bosses have been to see me to find out if he *could come* back" (8080)
(*c*) "I told him —— wouldnt be 18 untill october but he *could go* for one year Mr —— ask me to sign the blank and he would fill it out for one year so he filled it out for 3 years and sent it in so I got a telegram from —— to give my consent so I answered that for one year" (8244)
(*b*) "Maybe you *could know* if he can come home" (8038)

must

STANDARD ENGLISH

(*d*) "It is my opinion . . . that even though he reaches his majority afterwards yet he *must be discharged*" (8183)
(*g*) "we thought she *must be receiving* treatment" (8240)
(*c*) "you *mustn't tell* him that I wrote to you" (5231)
(*d*) "his policy being that everything . . . *must reach* —— through ——" (9000)

VULGAR ENGLISH

(*d*) "We *must fight* for them" (8005)

ought

STANDARD ENGLISH

(*d*) "he is reported as not being out with his organization at times I thought he *ought to be* out." (7340)

VULGAR ENGLISH

(*f*) "or do something *I had* not *ought to do*" (8038)
(*f*) "that *ought to be* enough" (8157)
(*d*) "any one *aught to know* as much" (8067)

Although, in most cases, there are not enough instances to make the figures of statistical value, there do appear some facts that seem significant.

1. The common statement that "the difference between *should* and *would* is in general the same as that between *shall* and *will*"[46] is

[46] W. D. Whitney, *Essentials of English Grammar* (Boston, Ginn and Co., 1877), p. 121. See also Garland Greever and Easley S. Jones, *The Century Collegiate Hand-*

hardly accurate and by no means an adequate description of the uses of these two function words. The examples found show that the notions of "obligation" are still strong in many uses of *should* and those of "wish" or "willingness" likewise strong in the uses of *would*. There is, in this respect, not the overlapping that was found in the cases of *shall* and *will*.[47] On the other hand, the strength of these full word senses of *should* and *would* causes greater complications in the uses of *should* and *would* as function words.

2. *Should* seems to be used very infrequently in the Vulgar English materials—much less frequently than in the Standard English letters and *would* proportionately more frequently. In the Vulgar English letters *should* appears in only 4.5 per cent of the instances as against 95.4 per cent of *would*. In the Standard English materials *should* is used in 26.6 per cent as against 73.4 per cent of *would*.

3. In both the Standard English letters and those of Vulgar English *would* frequently appears with the first person in sentences like the following:

> "I *would* be pleased if you will kindly forward to me . . ." (8294)
> "I *would* like to locate a white canvas bedding roll" (9053)
> "I *would* appreciate it very much if . . ." (9016)
> "It is quite possible that I *would* not receive a reply" (9005)
> "I *would* like to hear something . . ." (8029)
> "I did not think for one minute that I *would* be where I am now" (8265)

4. *May* seems to be much less frequently used in the Vulgar English letters in proportion to *can* than it is in the Standard English materials. (Vulgar English *may*, 10.2 per cent; *can*, 89.8 per cent. Standard English *may*, 52 per cent; *can*, 48 per cent.)

5. The so-called adverbial *maybe* as in "Well *maybe* I will be there" (8039), which has been in the English language since the early part of the fifteenth century, appeared only in the Vulgar English letters.

6. Comparatively few instances of *might* appeared in the Standard English letters (eleven in all), but only one instance in the Vulgar English materials.

7. Very few instances of either *must* or *ought* appeared in any of the materials examined. Two of the four instances from the Vulgar

---

book (New York, D. Appleton-Century Co., Rev. ed., 1939), p. 64: "The ordinary distinction between *should* and *would* is like that between *shall* and *will*."

[47] See above, pages 162 and 163.

English letters were of *had ought*,[48] a construction which did not occur in the Standard English letters.

II. FUNCTION WORDS USED WITH THE PARTICIPLES

As indicated above (pages 128, 129) function words are used not only with the infinitives or verbal "substantives" but also with the participles or verbal "adjectives." The constructions that are to be discussed in the rest of this chapter are those in which the words *be, get, keep, have* are followed by these verbal adjectives or participles. As a matter of fact no "clear line can be drawn between verbal adjectives and other adjectives," [49] and it is often very difficult to decide whether the participle is to be taken as a simple predicate adjective and the *be* or *have* with full word sense or the *be* or *have* are to be regarded as function words closely joined with a participle to make a so-called "verb phrase"—an "expanded tense" or a "passive voice." It is hard, for example, to demonstrate any real distinction between "She *is dependent* upon him for support" (8234), and "She *is depending* upon him for support" or "They *were depending* on him for their bread" (8004); between "M——'s presence at home *is* not *necessary*" (8027); and "his presence at home *is needed*" (8137). There are, however, those instances in which the verbal character of the participles seems to stand out prominently and the various forms of *be* or *have* used with them to become unstressed function words. These are the instances that need special discussion here.

1. Be *in its various forms, with the present participle, the so-called "progressive form"*

The combination of the verb *be* with the present participle was used, but very infrequently, in Old English. Åkerlund [50] counted

[48] The *Oxford Dictionary* records the past participle *ought*—
a. in the sense of *owed*, 1375 to 1672.
b. in the sense of *possessed* (modern Scots), 1560, 1800.
c. in the sense of *been obliged*, 1836, 1895.

[49] See K. Brugmann, *Comparative Grammar of the Indo-Germanic Languages*, Vol. IV, Part III, § 1099, p. 605. See also *ibid.*, Vol. II, Part I, § 144, p. 456:
"An adjective can be used to denote not only a quality inherent in the nature of the thing, but as a transitory attribute defined in regard to time according to the standpoint of the speaker; thus it comes to have somewhat a verbal character, in other words it becomes a participle (μετοχή)."

[50] Alfred Åkerlund, *On the History of the Definite Tenses in English* (Lund, 1911), p. 6.

only three examples in *Beowulf* and but twenty four in the whole of the *Anglo-Saxon Chronicle.* In Aelfric's *Lives of the Saints,* a lengthy work, he found about a hundred. It is only in the Modern English period after the time of Shakspere [51] that this combination of *be* with the present participle has become fairly frequent.[52]

In the older periods of the English language this present participle of the verb was added only to the simple present or past tense forms of the verb *to be,* as in "hio him beforan *hleapende wæs* and hi hyre æfter *fyligende wæron.*" No examples appear of *be* with the present participle following such other words as *will, would, must be, have,* etc., as in the following Modern English examples:

"A general dissatisfaction . . . *will soon be impairing* any value I might be to the service" (9061)
". . . or I *would not be trying* to get him home" (8067)
"he thought she *must be receiving* treatment" (8240)
"an immense new structure which *is being erected*" (8139)
"they *have been trying* to locate him" (8160)
"she *had been staying* at places where . . ." (8296)

The Modern English use of this combination is not only more frequent than it formerly was; it also extends into many more forms of the verb and thus has a wider range of use. In many cases the adjective character of the present participle seems especially prominent, as in the following examples:

"the pain in the groin *was excruciating*" (9006)
"I *was* in Columbus *arranging* for rental of quarters" (9054)
"The indictments *are* probably still *pending*" (8017)
"and any which *are lacking* to complete my record will be given my prompt attention" (9027)

[51] *Ibid.,* p. 62:
"Shakespeare has perhaps favoured the construction more than most of the authors belonging to the period; but still it must be said that the difference is great between the frequency in his works and in such as belong to our days."

[52] Otto Jespersen, who formerly believed that the Modern English *I am reading* is an aphetic form of *I am a-reading* "where *a* represents the preposition *on,* and the form in *-ing* is not the participle but the noun," now holds that these forms are "a continuation of the old combinations of the auxiliary verb and the participle in *-ende;* but after this ending had been changed into *-inge* and had thus become identical with that of the verbal substantive, an amalgamation took place of this construction and the combination *be on* + the sb, in which *on* had become *a* and was then dropped. . . . This amalgamation accounts . . . for the greatly increasing frequency of the construction . . . as well as for such peculiarities as the frequency of the prep. *of* before the object."—Otto Jespersen, *A Modern English Grammar,* Vol. IV (Heidelberg, 1931), pp. 168–169.

"I *am willing* to defray all expense" (9059)
"He *was missing* from home two weeks" (8257)
"Because of the age of Mrs. —— and the fact that her memory *is failing*, our visitor was unable . . ." (8095)

On the other hand, in most of the instances the verbal character of the participle stands out and the part of the verb *to be* used in combination with it seems to be an unstressed function word acting as the tense bearer for the whole expression. Some examples are

"I *am writing* you again . . ." (8023)
"The son *is making* $21.00 per month" (8064)
"She *is* no longer *living* at ——" (8144)
"He *is applying* for discharge" (8027)
"I *was doing* the best work of my career" (9033)
"I *was participating* in a baseball game" (9042)
"she *was* then *taking* insulin" (8240)
"he and his mother *were living* at ——" (8095)
"I *have been training* polo ponies" (9015)
"The regiment *was being divided*" (9019)
"This account *is being paid*" (9033)

Perhaps the best way to demonstrate the use of the combination of *be* + present participle is to place side by side for comparison the examples here given both with the expanded verb form and with the simple verb form.

1. I *am writing* you again.	I *write* you again.
2. The son *is making* $21.00 per month.	The son *makes* $21.00 per month.
3. She *is* no longer *living* at ——.	She no longer *lives* at ——.
4. He *is applying* for discharge.	He *applies* for discharge.
5. I *was doing* the best work of my career.	I *did* the best work of my career.
6. I *was participating* in a baseball game.	I *participated* in a baseball game.
7. She *was* then *taking* insulin.	She then *took* insulin.
8. He and his brother *were living* at ——.	He and his brother *lived* at ——
9. I *have been training* polo ponies.	I *have trained* polo ponies.
10. This account *is being paid.*	This account *is paid.*
11. The regiment *was being divided.*	The regiment *was divided.*

From this comparison the following statements seem justified:

a. In most of the instances, the form of the present participle with *be* expresses a "definite" time as opposed to the "indefinite" time of the simple tense form.[53] This seems to be particularly true in respect to sentences 1, 5, 6, 7, 8.

b. There is often a contrast between the completed action expressed by the form without the present participle and the incompleted action or "action in progress" expressed by the form with the present participle. This is particularly true of sentences 10 and 11.

c. At times there seems to be practically no difference between the form with the present participle and the simple tense form. See, for example, sentences 2 and 3.

d. At times the form with the present participle does not seem to have a satisfactory parallel in the simple tense form. See, for example, sentence 4. This is, of course, especially true of those instances also in which the adjectival quality of the present participle is most prominent. Such sentences are

"I *am willing* to defray all expenses" (9059)
"He *was missing* from home two weeks" (8257)
"Her memory *is failing*" (8095)
"The indictments *are* probably still *pending*" (8017)

There do not seem to be any differences in use in the instances from Standard English and those from the Vulgar English materials. The actual number of instances of the various forms of *be* with the present participle, appearing in our materials, is given in Table XXVI.

Although the total number of instances is not great enough to draw any valid statistical conclusions, the following statements seem justified:

1. Although more instances of this combination of *be* + present participle appear in the Vulgar English materials than in the Standard English letters, there is in the former a much narrower range of use than in the latter. As a matter of fact, 96 per cent of the Vulgar English instances are of the simple present and simple past tense form

[53] "The essential thing is that the action or state denoted by the expanded tense is thought of as *a temporal frame encompassing* something else which as often as not is to be understood from the whole situation. The expanded tenses therefore call the attention more specially to time than the simple tenses, which speak of nothing but the action or state itself."—Otto Jespersen, *A Modern English Grammar,* Vol. IV (Heidelberg, 1931), p. 180.

TABLE XXVI

Standard English		*Vulgar English*	
am, is, are + pres. part. *Sing.* *Pl.* 1. 27 1. 3 2. 0 2. 0 3. 24 3. 6 Total 60	*am,* etc. + *being* + past part. *Sing.* *Pl.* 1. 2 1. 0 2. 0 2. 0 3. 10 3. 2 Total 14	*am, is, are* + pres. part. *Sing.* *Pl.* 1. 74 1. 5 2. 1 2. 0 3. 35 3. 4 Total 119	*am,* etc. + *being* + past part. Total 0
was, were + pres. part. *Sing.* *Pl.* 1. 5 1. 0 2. 0 2. 0 3. 12 3. 2 Total 19	*was, were* + *being* + past part. *Sing.* *Pl.* 1. 0 1. 0 2. 0 2. 0 3. 1 3. 0 Total 1	*was, were* + pres. part. *Sing.* *Pl.* 1. 8 1. 1 2. 0 2. 0 3. 13 3. 0 Total 22	*was, were* + *being* + past part. Total 0
have + *been* + pres. part. *Sing.* *Pl.* 1. 3 1. 0 2. 0 2. 0 3. 2 3. 1 Total 6	*have* + *been* + *being* + past part. *Sing.* *Pl.* Total 0	*have* + *been* + pres. part. *Sing.* *Pl.* 1. 1 1. 1 2. 0 2. 0 3. 1 3. 0 Total 3	*have* + *been* + *being* + past part. Total 0
had + *been* + pres. part. *Sing.* *Pl.* 1. 0 1. 0 2. 0 2. 0 3. 3 3. 0 Total 3	*had* + *been* + *being* + past part. *Sing.* *Pl.* Total 0	*had* + *been* + pres. part. *Sing.* *Pl.* Total 0	*had* + *been* + *being* + past part. Total 0
will, etc. + *be* + pres. part. *Sing.* *Pl.* 1. 1 1. 0 2. 0 2. 0 3. 1 3. 0 Total 2	Total 0	*will,* etc. + *be* + pres. part. *Sing.* *Pl.* 1. 2 1. 0 2. 0 2. 0 3. 1 3. 0 Total 3	Total 0
Inf. *to be* + pres. part. Total 2	Total 0	Total 0	Total 0
Total 92	15	147	0
Grand Total	107	147	

of the verb *to be* with the present participle, i. e., of *am, is, are* + present participle, or *was, were* + present participle. In the Standard English materials 74 per cent of the instances are of this kind. Here again Vulgar English shows itself more conservative than Standard

English, for these were the only forms with the present participle that occurred in the older stages of English.

2. Fourteen per cent of the instances appearing in the Standard English letters are of the so-called "passive" voice. Not a single instance of this type appeared in the Vulgar English letters.

J. Get, *in its various forms, with the present participle, expressing inchoative action*

As indicated above (pages 170–171) the word *get,* like other words of "possession," has not only taken on a great variety of meaning but has tended to become a function word used with both the present and the past participles and the infinitive form of verbs. In its use as a function word with the present participle it is recorded by the *Oxford Dictionary* from the early part of the eighteenth century.[54] The combination appears to express inchoative or beginning action. Only one instance appeared in our materials and that in the Standard English letters.

"A number of years ago this soldier *got fooling* with liquor" (8296)

K. Keep, *in its various forms, with the present participle, expressing continuous or repetitive action*

Keep, another word having to do with possession, has also developed a wide range of meaning. The *Oxford Dictionary* gives forty one separately numbered senses and seventeen combinations with prepositions, that have specialized meanings. As a function word used with the present participle form of a verb to express continuous or repetitive action, it is recorded from the end of the eighteenth century.[55] Only two examples appeared in our materials, one from the Standard English letters and one from those of Vulgar English.

"—— *kept muttering* to himself during the whole trial" (7451)

"The reason I left —— was to come here to get my Wife to come

[54] Two of the quotations given by the *Oxford Dictionary* are

"Instead of looking at the sun, I *got thinking* about the dry bed of the stream, just beneath." Ruskin *Fors Clav.* xix. 10.

"When they *got talking* together it was Greek to me." Mrs. H. Martin *Common Clay* III. ix. 144.

[55] Three quotations from the *Oxford Dictionary* are

"Niagara . . . *keeps pouring* on forever and ever." Hawthorne *Fr.* and *It. Jrnls.* I. 124.

"He *kept changing* his plans." T. F. Tout *Hist. Eng.* 134.

"She *kept tumbling* off her horse." *Temple Bar Mag.* (1892) Feb. 198.

with me but when I got here why she *kep putting* it off until Sunday night" (8243)

L. Be, *in its various forms, with the past participle, the so-called "passive voice"*

The usual statement in the common school grammars of the combination of *be,* in its various forms, with the past participle is fairly represented by the following quotation:

"We called . . . the past participle also the 'passive' participle, because it usually marks the thing described by it as 'suffering,' or 'enduring,' or being the object of, action defined by the verb. . . . Now, by putting this passive participle along with all the various forms, simple and compound, of the verb *be,* we make a set of verb-phrases which are usually called the *passive conjugation* of the verb, because by means of them we take what is the object of any verbal form in the ordinary conjugation, and turn it into a subject, representing it as enduring or suffering the action expressed by that verbal form." [56]

One difficulty with such a statement is the fact that there are many examples in English at every stage in its history in which the past participle remains fully adjectival and does not form the so-called passive voice. Examples from the materials examined for this study are

"he *was gone* for some little time" (8114)
"the other countries of Europe *were unprepared*" (9017)
"he *is inclined* to cross bridges before they are reached" (9000)
"signed by —— and —— who *are* entirely *disinterested*" (8203)
"My military education *is limited* and has been largely self-acquired" (9021)

[56] W. D. Whitney, *Essentials of English Grammar* (Boston, Ginn and Co., 1877), pp. 126–127.

See also G. P. Krapp, *The Elements of English Grammar* (New York, Charles Scribner's Sons, 1908), pp. 145–146; and the following from Grattan and Gurray, *Our Living Language,* p. 212:

"In some languages (for example, Latin, Greek) the Passive Voice is distinguished from the Active by inflexions: in English it finds its expression in the union of a Form-Word with a Full-Word, the union of the Auxiliary verb *to be* with an ordinary verb."

A stimulating discussion of "The Relations Expressed by the Passive Voice," by E. T. Owen, appears in the *Transactions of the Wisconsin Academy,* Vol. VII, Part I, 17–148.

See below (p. 194) for comment on the use of *be* and *have* with intransitive verbs, especially with verbs of "motion."

"both of the parents *are advanced* in years" (8183)
"Mr. —— *was* very greatly *attached* to his children" (8296)
"her son *was connected* with an express company" (8095)
"Men who serve in the Army . . . *are* more *interested* in their government and the welfare of the nation" (9012)
"he *is colored* and his age is . . ." (8314)
"he *is mistaken* about C—— being his birth place" (8151)
"they *are* so *devoted* to each other" (8028)
"he *was gone* a little over 7 months" (8246)
"I *am* so *disheartened* when I think of what . . ." (8153)
"I *am crippled* in my limbs and not able to work" (8201)

The difference between a past participle which remains a predicate adjective after the verb *to be* and one that can be looked upon as forming a passive with the function word *be* may be illustrated by the sentence, "The man *was lost* in the woods." If the context is such that the attention centers upon the fact of the man's situation (the fact that he is in the *lost* condition), the *lost* is a predicate adjective; if, however, the context is such that the attention centers upon an antecedent activity "that some one or some thing *caused* this situation," then the expression can be looked upon as a "passive." The so-called "passive," then, is largely a matter of *context,* not a matter of *form.*

Another difficulty with the statement quoted is the fact that it does not seem to cover the especially significant use of this combination of *be* with the past participle. This function word *be* with the past participle of a full word verb is a device which makes possible a certain freedom within the fixed word order of expressing an actor-action-goal construction. As will be shown below (Chapter X), the distinguishing of the substantive that is actor from that that is goal in Modern English rests solely upon word order. The difference between the "The man struck the bear" and "The bear struck the man" depends upon the fact that in the first instance the word *man* is shown to be the "starting point" of the action by its position before the verb, and the word *bear* is shown to be the "ending point" by its position after the verb. It is not possible to reverse the relative positions of the two substantives and maintain the same relations for these substantives if one keeps the same verb word or the same verb form. One can in many cases, however, because of the existence in English of many contrasting pairs of verb words, reverse the order and use a contrasting verb. For example,

> The water wet the sponge.
> The sponge absorbed the water.

In these two sentences the actual fact that is stated seems to be the same. In the first, however, *water* is the "starting point" of the construction and *sponge* the "ending point" or "goal." In the second, *sponge* is the "starting point" and *water* is the "ending point." This shift of order and therefore of point of view while maintaining the expression of the same fact is accomplished by using a contrasting verb word.[57] In many cases contrasting pairs of words make possible such an easy shifting of order and point of view.

> The soldier followed the captain.
> The captain $\left\{\begin{array}{l}\text{preceded}\\ \text{led}\end{array}\right\}$ the soldier.

But the language does not depend upon the existence of such word pairs to effect this shifting of word order and point of view in the actor-action-goal construction. For each verb that can be used in this construction there are in Modern English two forms, and these also make possible this shifting of word order and point of view. The first is the "simple" verb form; the second is the past participle of this verb preceded by the function word *be* as the tense bearer.

> The water wet the sponge.
> The sponge is (was, etc.) wet.
>
> The man gave the boy the money.[58]
> The boy was given the money.
> The money was given the boy.

As shown above, this shift of order and point of view by means of this particular function word and verb form implies a "passive" only in certain contexts.

The following are some examples of the function word *be* + the past participle that appeared in the letters examined for this study:

[57] The terms "subject" and "object" as applied to sentences do not signify the actual relations of things in the world itself; they refer solely to the grammatical point of view of a particular utterance.

[58] By this device either of the two nouns following the verb can be made the "starting point" or "subject," the "dative" object as well as the "accusative" object.

STANDARD ENGLISH

"I am aware that I *am* not *accounted for* on June 30 ——" (9007)
"I *was* personally and intimately *acquainted* with him" (8060)
"We *were told* that Mrs. —— . . ." (8240)
"I *am* physically *qualified* to resume flying" (9031)
"I *am convinced* of the justice of . . ." (8234)
"I personally *am opposed* to connecting . . ." (9032)
"I *am* not *interested* in the future" (9061)
"I *am informed* Mr. —— is in failing health" (8163)
"If I cannot *be granted* this . . ." (9024)
"I *am given* to understand that . . ." (7321)
"I should have *been consulted* . . ." (9010)
"a letter from —— *was sent* me" (9050)
"Register cards *are made* in all cases" (9002)
"the address in pencil *was mistaken*" (9063)
"A very limited experience *was had* in the basic duties of . . ." (9019)
"my middle name in the commission *is misspelled*" (9036)
"The room *is* poorly *furnished* . . ." (8095) (8027)
"Twenty-five days of leave *are accrued* to my credit" (9019)
"his resignation *was* very reluctantly *accepted*" (9013)
"He stayed on the job until these supplies *were obtained*" (9009)

VULGAR ENGLISH

". . . and help me here at —— where I *am* well *known*" (8094)
"I am to *be sent* to ——" (8198)
"I *was obliged* to give up work" (8265)
"i *was hit* with automobile laste weeke" (8133)
"I *was apointed* his gardine" (8025)
"I *was told* to write to you" (8074)
"I *am married* now" (8112)
"Lately his father *was ruptured* and . . ." (8233)
"I *was* very much *displeased*" (8285)
"his Mother *is* sick and *worried* since he left home" (8101)
"my health *is failed* from over work" (8235)
"my employment *is shut* down" (8079)
"all mail *is returned* uncalled for" (8149)
"The work his step Father followed *is done* now" (8218)
"he will never *be allowed* to vote or . . ." (8038)
". . . how much a month he *was paid*" (8218)
"—— *was born* here in . . ." (8151)

The actual number of instances of this *be* + past participle found in our materials is given in Table XXVII.

TABLE XXVII

Standard English				Vulgar English			
With subject in				With subject in			
1st person		156	21.9%	1st person		27	23%
2nd person		3		2nd person		0	
3rd person				3rd person			
Persons	150			Persons	73		
Neuters	403	553	77.6%	Neuters	17	90	77%
Total		712		Total		117	

From these figures the following statements seem justified:

1. The function word *be* + past participle is used much more frequently in the Standard English materials than in those of Vulgar English. In fact there were found just six times as many instances in the former as in the latter.

2. This construction appeared very rarely with a subject in the second person (three instances in Standard English; none in Vulgar English).

3. The difference in distribution of the instances found in the two sets of material was striking. In both the Standard English materials and in those of Vulgar English there is approximately the same percentage of instances with a subject in the first person (21.9 per cent in Standard English; 23 per cent in Vulgar English) and with a subject in the third person (77.6 per cent in Standard English; 77 per cent in Vulgar English). But when the instances with a subject in the third person are separated into those in which the subjects are "persons" and those in which the subjects are "things" (neuters) the contrast between the two sets of materials is great. In the Standard English materials, 150 or 27 per cent are instances in which "persons" are subjects and 403 or 73 per cent in which "things" (neuters) are subjects. In the Vulgar English letters, however, seventy three or 81 per cent are instances in which "persons" are subjects and only seventeen or 19 per cent are instances in which "things" (neuters) are subjects.

M. Get, *in its various forms, with the past participle*

Get as a function word with the past participle form of the verb is recorded by the *Oxford Dictionary* from the middle of the seventeenth century.[59] As in the case of the other uses of *get* (see above

[59] Four quotations from the *Oxford Dictionary* are
"His Lordship was voted a bore, and *got shelved.*" Disraeli, *Viv. Grey* II. 1.

pages 170 and 171 this particular combination of *get* with the past participle appears in both the Standard English materials and those of Vulgar English. Again, however, it occurs more frequently in Vulgar English. Ten instances, in all, were found; three from the Standard English letters and seven from those of Vulgar English.

STANDARD ENGLISH

"The fact that my pay will soon be reduced is going to make it difficult . . . for me to *get settled*" (9033)
"I was in Columbus arranging for . . . and *getting settled*" (9033)
"but should I ever *get detailed* in that department, I would feel very pleased to . . ." (7512)

VULGAR ENGLISH

"my crop *got* all *washed* away" (8037)
"I *got crippled* with a horse" (8037)
"he *got killed* last fall driving a truck" (8246)
"if he *gets discharged* I no I would have help" (8205)
". . . nothing could be done until he *got tried*" (8153)
"and help us to *get located* at a home of our own" (8094)
"and come to me . . . and *get acquainted* with our Relatives" (8094)

N. Have, *in its various forms, with the past participle, forming the so-called "perfect tenses"*

The use of *have* as a function word with the past participle seems to have arisen out of *have* in its full word meaning of "possession" followed by an object substantive modified by the past participle of a transitive verb. This participle often carried the accusative case inflection as in the following sentence:

hie hæfdon hira cyning aworpenne
(they had their king deposed)

This use of *have* with the participle is much like such Modern English sentences as the following:

"because they *had* a child *born* about the same time" (8203)
"I *have* two months leave *accrued*" (9058)

" 'The taste . . . . is peculiar . . . . but one soon *gets used* to it.' " J. H. Newman *Loss & Gain* 264.
"I . . . . *got caught* in a storm." Rider Haggard *Jess* vi.
"It may leave on your readers an impression unfair to Prof. Royce if nothing more *gets said.*" *Nation* (N.Y.) 19 Nov. (1891) 389/3.

"she *had* her hand *caught* in the door of a street car" (8095)
"so as not to *have* my pay *held up*" (9030)

Somewhat similar, too, are those instances in which the word *have* is used in the sense of "to cause, procure, or oblige (something to be done)" and is followed by a substantive and the past participle of a transitive verb.

"They will *have* the papers *prepared* that you require" (8160)
". . . do my best to *have* this account *settled*" (9033)
"We are *having* a cataract operation *performed* on Mr. ——" (8207)
"I would like to *have* them *returned*" (9027)

Even in Old English, however, there are instances in which the *have* is followed immediately by a past participle of a transitive verb in conditions that appear to be equivalent to our present-day "perfect tense."

Augustinus hæfde genumen wealhstodas of Francena rice.
(Augustine had taken interpreters from [the] Franks' kingdom)

But in general in Old English the *have* was used only with the past participles of transitive verbs. With intransitive verbs the verb *be* was used especially with verbs of motion. In early Middle English, however, the word *have* is found with verbs of action without an object and then with intransitive verbs, especially with the verb *be*. Verbs of motion long continued to have the verb *be* rather than *have* to express "completed" action. "He *is* gone" and "he *was* gone" are common in Present-day English as well as "he *has* gone" and "he *had* gone."

That *have* (when joined with the past participle) has lost its full word meaning and has become a function word for the expression of completed action seems clear from the not infrequent instances of its use with the participle *had* (about 8 per cent of the total number of instances).

"It is true that I *have had* a days leave for which I . . ." (9007)
"I . . . *have had* the opportunity . . ." (9005)
"I *have had* the misfortune to . . ." (9001)
"and he *has had* charge of . . ." (6410)
"we *had had* no report . . ." (6415)
"he *had had* no experience in . . ." (6418)
"I *have had* the care of . . ." (8077)

"his father *has had* an accident" (8255)
"We *have had* conclusive proof of this in recent years" (8063)
"The only support I *had had* was from . . ." (8079)

The number of instances of the function word *have* + the past participle that occur in our materials is given in Table XXVIII.

TABLE XXVIII

Standard English			*Vulgar English*		
Have + past part. of "transitive" verb:			*Have* + past part. of "transitive" verb:		
have + *had*	39	8.8%	*have* + *had*	16	7.8%
have + *been* + p.p.	88	20.0	*have* + *been* + p.p.	16	7.8
have + p.p. of other "transitive" verbs	232	52.4	*have* + p.p. of other "transitive" verbs	104	50.3
Total	359	81.2%	Total	136	66.3%
Have + past part. of "intransitive" verb:			*Have* + past part. of "intransitive" verb:		
have + *been*	49	11.0%	*have* + *been*	54	26.4%
have + p.p. of other "intransitive" verbs	34	7.8	*have* + p.p. of other "intransitive" verbs	15	7.3
Total	83	18.8%	Total	69	33.7%
Grand total	442		Grand total ...	205	

From this survey the following facts seem especially interesting:

1. *Have* + past participle was used much more frequently in Standard English than in Vulgar English. As shown earlier in this book (page 68) the past participle occurs nearly four times as frequently in the Standard English letters as in those of Vulgar English. *Be* + past participle (see page 192) occurs more than six times as frequently in Standard English as in Vulgar English. But *have* + past participle occurs only twice as frequently in the former as in the latter (442 in the Standard English letters as against 205 in those of Vulgar English). Here again Vulgar English shows itself to be more conservative than Standard English.

2. The facts concerning the distribution of the instances that occur in the two sets of material are especially interesting. Remarkable similarity between the two shows itself in three situations.

a. Have + *had.* In Standard English 8.8 per cent of the instances are of this kind; in Vulgar English 7.8 per cent.

b. Have + past participles of "other transitive verbs." In Standard English 52.4 per cent of the instances; in Vulgar English 50.7 per cent. The *have* + past participle of "transitive" verbs was the earliest form in which this combination appeared in English, and it still accounts for more than half of the instances.

c. Have + past participle of "other intransitive verbs." In Standard English 7.8 per cent of the instances; in Vulgar English 7.3 per cent.

3. The two sets of material differ sharply in two situations.

a. Have + *been* + past participle. Here the number of instances in the Standard English letters greatly exceeds that of the instances from the Vulgar English materials (in Standard English 20 per cent of the instances as against 7.8 per cent of the instances in Vulgar English).

b. Have + the past participle *been*. Here is the one situation in which the number of instances from the Vulgar English letters exceeds that of the instances from the Standard English materials. (In Standard English only 11 per cent of the instances as against 26.4 per cent of the instances in Vulgar English.)

Some examples of these uses of *have* + past participle are the following:

1. Have + *Past Participle of "Other Transitive Verbs"*

STANDARD ENGLISH

"He *has written* you the enclosed letter" (8144)
"they *have* not *paid* the taxes for this year" (8283)
"I *have taken* a personal interest in this case" (8267)
". . . how long we *have lived* there" (8280)
"he *had* never *received* any pay for this visit" (8240)
"she *had* already *prepared* affidavits" (8240)
"we *had talked* it over" (9040)

VULGAR ENGLISH

"he *has* always *minded* me" (9025)
"i *have lost* the use of . . ." (8281)
"I *have* not *received* an answer" (8259)
"we *have raised* him ever since . . ." (8084)
"saying he *had passed* the last board" (8038)
"as I *had* previously *asked* him" (8070)

2. Have + *Past Participle of "Other Intransitive Verbs"*

STANDARD ENGLISH

"It *has* just *come* to my attention" (9051)
"her husband *has become* helpless" (8189)
"the trunk *has* not *arrived* at ——" (9052)
"*Had* my wife *remained at* ——" (9052)
"if any question *had arisen*" (9010)
"my name *has* never *appeared* in . . ." (9022)
"an infection *had set* in" (6406)

VULGAR ENGLISH

". . . would see what *has became* of my son" (8015)
"that poor mother *has went* and got a job" (8005)
"health . . . *has become* worse" (8251)
"I *have come* to a point . . ." (8079)
"we did not know where he *had gon* to" (8193)
". . . sorry such a thing *has happened*" (8281)

3. Have + been + *Past Participle*

STANDARD ENGLISH

"I *have been informed* that I would shortly . . ." (9033)
"my duties . . . *have been* very *limited*" (9019)
"my earned leave *will have been* nearly all *used*" (9001)
"If this account *has* not *been paid*" (9057)
"the solution that *had been proposed*" (9057)
"this authority *had been requested* and *granted*" (9040)
"the requisition *had been* previously *submitted* to . . ." (9040)
"that I *had been granted* the remainder of the month . . ." (9007)

VULGAR ENGLISH

"I *have been devorced* for several years" (8259)
"He *has been discharged* since we were married" (8127)
"His mother *has been worried* about him" (8136)
"I *have been transferred* back" (8039)
"a couple of his classmates *had been informed*" (8251)

4. Have + *the Past Participle* been

STANDARD ENGLISH

"he *has been* out of employment for . . ." (8283)
"he *has* always *been* lenient with her" (8144)
"my service *has been* continuous" (9022)
"he *had* not *been* home for eight months" (8142)

VULGAR ENGLISH

"He *has* not *been* in good health" (8072)
"—— *has* always *been* a good boy" (8074)
"his Mother *has Bin* Did 3 years" (8277)
"i *have Bin* sick for over a year" (8155)
"until he *had been* in there for sometime" (8067)
"If he *had been* well enough to come" (8193)

IX

THE USES OF FUNCTION WORDS: WITH ADJECTIVES AND WORD GROUPS
THREE MISCELLANEOUS FUNCTION WORDS

As may be seen from the two chapters preceding this one, the function words have become for Modern English an exceedingly important grammatical device. They are used freely with nouns to indicate a great variety of relationships that formerly were expressed by inflections or the forms of words. With verbs, the function words play an even more important rôle and are used to signal a number of aspects of verbal action, and attitudes toward that action, that do not seem to have formal expression in the earlier stages of English. There are, however, still other uses of function words in Modern English, and these will be considered in this chapter. These are

I. Function Words Used with Adjectives
II. Function Words Used with Word Groups, the So-Called Conjunctions
III. Three Miscellaneous Function Words: *it, there, one*

I. THE FUNCTION WORDS USED WITH ADJECTIVES

In a former chapter (pages 96–101) we have already touched the matter of the function words used with adjectives in connection with the topic "The Comparison of Adjectives." There it was shown that the inflections for comparison *-er* and *-est* have in some measure been supplanted by the function words *more* and *most* acting somewhat as inflection equivalents. The actual situation in respect to this development of the function word is given in Table XXIX.

In general, the function word rather than the inflection is used with the less familiar and more learned words,[1] although there

[1] See above pages 98 and 99, for examples from our materials.

TABLE XXIX

Standard English				*Vulgar English*			
Inflection		Function word		Inflection		Function word	
-er	56.4%	*more*	43.6%	*-er*	90%	*more*	10%
-est	47.0%	*most*	53.0%	*-est*	89%	*most*	11%

are many words with which either method of comparison is possible.[2] As the figures show, the use of the function word seems to be especially characteristic of Standard English, for approximately half of the instances from the Standard English letters appear with the function word and but one tenth of the instances from the Vulgar English materials. Here again Vulgar English is more conservative than Standard English, for from the Early Modern English period the drift in English has been slowly toward an increasing proportion of instances that use the function word rather than inflection for comparison.

The use of the function word in the matter of comparison, however, is not the only use of the function word with the adjective in Modern English. There are those function words that have been called "intensives" and "down-toners," [3] or sometimes "adverbs of degree." In general the process of their development seems to be as follows. If two adjectives stand next to one another as in "the *dark green* house," the first tends to become a modifier of the second. The active force in this process seems to be the pressure of word order for modification. As will be shown below (pages 270–277), the pattern of Modern English is that single words modify the words immediately following.

The force of this word order pattern has shown itself in a great variety of instances. Thus *very,* originally in English an adjective meaning "true," as in Chaucer's description of the knight, "a *verray* parfit gentil knight" (= a *true,* perfect, well-born knight) or in his "And if that it a *verray* angel be" (= and if that it a *real* angel be), wherever it stood before another adjective tended

[2] For the usage with various types of adjectives see the dissertation by Anny Rohr, *Die Steigerung des neuenglischen Eigenschaftswortes im 17. und 18. Jahrhundert mit Ausblicken auf den Sprachgebrauch der Gegenwart* (Giessen, 1929).

[3] See C. Stoffel, "Intensives and Down-toners," *Anglistische Forschungen,* Heft 1 (Heidelberg, 1901).

to lose its full word meaning of "true," "real," "genuine," and become a function word of degree. *Very* is in Present-day English the most frequently used function word of degree. In similar fashion *pretty*, an adjective originally meaning "cunning" or "crafty," then "clever," "skilful," and later "pleasing," "comely," wherever it stood before another adjective has since the sixteenth century tended to lose its full word meaning and become a function word of degree as in the following quotations: [4]

pretty

"I'll take *pretty* good care of you." Sheridan *St. Patr. Day* II. ii.

"I gave you, I remember, a *pretty* full account of all but her name, in my letter." Shaftesbury *Characteristics* I. 48.

"If such be the law, we are *pretty* sure it is not the law Parliament intended to make." *Law Q. Rev.* (1896) July. 201.

Very similar has been the development of the word *mighty*. From an adjective meaning "powerful," *mighty* (and *almighty*) like *very* has become an intensifying function word.

mighty

"Tomorrow . . . wyll I cause a *mightie* greate hayle to rayne." Coverdale *Exod.* ix. 18.

"You are a *mighty* good obedient thing." De Foe *Fam. Instruct.* (ed. 1841) I. iv. 91.

"This is all *mighty* fine." Dickens *O. Twist* xlix.

"a *mighty* late hour" Stevenson *Men & Books* 206.

"The coffee is *almighty* hot." Henry James *The American* I. 79.

Examples of other words used as intensifying function words or function words of degree with the full word meanings fading out under the pressure of the word order pattern for modification are the following:

right

"the *right* gentell, *right* graciouse, and *right* confortable lettres" *Paston Letters* I. 72.

"There is also a *ryght* good exercise, which is also expedient to lerne." Sir Thomas Elyot *The Governor* I. xvii. 201.

"I was *right* glad . . . to see your writing again." Coleridge *Lett.* (ed. 1895) 336.

"And *right* interesting it is to observe . . ." Lytteil *Landmarks* III. viii. 142.

[4] Most of the quotations given here and in the immediately following pages are taken from the *Oxford Dictionary*, O. Jespersen's *A Modern English Grammar*, Vol. II, pp. 366–377, and C. Stoffel's *Intensives and Down-toners*.

Similar also is *right* in forms of address such as "Right Reverend," "Right Honorable," etc.

real

"An opportunity of doing a *real* good office . . ." J. Fox *Wanderer* No. 17. 116.

"The burning of three *real* good and substantial houses in this town . . ." Mrs. Griffith *Hist. Lady Barton* II. 283.

"Last Friday was a *real* fine day." R. H. Froude *Rem.* (ed. 1838) I. 448.

"It looks *real* nice." G. Allen *Babylon* vi.

"*real* wicked . . . *real* stubborn" Hall Caine *The Christian* 75.

stark

"Everybody was, for the moment, *stark* mad on the subject of Porteous." Scott *Hrt. Midl.* vi.

"It fell *stark* calm." W. Scoresby *Jrnl.* 390.

"And, *stark* awake, with beating heart He put the hawthorn twigs apart." Morris *Earthly Par.* II. III. 45.

dead

"We were *dead* silent on that head." Carlyle *Reminiscences* I. 157.

"let a stockbroker be *dead* stupid about poetry" Stevenson *Virginibus Puerisque* 241.

"I thought it was a *dead* sure thing." Gilbert Parker *The Right of Way* 36.

"In a few minutes it fell *dead* calm." R. H. Dana *Bef. Mast* x. 24.

"Her engines were going *dead* slow." *Times* [London] 25 July (1881) 4/5.

precious

"While on the Continent I have received *precious* few letters." Asa Gray *Lett.* (ed. 1893) I. 268.

"I . . . took *precious* good care to have it." Thackeray *Fatal Boots* viii.

"society makes *precious* short work of the cads" Shaw *Plays Unpleasant* 213.

"life is a dream, a *precious* poor dream at times" H. G. Wells *The Time Machine* 147.

terrible

"The weather being *terrible* hot . . ." Sir T. Herbert *Trav.* 5.

"We were so *terrible* good as to take James in our carriage." Jane Austen *Lett.* (ed. 1884) I. 126.

"your ale is *terrible* strong" Swift *Polite Conversation* 159.

Similar to *terrible* is the development of *awful,* with the later form also, *awfully.*

awful

"He will have made an *awfully* bad choice if he comes to be sentenced to be hanged." Gen. P. Thompson *Exerc.* (ed. 1842) I. 238.

"In the way of money-making . . . he is *awfully* clever." Lang *Wand. India* 154.

"You'll be *awfully* glad to get rid of me." Black *Green Past,* ii. 15.

devilish

"The cur is *divelishe* hungrie." Massinger *Beleeve as you list* IV. iii.

"Taking *devilish* long strides" De Foe *Crusoe* (ed. 1840) I. xx. 353.

"I have seen *devilish* little of the man." Stevenson *Dr. Jekyll* ii.

"I've been *devilish* annoyed about it." Thackeray *The Newcomes* 303.

It is by this process also that the word *damned* originally meaning "condemned" and "accursed" has become an intensifying function word.

damned

"I believe she's *damned* fond of me" Thackeray *Van. Fair* xiii.

"Damn'd's the superlative degree; Means that alone and nothing more. . . . Examples we may find enough, *Damn'd* high, *damn'd* low, *damn'd* fine, *damn'd* stuff." Lloyd *Satyr & Pedlar* Poet. Wks. I. 57.

The adjective *good* also becomes an intensive function word as in the following quotation:

good

"It will take a *good* long time to bring them right." *Daily News* [London] 16 July (1885) 4/7.

But with the word *good* and the word *nice* the process extends even farther, for in sentences in which *good* or *nice* is joined by *and* with another adjective, the *good and* and the *nice and* together become the intensive function word.

good and, nice and

"when it was *good and* dark" Mark Twain *Huckleberry Finn* l. 78.

"I was *good and* tired" *Ibid.* l. 152.

"You'll be *nice and* ill in the morning" D. Jerrold *Mrs. Caudle* ii.

"The boy was bad. Yes! He was *good and* bad."

In general, it seems fair to say that any adjective no matter what its original meaning, if placed immediately before another adjective, will tend, because of the pressure of the word order pattern to indicate the direction of modification, to lose its full word meaning and become an intensifying function word. There is, afterward, it seems, considerable pressure to add an *-ly* ending to such "adverbs" of degree, and "*awful* good" becomes "*awfully* good," "*tremendous* large" becomes "*tremendously* large," "*real* wicked" becomes "*really* wicked," and so on.

The instances of intensifying modifiers that occur in the letters examined here can be grouped as follows. *More* and *most* which have been dealt with above (pages 98 and 99) are not included here.

A. INTENSIFIERS WITH "-LY" ENDING + ADJECTIVE

Standard English	*Vulgar English*
"*absolutely* truthful" (9007)	"*entirely* alone" (8094)
"*considerably* larger" (9033)	"*hardly* able" (8052)
"*duly* grateful" (9023)	"*nearly* three weeks" (8265)
"*especially* fit" (7231)	"*nearly* 50 years" (8187)
"*extremely* careful" (9006)	"*perfectly* able" (8256)
"*fairly* accurate" (9003)	"*really* necessary" (8152)
"*largely* self-acquired" (9021)	
"*nearly* continuous" (9001)	
"*nearly* all" (9001)	
"*palpably* inappropriate" (9010)	
"*practically* abandoned" (9030)	
"*practically* unchanged" (9006)	
"*strongly* otherwise" (9030)	
"*terribly* disappointed" (9019)	
"*widely* scattered" (9010)	
Etc.	
Total 22	Total 6

B. INTENSIFIERS WITHOUT "-LY" ENDING + ADJECTIVE

Standard English	*Vulgar English*
"*almost* necessary" (9063)	"*all* right" (8039)
"*better* satisfied" (9020)	"*almost* crazy" (8204)
"*better* qualified" (9042)	"*almost* dead" (8288)
"*far* distant" (9089)	"*awful* bad" (8016) (8087) (8021)
"*far* reaching" (9063)	"*ofel* hard" (8205)
"*much* excited" (9000)	"*awful* sorry" (8024)
"*much* interested" (9014)	". . . has been *bad* sick" (8016)
"*quite* sure" (9018)	"*better* satisfied" (8082)
"*quite* presentable" (9018)	". . . is *but* eighteen years" (8257)
"*quite* possible" (9005)	
"*so* glad" (9018)	

Standard English	*Vulgar English*
"*somewhat* straitened circumstances" (9023)	"the —— is *but* seventeen years" (8097)
"*too* bad" (9011)	"*little* more" (8246)
"*very* successful" (9008)	"*mighty* hard" (8152)
"*very* exceptional" (9009)	"*much* longer" (8072) (8265)
"*very* minor" (9007)	"*part* dependent" (8036)
"*very* desirous" (9029)	"*pretty* bad" (8087)
"*very* necessary" (9027)	"*pretty* good" (8251)
"*well* fitted" (9020)	"*pretty* well" (8053)
"*well-nigh* impossible" (9032)	"*quite* necessary" (8072)
Etc.	"*real* bad" (8016)
	"*right* good" (8324)
	"*so* old" (8005)
	"*so* bad" (8244) (8246)
	"*so* thankful" (8028)
	"*such* hot climate" (8250)
	"*too* long" (8038)
	"*too* young" (8218) (8270)
	"*very* thin" (8250)
	"*very* ill" (8288) (8024)
	"*well* disciplined" (8063)
	Etc.
Total 47	Total 157

C. Adjective + "Enough"

Standard English	*Vulgar English*
"good *enough*" (9011)	"old *enough*" (8067) (8084) (8176) (8264)
	"large *enough*" (8251)
Total 1	Total 5
Grand Total 70	Grand Total 167

Some points of difference between the practice of Standard English and that of Vulgar English as revealed in our materials are as follows:

1. The pressure to add *-ly* to intensifiers modifying adjectives is especially strong in Standard English.

2. The use of intensifiers without the *-ly* ending, although it appears in both sets of materials, is much greater in Vulgar English. There are not only more than three times as many instances in Vulgar English, but also a much greater variety of separate words. Some of the words that appeared in the Vulgar English materials and not

in Standard English are *all, awful, bad, but, mighty, part, pretty, real, right, such.*

3. *So* as an intensifier modifying an adjective, not followed by a *that* clause, is found in both Standard English and Vulgar English.[5]

II. THE FUNCTION WORDS USED WITH WORD GROUPS —THE SO-CALLED CONJUNCTIONS

A conjunction is often defined as "a word that joins together sentences or parts of a sentence." [6] Conjunctions are therefore also words whose chief meanings lie in the grammatical functions they indicate, and, in spite of the fact that there is considerable independent "meaning" in some of them, we shall include them all here as "the function words used with word groups." The particular word groups with which these function words are used are sentences and those "parts of a sentence," frequently called "clauses," which also have the formal characteristics of sentences. The word groups, then, with which we are concerned here are those in which there are two essential elements, (*a*) a word with the formal marks of a substantive, and (*b*) a word with such a tense form as marks a finite verb. Table XXX gives the complete list of these function words that were found in the letters examined for this study and the number of occurrences of each.

TABLE XXX

FUNCTION WORDS WITH WORD GROUPS

In the Standard English Materials			*In the Vulgar English Materials*		
and	474	485	and	707	716
and also	4		and also	3	
and then	2		and then	2	
and consequently	3		and consequently	0	
and so	1		and so	1	
and therefore	1		and therefore	1	
and still	0		and still	2	

[5] The finding here corroborates that of Russell Thomas in his article "Language Attitude," *The English Journal,* Vol. 19, 1930, pp. 557–560.

[6] G. O. Curme, *Parts of Speech and Accidence* (Boston, D. C. Heath and Co., 1935), p. 92.

The Oxford Dictionary gives the following definition for the word *conjunction* in its grammatical sense: "an uninflected word used to connect clauses or sentences, or to coördinate words in the same clause."

TABLE XXX (*Continued*)

In the Standard English Materials		*In the Vulgar English Materials*	
also	3	also	0
nor	2	nor 0	
		or 1	1
but	66	but	87
yet	1	yet	0
then	3	then	4
therefore	6	therefore	2
however	9	however	0
Total	575	Total	810
after	9	after	6
although 2		although 1	2
though 5	7	though 1	
as	88	as	138
because	3	because 6 cause 1	7
before	6	before	10
for	1	for	53
how	3	how	19
if	102	if	171
like	1	like	5
provided	3	provided	0
since	12	since	23
so	17	so	105
than	2	than	3
that	414	that	185
unless	4	unless	6
until	7	until 12 till 3	15
what	19	what	44
when	36	when	48
where	19	where 25 everywhere 1	26
whether	10	whether	2
which	121	which	31
while	25	while	7
who	79	who	47
why	6	why	6
Total	994	Total	959
in case 7			
in as much as 8			
in order that 6			
in the event that 4			
in so far that 1	26		
GRAND TOTAL	1595	GRAND TOTAL	1769

From the Standard English Materials		*From the Vulgar English Materials*	
Clauses with no function word, in which *that* might be used	78	Clauses with no function word in which *that* might be used	206
Conditional clauses with no function word but with inverted word order	5	Conditional clauses with no function word, but with inverted word order	0

Some significant facts in the figures of this table seem to be the following:

1. Of the thirty two function words here listed for the Standard English materials seven account for 1,353 or 84.9 per cent of the instances, and five more, or twelve in all, account for 92.2 per cent of the instances. These particular function words are

and	485	instances	
that	414	"	
which	121	"	
if	102	"	
as	88	"	
who	79	"	
but	66	"	
	1355	"	or 84.9%
when	36	"	
while	25	"	
what	19	"	
where	19	"	
so	17	"	
	1471	"	or 92.2%

2. Strikingly similar in totals are the figures for the Vulgar English materials, although the figures for the various words differ significantly. Here again seven words account for 1,455 or 82.2 per cent of the instances, although they are not the same seven words as appeared most frequently in the Standard English letters. In the Vulgar English letters twelve words also accounted for 93.3 per cent of the total instances.

and	716	instances	
that	185	"	
if	171	"	
as	138	"	
so	105	"	
but	87	"	
for	53	"	
	1455	"	or 82.2%

when	48	"	
who	47	"	
what	44	"	
which	31	"	
where	26	"	
	1651	"	or 93.3%

3. The very figures show certain differences between the Standard English materials and those of Vulgar English.

a. Although the two lists of the twelve most frequently used function words differ only in one word (*while* in the Standard English list does not appear in the Vulgar English list, and *for* of the Vulgar English list does not appear in that for Standard English), the order in which these words occur in the list differs in respect to the words *so, which,* and *who. So* appears about six times as frequently in the Vulgar English letters as in those of Standard English. *Which* appears about four times as frequently in the Standard English materials as in those of Vulgar English; and *who* about twice as often.

b. As might be expected, the word *and* appears about 50 per cent more frequently in the Vulgar English materials than in those of Standard English.

c. The actual total numbers of instances of the so-called "subordinating" conjunctions in the two sets of material are approximately equal. The usual assumption that Vulgar English does not use "complex" sentences with "subordinate" clauses is not borne out by these figures.

d. Especially noticeable is the greater frequency in Vulgar English of the use of *as* and *so*. As will be shown later, *as* is used in the Vulgar English letters especially as a "causal" conjunction. In this use it is two and one half times as frequent as it is in Standard English. *So* is used in Vulgar English especially in the sense of a loose *therefore.*

e. *That* appears to be used much more frequently in Standard English than in Vulgar English. In this connection one should point to the figures for those clauses in which no function word appears but in which a *that* might be used. There were 414 instances of *that* in the Standard English letters and but 185 instances of *that* in those of Vulgar English. On the other hand there were in the Standard English letters only seventy eight instances of clauses without a function word in which *that* might have been used, as against 206 such instances in the Vulgar

English letters. If these figures are put together, one would have 492 for Standard English and 391 for Vulgar English—not a very significant difference.

f. *If* appears more frequently in the Vulgar English letters, but the difference does not seem to be significant. In this connection one should point out that the conditional clauses with no function word *if*, but with inverted word order, appeared only in the Standard English letters.

g. For some reason that is not apparent, *for* as a causal function word appeared fairly frequently in the Vulgar English letters (fifty three instances), and but once in those of Standard English.

h. *Till,* rather than *until,* and *cause* rather than *because* appeared only in the Vulgar English materials. *Provided, yet,* and *however* appeared only in those of Standard English.

It is usual to classify these function words that are used with clauses into what are called "coördinating" conjunctions and "subordinating" conjunctions, and, in accord with that common practice, the conventional two groups have been kept separate in the table. Although one can easily distinguish those clauses that stand at the extreme of the coördinate group from those that stand at the extreme of the subordinate group, it is difficult to draw a distinct line to separate the two. Where, for example, would one mark the division between coördinate and subordinate clauses in the following series? And why?

a.	The house is large	*and*	the location will suit it.
b.	The house is large	*and consequently*	the location will suit it.
c.	The house is large	*thus*	the location will suit it.
d.	The house is large	*but*	the location will suit it.
e.	The house is large	*still*	the location will suit it.
f.	The house is large	*yet*	the location will suit it.
g.	The house is large	*therefore*	the location will suit it.
h.	The house is large	*however*	the location will suit it.
i.	The house is large	*so*	the location will suit it.
j.	The house is large	*so that*	the location will suit it.
k.	*As*	the house is large	the location will suit it.
l.	*Because*	the house is large	the location will suit it.
m.	*Since*	the house is large	the location will suit it.
n.	*Although*	the house is large	the location will suit it.
o.	*If*	the house is large	the location will suit it.
p.	*Provided*	the house is large	the location will suit it.

q. *Unless* the house is large the location will not suit it.
r. *In case* the house is large the location will suit it.
s. *In as much as* the house is large the location will suit it.

The difficulty of finding a reasonable set of criteria by which to separate coördinate from subordinate clauses and thus coördinating function words from those that are subordinating, argues that, in English, this distinction is really of practically no importance. Each of these function words signals a particular set of relationships between the clauses which it joins and the precise nature of the relationship is vitally important. Whether we further classify that relationship as a "coördinate" one or a "subordinate" one makes no difference whatever.

Another classification of these function words, however, does seem to have importance. It will be observed that in the series of sentences given above, the function words in the sentences *a* to *j* stand between the two clauses that are joined, but that those in the sentences *k* to *s* stand before the first of the two clauses that are brought together. Certain of these function words, notably those given in the sentences *a* to *j* and *that* in such uses as "He knows *that* it is not safe," *than* in comparisons, *for*, and the relative pronouns, appear only *between* the two clauses that they join. The rest of the function words listed, notably those in sentences *k* to *s*, may appear *either between* the two clauses joined or *before* the first of the two clauses that are brought into relationship. For example, sentences *k* to *s* might also have had the following order:

The location will suit the house *as* the house is large.
because
since
although
if
provided
in case
in as much as
The location will not suit the house *unless* the house is large.

Some of the other function words that can appear either between the two clauses that are joined or before the first of the two related clauses are *after, before, like, until, when, while, where, in order that.*

Most of the words in our list of function words with word groups will need no special comment. It will be sufficient for the following words simply to give typical examples for each from the materials covered in this study: ***also, nor, but, yet, then, therefore, however, after, although, because, before, for, how, provided, than, unless, until, whether.*** For the following fourteen words, however, some comment seems necessary to indicate the variety of their use and they will be discussed below: ***and, as, if, like, since, so, that, what, when, where, which, while, who, why.***

A. Examples of eighteen function words used with word groups

also

STANDARD ENGLISH

"... I have completed four years of college work with . . . degrees. *Also* I graduated in Business and Accounting from —— College" (9029)

"I will be called upon to take charge of . . . demonstrations; *also* will make some demonstrations myself" (9031)

VULGAR ENGLISH—NO EXAMPLES

nor

STANDARD ENGLISH

"he is not able to work *nor* does he send her any money" (8144)

"his married sister denies having signed her consent to his —— papers *nor* had she any legal right to do so" (8234)

VULGAR ENGLISH—NO EXAMPLES

but

STANDARD ENGLISH

"His education is limited, *but* I have not at any time had cause to doubt his integrity" (8296)

"—— appears very much excited at the idea of being left alone in the office for a while *but* being inclined to cross bridges before they are reached, I am of the opinion he will by actual practice find it can be done" (9000)

VULGAR ENGLISH

"I dont ask Him to come back here to live *but* I want to go where he is liveing" (8151)

"Mother needs me at home *but* she had too much pride to say so" (8026) *yet*

STANDARD ENGLISH

". . . even though he reaches his majority afterwards, *yet* he must be discharged for the reason that . . ." (8183)

VULGAR ENGLISH—NO EXAMPLES

then

STANDARD ENGLISH

"At first —— stated that after a thorough search he could find no record of my enlistment, *then* later he found where I had enlisted . . ." (9030)

". . . he promised to let it alone and for a number of months he did so. *Then,* through planted evidence . . . he was arrested" (8296)

VULGAR ENGLISH

"I used to wash for a living *then* kept boarders" (8235)

"he was there several weeks *then* they sent him on to ——" (8193)

therefore

STANDARD ENGLISH

"His parents being rather poor could not help him as much as he deserved, *therefore,* what he is he has made himself" (8060)

"These people had been educated to the belief, that the Emperor was first and supreme even before God, *therefore* they were willing to be led by such a man" (9017)

VULGAR ENGLISH

"I am sickly and not able to do any work myself, *therefore,* I earnestly request . . ." (8127)

"I had previously asked him, *therefore* I decided . . ." (8070)

however

STANDARD ENGLISH

". . . I had absolutely no motive in not entering them, as all repairs . . . were to my mind necessary and I believe were obvious to ——, as we had talked over the things needed several times. *However,* my omission was due to carelessness on my part and to nothing else" (9040)

"Owing to a change in my address said document was not received until Mar. 29. *However* I accept with pleasure the commission" (9042)

VULGAR ENGLISH—NO EXAMPLES

after

STANDARD ENGLISH

"These people took this boy *after* his mother died" (8160)
"Father's death occurred *after* the boy enlisted" (8303)
"*even after* he confessed rather than have a trial, he was sentenced . . ." (8296)
"*After* you are through with the passport, kindly return it" (8267)

VULGAR ENGLISH

". . . heard from him one time *after* he arrived there" (8117)
"*After* my devorce was granted I resumed my maden name" (8259)
"*After* a man gets past 50 years old he cant get a job" (8246)

although, though

STANDARD ENGLISH

". . . I would have supposed that he had arranged the matter correctly, *even though* I did not freely understand the proceedure" (9007)
"*although* I fully realize the great importance of the work being done . . . I feel that the long period . . ." (9064)
"they will not be inspired to become leaders or thinkers, *though* they are naturally bright" (8296)

VULGAR ENGLISH

"his Mother is sick and his Father unable to get any work *although* he has been trying every day" (8270)
"it takes quite a good bit *even though* I try to be careful" (8251)

because, (cause)

STANDARD ENGLISH

"I am taking the liberty of writing you a personal letter *because* I believe that the situation warrants such action" (9001)
"If this account has not been paid, it is *because* the bill never reached me" (9057)
"—— is having trouble with his eyes, and *because of this* has been recommended for discharge" (9011)[7]

VULGAR ENGLISH

"The reason we would like to find it out is *because* he has a big board bill to pay" (8088)
"I wish you could help me *cause* I want —— with me if its possible" (8107)
"I am doing so *because* I feel it is my duty towards my son" (8153)

[7] This instance is included here because the words "because of this" inserted *between* the two clauses which would otherwise have been "—— is having trouble with his eyes and has been recommended for discharge" operate as a "because" would *before* the first clause. See also below comments on *and.*

before

STANDARD ENGLISH

"My parents moved to Ohio *before* I graduated" (9053)
"he was gone for some little time *before* she knew" (8114)

VULGAR ENGLISH

"please let me here at once *before* I take other steps" (8025)
"he was making $17.00 a week *before* he went . . ." (8053)
". . . if I had this to do over again I would quit *before* I started" (8039)

for

STANDARD ENGLISH

"Were I to advise —— I would say to him not to return . . . *for* the same influence . . . will continue to make his life unbearable" (8296)

Examples of what might be called an expanded function word with *for* as the first element of the compound function word (See also pages 115 and 116 above) are the following:

"—— is applying for Joe's release *for the reason that* the father has become disabled" (8073)
"—— must be discharged *for the reason that* he was a minor at the time of his enlistment" (8183)

VULGAR ENGLISH

"please get him out *for* I need his help" (8280)
"you can get his Birth date in —— *for* he quit school and got a paper to go to work" (8280)
"We will have to go to the County farm *for* we we have no Way of suport" (8155)

how

STANDARD ENGLISH

"I do not understand *how* this came about" (9010)
"—— does not know *how* she will pay for fuel, light, gas. . . ." (8260)
"I cannot say *how* it was worded" (9007)

VULGAR ENGLISH

"I cannot see *how* he ever passed the examination" (8021)
"let me know *how* soon he can come home" (8133)[8]
"give me some information of *how* I can get my son out" (8171)
"I have explained everything *how* we are at this time" (8005)

[8] Other similar examples with *how much* are in 8168, 8250, 8094, with *how long* in 8280.

"The thing now is *how* he could get in through a lawyer" (8218)
"it will be a matter of Great importance *how* soon I can have him discharged" (8238)

provided

STANDARD ENGLISH

"I request information as to . . . in order to arrange for leave *provided* I am likely to go to Japan" (9061)
"I was given verbal information that I could proceed *provided* the trip would be continuous" (9065)
"*Provided* this detail is given me, I am willing to give up my leave" (9028)

VULGAR ENGLISH—NO EXAMPLES

than

STANDARD ENGLISH

"Due to my financial condition, I am more constrained *than* I otherwise would be to ask for . . ." (8056)
"Mother . . . states that dependency on him exists more at the present time *than* when he enlisted" (8081)

VULGAR ENGLISH

"I knead him even more *than* the service does" (8187)
"I dont think I could send better Proofs *than* I have of the way . . ." (8072)

unless

STANDARD ENGLISH

"Regulations require that she be vaccinated against Typhoid and Paratyphoid, *unless* she can present evidence that she has received two complete vaccinations" (9055)
"*Unless* —— comes home, Mrs. —— does not know how she will pay for . . ." (8260)

VULGAR ENGLISH

"it is all I can do under the circumstances *unless* I was where he was borned" (8280)
"*unless* I have my boy I will have to give up my home" (8080)

until

STANDARD ENGLISH

"He . . . works untiringly *until* his object is accomplished" (9009)
"he had attended school *until* he was probably eighteen years of age" (8095)

VULGAR ENGLISH

"I will close *until* I get news from you" (8270)
"I always told him to waite *until* he was twenty-one" (8288)

"his mind is bad *untill* he dont remember his age" (8254)
"I held of *until* I could indure no longer" (8024)
"they Kept him in —— *till* he rote for my consent" (8244)
"we did not know anything *till* we got telafone that he is going . . ." (8178)

whether

STANDARD ENGLISH

"A board of medical officers is appointed to determine the degree of disability and *whether* it originated in line of duty" (9002)
"it is doubted *whether* her son —— would return to his home" (8017)
"*Whether* it was received during a demonstration of a physical drill, or in lifting a gun trail is not known" (9006)
"*Whether* or not it be adopted, the fact that it is presented . . . should obtain . . . much newspaper publicity" (9036)

VULGAR ENGLISH

"the party did not say *whether* —— could or could not come home" (8038)
"I do not know *whether* he is in —— or not" (8186)

B. Discussion of fourteen function words most frequently used with word groups

The fourteen function words to be discussed now are the twelve that were shown above to be those that accounted for approximately 93 per cent of the instances in the materials examined and two others, *like*, and *since.*

and

The function word *and* is often looked upon as the one conjunction that is strictly coördinate, acting simply as a plus sign to add together two sentences or clauses or other word groups (or even separate words) that are exactly alike in structure or function. And it is true that most of the instances of the use of *and* are "additive." There are, however, a fair number of instances in which the context clearly shows that the actual relationship of two word groups that are joined by *and* is not that of simple addition. The following examples illustrate the various relationships found in our materials for which *and* is the function word used.

1. *Additive.* The word *and,* alone, frequently has the function of a mere plus sign, but at times it seems to be felt necessary to

emphasize or to make clearer the additive quality of this function word and an *also* or some other word of similar meaning is used with the *and*.

STANDARD ENGLISH

"the father has been out of employment for the past four months, *and also* is in poor physical condition" (8283)

"the leave is necessary to allow me to attend to personal business on the Pacific Coast *and also* to enable me to place myself in the best physical condition . . ." (9066)

"Mrs. —— keeps the home *and in addition* raises chickens" (8027)

"You already have in your possession the affidavit of the parents of —— *and also* the baptismal certificate of the parish . . ." (8183)

VULGAR ENGLISH

"Do you think any mother would Sign any . . . to have her son scent away knowining that we couldnt get along without the Boys help *and also* knowing she would halft to go to Work . . ." (8005)

"I had wanted to join . . . *and also* knew that my father would not sign any papers . . ." (8070)

2. *Adversative, contrasting.* Sometimes the two word groups joined by *and* are in opposition or contrast. This opposition or contrast is at times emphasized by adding words such as *still* or *yet* to the *and*.

STANDARD ENGLISH

"Plain surveying is the measurement of straight lines *and* geodetic surveying is taking into consideration the curvature of the earth's surface in the measurement of the lines" (9003)

". . . my middle name in the Commission is misspelled. It reads —— *and* should read ——" (9036)

"I have been single-handed with the . . . since my arrival *and* believe that I am safe in saying the organization and work of the office has increased ten foal . . ." (9000)

VULGAR ENGLISH

"I cood not change his Mind *and* his Father thought he cood" (8285)

"My son has Joined the . . . *and* I did not want him to Join" (8261)

"I feel that he has suffered *and* it has been a good lesson to him" (8153)

"my mother has to take in washings *and still* they been getting in debt" (8129)

3. *Introducing a consequence or result.* Sometimes the word group that follows an *and* expresses a fact that not only follows in time that which is expressed in the preceding word group but also follows it as a consequence, sequel, result, or effect. This relationship is at times definitely expressed by adding *consequently, so,* or *therefore* to the function word *and.*

STANDARD ENGLISH

"they have become impatient *and* forwarded this account to . . ." (9033)

"in order that I may again become an active pilot *and* keep up to date upon the new machines" (9031)

"he had made a failure of business *and* was not able to support her" (8076)

"he was living in hell all the time *and* had to drink to keep from going crazy" (8296)

"I do not feel justified in submitting to . . . *and therefore* beg leave to withhold authority to . . ." (9007)

"Mr. ——'s father . . . suspected that he might join . . . *and so* the father wrote to your office and learned . . ." (8076)

"My duties . . . take me to very remote places *and consequently* mail is often delayed" (9004)

VULGAR ENGLISH

"He didnt like his name D—— *and* he named his self R——" (8151)

"I am his wife *and* would like to know his whereabouts" (8030)

"I am a widow without means of support *and* need the aid of my son" (8261)

"The income my husband gets alone would not keep us *and so* I am asking his release" (8265)

4. *Introducing the concluding clause of a condition, the protasis of which is expressed imperatively.* Sometimes the relationship between the two word groups connected by *and* is that of a hypothesis expressed without an *if* and a conclusion.

STANDARD ENGLISH

"put in your request *and* I'll approve it" (9040)

"Let us know *and* we will try and obtain it" (8283)

VULGAR ENGLISH—NO EXAMPLES

5. *Introducing an explanatory or parenthetical clause.* Sometimes the relation between the two word groups joined by *and* is

very loose, the second group being only a parenthetical comment or explanation.

STANDARD ENGLISH

"The work of the office has increased ten foal since my arrival *and* not without difficulty on my part" (9000)

". . . based upon my experience in . . . with fourteen thousand on my hands *and* 25 per cent of these coast artillery" (9000)

VULGAR ENGLISH

"He then lost his job from a partial shut down of the factory *and* no falt of his" (8080)

"he was to get a furlough and now he cant get one as he is so far away *and* me his mother cant see him" (8020)

"I am nearly 50 years old with 5 little ones to support . . . *and* me with bothe knees all to pieces with Rheumatism" (8187)

6. *Connecting two verbs the second of which is logically subordinate to the first.*[9]

STANDARD ENGLISH

"she will try *and* get a statement to this effect" (8283)

"he can come home *and* support her" (8189)

VULGAR ENGLISH

"please try *and* let him come back home to his Mother" (8288)

"i want your department to try *and* locate him" (8154)

"So hurry up *and* get me out" (8096)

"let him come home *and* help us" (8244)

"if you will write *and* tell them" (8039)

In addition to the instances already listed in which the words or word groups connected by *and* are not simply in an additive relation to one another there are the following miscellaneous examples:

STANDARD ENGLISH

"—— has two other sons aged 18 *and* 20 years who are living . . ." (8142)

"if he be between 18 *and* 21 years of age he must have the written consent of his parent or guardian" (8056)

"—— has worked at this plant off *and* on" (8207)

"I have enjoyed my service here *and* as you are aware have been single handed since my arrival" (9000)

[9] See above, note 10, page 134.

Two instances in which the precise nature of the relation between the clauses is indicated by a phrase following the *and* are

"She knows that there is no hope for her *and for this reason* she is almost losing her mind" (8064)

"Germany by her ruthlessness . . . brought the rest of the allies down on her *and by this action* was finally forced to lay down her arms" (9017)

VULGAR ENGLISH

"we have two boy go to school 14 *and* 10 years old" (8178)

"I have been writing and Coaxing *and* well eny way I can or could to get him home" (8187)

"my husband *and* his father [these nouns refer to the same person] is unable to suport the Family" (8052)

Despite the fact that many more instances of *and* appear in the Vulgar English materials (485 in the Standard English letters and 716 in those of Vulgar English) the difference in use between the two sets of letters seems to be negligible. On the whole the same varieties of use appear in both except for the fact that there were no examples in the Vulgar English letters of those uses indicated in (4) above, in which *and* connects two word groups that are related as protasis and conclusion. One might suspect that the greater frequency of *and* in Vulgar English would be accompanied by a proportionate infrequency of the so-called subordinating conjunctions. But the actual figures show no such balance. In the so-called subordinating function words there are approximately a thousand instances in each of the two sets of material. In the Vulgar English letters there are, however, more sentences connected by *and* than there are in those of Standard English.

as

The function word *as* is used as the connective of two word groups that may be related to each other in a variety of ways, the chief of which are (1) the group introduced by *as* may state a cause or reason; (2) it may indicate a comparison; (3) it may indicate a point of time; (4) it may indicate a description or identification.

1. As *introducing a cause or reason.* This use of *as* occurred frequently. About half the instances from Standard English are

of this type and three fourths of the instances from Vulgar English. It occurs, therefore, much more frequently in the Vulgar English letters—two and a half times as often. In this use *as* may stand either between the two word groups or before the first one.

STANDARD ENGLISH

"the home will be lost *as* the mother cannot meet the payments" (8081)

"I should greatly appreciate knowing this information *as* I wish to cable him" (8075)

"*as* she is wholly unable to support herself she is badly in need . . ." (8023)

"*as* Mrs. —— is not able to speak English, her married daughter . . . acted as interpreter" (8144)

"*as* we received no reply we again wrote . . ." (8299)

VULGAR ENGLISH

"We need his support at home *as* My Husband is a cripple" (8128)

"please let me hear at once *as* i am so wearried a bout him" (8117)

"*As* I did not get an answer from my other letter. . . . I will again ask if . . ." (8270)

"*As* my famlie is all sick I am writing you . . ." (8179)

2. As *indicating a comparison, similarity, or parallelism.* The use of *as* to indicate a comparison or similarity is used more frequently in the Standard English materials than in those of Vulgar English.

STANDARD ENGLISH

"*As* the family expressed it, he is of a rather roving disposition" (8142)

"*As* I understand the law a person must be 21 years of age" (8156)

"for all who arrive *as* I did" (9060)

"The following are the facts *as* I recall them" (9052)

VULGAR ENGLISH

"*As* I told you in my first letter his Mother is sick" (8270)

"*As* you know me and some friends have been trying to get my son released" (8080)

"everything will be the same again, *as* it was before" (8233)

"though I try to be careful *as* I can" (8251)

In this group should also be included, perhaps, those expanded forms such as *as soon as, as quick as, as long as, as far as, as much as, as nearly as,* etc.

STANDARD ENGLISH

"The youths of our country should be required to register *as soon as* they reach the age of nineteen" (9012)
"—— will continue to occupy quarters on the post *as long as* it is practical to do so" (9017)
"the boy had really never worked anywhere *as far as* she knew" (8095)
"*As nearly as* I can understand the case, it appears that young —— is having trouble. . . ." (9011)

VULGAR ENGLISH

"Ill send the papers *as soon as* I get them" (8254)
"Just *as soon as* you get this letter I want you to ans right away" (8087)
"send him home to me *as quick as* you can" (8001)
"*as far as* I know he entered the . . ." (8281)
"I have tried to get along *as best as* I could" (8079)

3. As, *temporal.*

STANDARD ENGLISH

"*as* the piston starts back down a spark is introduced in the cylinder. . . ." (9027)

VULGAR ENGLISH—NO EXAMPLES

4. As, *relative.*

STANDARD ENGLISH

"I have waited until such time *as* I might be stationed . . ." (9058)

VULGAR ENGLISH

"But he had'nt a Devorce from me *as* I know of" (8186)

Some miscellaneous uses of *as,* especially in combinations, are

STANDARD ENGLISH

"No information has been received *as to whether* I would be recommended to attend this school" (9033)
"I am in doubt *as to which* Corps Area I belong" (9042)
"it would seem *as if* I had received both a . . ." (9018)
"it seems *as though* he could alleviate . . ." (8002)

VULGAR ENGLISH

"I don't know *as* my writing to you will help" (8038)
"if you want any references *as to what* kind of parents we are . . ." (8074)

if

The function word *if* introduces word groups that usually have one of two relations to the context in which they occur. They may be either the protasis of a condition or an indirect question. The two kinds of word groups appeared in about the same proportions in the two sets of material examined here. The conditions [10] were much more frequent in both, accounting for 84 per cent of the instances in the Standard English letters and 76 per cent of the instances in those of Vulgar English.

1. *Introducing a condition.*

STANDARD ENGLISH

"*If* these records are available I would like to have them returned" (9027)
"*If* you will kindly pass on this . . . I will appreciate it" (8183)
"a reconciliation may be brought about *if* it is the will of the parties" (8296)
"I would appreciate it very much *if* you would let me know" (8075)

VULGAR ENGLISH

"*if* you cant let him out on just what has been done and said already couldnt I get up more paper showing . . ." (8080)
"*If* you doubt what Im saying just drop a line to the priest of the place" (8107)
"probably —— will be sent with this bunch *if* something isent done soon" (8080)
"I am tryen to hear from him *if* i can" (8112)

2. *Introducing an indirect question.*

STANDARD ENGLISH

"When asked *if* he could get work here she stated . . ." (8139)
"I doubt *if* a Quartermaster would take the responsibility" (9060)
"I shall take up this matter . . . to see *if* the bill is correct" (9057)

VULGAR ENGLISH

"I was wondering *if* there was any way in your power to get . . ." (8129)

[10] Attention should probably also be called to the construction in which inverted word order is used rather than the function word *if*. A number of instances appeared in the Standard English materials but none in those of Vulgar English. Examples are
"*Had I noticed* them I would not have presumed to think myself correct . . ." (9007)
"he is assured employment *should he be* discharged" (8081)
"*Were I* to advise Mr. —— I would say to him . . ." (8296)
"*Should she do* so, we may be able to obtain . . ." (8144)

"will you please see *if* you can send my letter" (8087)
"Would you please find out *if* there was a man by the name of ——" (8310)

Some miscellaneous examples from the Standard English letters are the following:

"I am very sorry *if* my letter offended" (9033)
"*Even if* the mother were well the father needs his son" (8064)
"The total amount involved is beyond my means, *even if* refund is made in monthly payments" (9032)

like

Like as a function word introducing a clause has been used for more than four hundred years. Some early examples [11] of this use of *like* are the following:

"Ye have said *lyke* a noble lady ought to say." Ld. Berners *Arth. Lyt. Bryt.* (c. 1530) 520.
"*Lyke* an excellent Phisitioun cureth moste daungerous diseases, so doth a man that is valyant . . ." Elyot *Gov.* (1531) III. viii.
"*Like* an arrow shot from a well experienst Archer hits the marke his eye doth leuell at." Shaks. *Per.* (1608) I. i. 163.
"Unfortunately few have observed *like* you have done" Darwin *Life & Lett.* (1866) III. 58.

In the materials here examined *like* as a function word introducing a clause occurred once in the Standard English letters and five times in those of Vulgar English.

STANDARD ENGLISH

"He was so hurt to think he could not draw his pay *like* the others, that he threatened to enlist" (8002)

VULGAR ENGLISH

"I never received any money . . . *like* other mothers received" (8153)
"he is very sorry he left me *like* he did" (8152)

since

The word groups that are introduced by *since* have usually one of two relations to the word groups with which they are connected, either *causal* or *temporal*. The instances from the Standard English letters are about equally divided between these two types, but those from the Vulgar English letters are all temporal;

[11] From the *Oxford Dictionary, Like, adv.*, 6.

no instances of the causal relationship occur. In a few cases in both sets of material the temporal character of the relationship is stressed by the addition of the word *ever*.

1. *Causal*

STANDARD ENGLISH

"*Since* such does not appear to be the case, I request permission to . . ." (9007)
"*Since* my home was Falls City, Nebraska, I was directed to look to —— for further orders" (9050)

VULGAR ENGLISH—NO EXAMPLES

2. *Temporal*

STANDARD ENGLISH

"the father has become disabled *since* the boy enlisted" (8073)
"*Since* the boy joined . . . her husband has become helpless" (8189)
"I have been knowing Mr. —— *ever since* I was . . . Judge of the —— Circuit" (8064)

VULGAR ENGLISH

"He has been discharged *since* we were married" (8127)
"*Sence* he Joined —— his father has had an accident" (8255)
"his mother has been worried about him *ever since* he has been in ——" (8136)

so

The function word *so* is most frequently used to introduce two types of word groups. (*a*) There are those expressing a result or logical sequence. In these the *so* is moderately often supported by the addition of the word *that,* making the compound function word *so that.* (*b*) There are those expressing the conclusion for which the preceding clause is offered as a reason. In these the causative force may at times be very slight and the *so* indicate almost a mere sequence of time; at others the *so* is practically equivalent to a *therefore* or *for that reason.*

Although *so* is used in both types of connections in Standard English as well as in Vulgar English, its use in Vulgar English is much more frequent (six times as many instances). Most of the instances of the Vulgar English letters were of the second type; i. e., those in which the *so* is more or less equivalent to *therefore* and introduces a conclusion.

1. *Introducing a result*

STANDARD ENGLISH

"please rush this through *so* . . . he will not have to go back to . . ." (8138)

"she would like to have him home *so* she could look after him" (8114)

"This information is desired *so that* I may know where to report . . ." (9042)

"I hope you will find these papers in proper form *so that* we will be able to bring the matter to a conclusion" (8267)

VULGAR ENGLISH

"pleas let him out *so* he can come home" (8261)

"I am writing you *so* you can tell me what to do" (8258)

"see if you can send it *so* he will get it in a few days" (8087)

". . . are in need of clothing *so that* they can go to school" (8270)

"I am asking his release *so that* he can come home" (8265)

2. *Introducing a conclusion* (*equivalent to* therefore)

STANDARD ENGLISH

"she works by the day, *so* it was only recently we were able to have a personal interview" (8002)

"It was slow in so doing, *so* I was examined by Dr. ——" (9006)

"The time necessary for . . . would exceed my allowance of leave, *so for this reason* I am desirous of getting . . . as soon as possible" (9040)

VULGAR ENGLISH

"i cant stand it much longer *So* hurry up and get me out" (8096)

"i cant get one the Trace of him at all *So* i am writen you for help" (8120)

In the Vulgar English materials there are some instances in which the connection indicated by *so* is exceedingly loose indeed, as in the following examples:

"they said his licence were in the paper. And it was but I did not pay any attention to it until they told me about it. *So* then I went to the Licence Bureau Where he had gotten the Licence" (8186)

"he has had 3 Breaks Down in the Last 6 month *So* Why cant you Send me Paper to fill out . . ." (8168)

"he is now 20 years old he was Born January —— *So* i need his help home" (8168)

that

The function word *that* with word groups is used very frequently both in Standard English and in Vulgar English, but more than twice as many instances appeared in the Standard English letters. In general the same varieties of use appear in the two groups of letters.

TABLE XXXI

Type of clause introduced by that	*Number of instances*			
	Standard English		Vulgar English	
1. Object clause after such verbs as *advise, believe, certify, claim, feel, inform, know, notice, notify, request, say, suggest, think, wish, write*		255		103
2. After such adjectives as *certain, confident, sure*		8		6
3. Relative, modifying a substantive				
Neuters	91		29	
Persons	2		22	
Total		93		51
4. Predicate nominative		6		7
5. "Logical" subject with function word *it* in subject position		43		3
6. Result		9		9
7. Purpose		0		6
TOTAL		414		185

In these figures two matters that seem significant are

a. That as a relative pronoun for persons (introducing "restrictive" clauses) is used freely in Vulgar English but very rarely in Standard English.

b. The construction of the *that* clause as the "logical" subject with *it* in the subject position seems to be characteristic of Standard English rather than of Vulgar English.

Examples of the various uses of *that* are

1. *Introducing an objective clause*

STANDARD ENGLISH

"the court indicated *that* the right of the plaintiff to the divorce from bed and board was doubtful" (8296)
"She says *that* her brother and his family will remain" (8139)
"he suggests *that* I apply to you" (9027)

VULGAR ENGLISH

"you can see for your self *that* I am not lying to you people" (8133)
"He said to me to tell you sir *that* he lied about his age" (8288)
"to let youse know *that* I am in the ——" (8243)

2. *After adjectives*

STANDARD ENGLISH

"I feel certain *that* . . . I would not be handicapped" (9064)
"he is confident *that* . . . the boy will be able to continue" (9011)
"I am sure *that* any duties required of him will be . . ." (9013)

VULGAR ENGLISH

"I am sure *that* it is a fine place" (8121)
"I feel sure *that* he has change place" (8147)

3. *Relative, modifying substantives*

STANDARD ENGLISH

"the magic *that* you worked" (9018)
"mistakes *that* only made matters worse" (8296)
"He was one worthy of trust and one *that* has never failed in anything" (9029)
"I have never known any person *that* I could feel freer to endorse than ——" (9029)

VULGAR ENGLISH

"His pay *that* he received in —— is not sufficient" (8127)
"a trade *that* will be useful to him" (8113)
"him and this man *that* was with him was found" (8076)
"have sent the last two doctors certificate *that* have tended on him" (8072)
"I can give you people *that* have known us for years" (8074)

4. *Predicate nominative*

STANDARD ENGLISH

"My reasons for wanting to transfer are *that* I feel . . ." (9059)
"the possibilities are *that* he will never work again" (8027)

VULGAR ENGLISH

"the only reason he desires to stay in . . . is *that* he has already served . . ." (8057)
"one reason he went away was *that* he had no work . . ." (8218)

5. *"Logical" subject with function word* it *in subject position*

STANDARD ENGLISH

"It is presumed *that* eventually damages will be paid" (8139)
"it does not appear *that* the certificate referred to is desired" (9055)
"It is true *that* I have had a days leave" (9007)
"It is probable *that* this might easily be adjusted" (9007)
"It is on this account *that* we write to you" (8239)
"It is my understanding *that* . . . service in . . . does not count" (9055)
"It is only near the edges of the map *that* noticeable errors creep in" (9003)

VULGAR ENGLISH

"if it was not *that* we need the help of my son . . ." (8172)
"it looks like *that* I may have some help" (8037)
"it is necessary *that* we get him out . . ." (8270)

6. *Result*

STANDARD ENGLISH

"I so arranged his trips *that* he was able to live . . ." (9023)
"her condition had grown so much worse *that* she could not work" (8240)

VULGAR ENGLISH

"he has had so many fits for 13 years *that* his mind is bad" (8254)
"the mule that throwed him and cracked his skull has Engered his mind *that* he is not real bright at times" (8220)

7. *Purpose*

STANDARD ENGLISH—NO EXAMPLES

VULGAR ENGLISH

"Please send me a copy of . . . *that* I can show the same to the Court" (8157)
". . . advised me to write to you for a dismissal blank *that* he might be released immediately" (8251)

Because of the fact that the uses of the clauses with no function word, in which *that* might be used, parallel so closely the uses of the *that* clauses, the pertinent facts and figures concerning them are given here.

TABLE XXXII

Type of clause (no function word)	*Number of instances*			
	Standard English		Vulgar English	
1. Object clause after such verbs as *believe, claim, feel, know, say, think*		47		129
2. After adjectives		1		7
3. Modifying a substantive—				
Neuters	26		52	
Persons	1		13	
Total		27		65
4. Predicate nominative		1		1
5. "Logical" subject with function word *it* in subject position		2		1
6. Result		0		3
TOTAL		78		206

1. *Object clause*

STANDARD ENGLISH

"he will find by actual practice *it can be done*" (9000)
"the mother said *she had given her consent*" (8144)

VULGAR ENGLISH

"I trust *it will Satfie you*" (8000)
"I hope *I haint don any thing wrong*" (8005)

2. *After adjectives*

STANDARD ENGLISH

"I shall be quite sure *you are right*" (9018)

VULGAR ENGLISH

"I am very shure *he would be found in* . . ." (8151)
"I am sure *you will not* . . ." (8153)

3. *Modifying a substantive*

STANDARD ENGLISH

"any news *you can give me*" (8075)
"the data *I have submitted*" (8023)
"the children *she brought with her*" (8276)

VULGAR ENGLISH

"the only thing *he can get to do*" (8218)
"do some thing *I had not ought to do*" (8218)
"now is the time *I need it*" (8235)

"my boy . . . is the only one *I can depend on*" (8272)
"I have a son in Law *has served 7 years* . . ." (8258)

4. *Predicate nominative*

STANDARD ENGLISH

"The fact is, *it is constantly getting worse*" (8064)

VULGAR ENGLISH

"his answer was *B—— was treated with fairness*" (8038)

5. *"Logical" subject with function word* it *in subject position*

STANDARD ENGLISH

"it is feared *it will become serious*" (8065)

VULGAR ENGLISH

"It seems to me *he is very young*" (8167)

6. *Result*

STANDARD ENGLISH—NO EXAMPLES

VULGAR ENGLISH

"times is so hard *work is hard to get*" (8293)
"we need him so bad *I would be so glad if you would* . . ." (8244)

what

There seem to be no significant differences in the uses of the function word *what* in the two sets of material examined here. Examples of the various uses of *what* are

STANDARD ENGLISH

a.

"*What* makes it more horrible it is on her face" (8064)
"*What* he is he has made himself" (8060)

b.

"he is sorry for *what* he has done" (8144)
"He has no income whatever except *what* he makes on a rented farm" (8064)

c.

"Her only income is *what* small help her married children are able to give her" (8240)

d.

"She wants to know *what* steps to take" (8189)
"let me know *what* steamer he is coming on" (8075)

VULGAR ENGLISH

a.

"please do *what* you can for me" (8186)

". . . hopes you will think over *what* I am asking you" (8187)

b.

"when I think of *what* the Doctor's testified at the trial . . ." (8153)

c.

"Can you inform me . . . *what* time he was Discharge" (8109)

d.

"let me know *what* to do about it" (8084)

"I would like to know *what* the delay is" (8135)

"I Wounder *what* you are mad with me a bout" (8179)

when

The distribution of the various uses of *when* is shown in Table XXXIII.

TABLE XXXIII

Type of clause introduced by when	*Number of instances*	
	Standard English	Vulgar English
1. Temporal, definite	24	32
2. Temporal, indefinite, or conditional	7	6
3. Indirect question	2	5
4. Modifier of noun	4	4
5. Concessive	0	1

Examples of the various uses of *when* are as follows:

STANDARD ENGLISH

1. *Temporal, definite*

"*When* I changed stations in . . . I left a half dozen articles" (9058)

"*When* I boarded the train I was unable to get transportation" (9016)

2. *Temporal, indefinite, or conditional*

"*When* the piston starts up on the compression stroke the intake is closed" (9027)

"Then *when* they are discharged they remain interested" (9012)

"*When* an enlisted man is permanently unfitted . . . he is discharged . . ." (9002)

3. *Indirect question*

"kindly inform me by telegraph . . . *when* he may be expected to arrive . . ." (8075)

"I am . . . most anxious to know *when* he will be in ——" (8075)

4. *Modifier of noun*

"the time . . . *when* he . . . could conquer" (9017)

"any record of his next step *when* he left the coast" (8075)

VULGAR ENGLISH

1. *Temporal, definite*

"*When* we last heard from him he was stationed at ——" (8149)

"My nephew's Mother and Father died *when* he was nine weeks old" (8084)

2. *Temporal, indefinite, or conditional*

"*when* a man gets so old working in the mines they kick him out" (8005)

"I am so disheartened *when* I think of what the Doctor's testified . . ." (8153)

3. *Indirect question*

"*When* he is discharged will you please give him his ticket" (8118)

"they Knew *when* he was borned" (8254)

"I want to know *when* he will get his discharge" (8001)

4. *Modifier of noun*

"In the days *when* the public would not associate with . . ." (8057)

". . . at times *when* he takes cool or gets to hot . . ." (8190)

5. *Concessive*

"I have sacrificed to let him . . . *when* I needed him at home" (8153)

where

The distribution of the various uses of *where* is shown in the following table:

TABLE XXXIV

Type of clause introduced by where	*Number of instances*	
	Standard English	Vulgar English
1. Relative, modifying a noun	14	9
2. Adverbial, indefinite, equivalent to *wherever,* or conditional	2	7
3. Indirect question	3	7
4. Miscellaneous	0	2
Total	19	25

Examples of the various uses of *where* are

STANDARD ENGLISH

1. *Relative, modifying a noun*
   "The community *where* he lived considers him . . ." (8017)
   ". . . in the northern states *where* it was read extensively" (9012)
   "This appears to be a case *where* the mother is much in need of . . ." (8239)
   "A promising opportunity *whereby* I feel I can better myself" (9061)
2. *Adverbial, indefinite, equivalent to* wherever, *or conditional*
   ". . . is used . . . *where* exactness is demanded" (9037)
   ". . . there is no travel pay available *where* a preference of this kind is taken" (9029)
3. *Indirect question*
   ". . . to know *where* I am . . ." (9060)
   "he found *where* I had enlisted" (9030)

VULGAR ENGLISH

1. *Relative, modifying a noun*
   "the priest of the place *where* my son was born . . ." (8107)
   "I went to the Licence Bureau *Where* he had gotten the Licence" (8186)
   "you can write to —— and get my papers *where* I was apointed his gardine" (8025)
2. *Adverbial, indefinite, equivalent to* wherever, *or conditional*
   "I have to carry her *where* she goes" (8291)
3. *Indirect question*
   "let me know *where* he is" (8147)
   "no one ever told me *Where* he was" (8201)
4. *Miscellaneous*
   "I see *where* . . . can be released if . . ." (8080)
   "I was gone about 5 hours and got 7 years *where* if it was another man they would have got 1 month" (8039)

Instances such as these in 4 in which *where* is equivalent to *that* or to *where as* appeared only in the Vulgar English materials.

which

Although there are four times as many instances of *which* in the Standard English letters as there are in the Vulgar English letters, there seem to be no significant differences in the uses of this function word in the two sets of examples, except for the following four instances which come from Vulgar English:

> "we have two boy go to school one 14 and 10 years old *which* you see they need edycation" (8178)

"his Father being a man of 57 years and has Rupture in Both Sides ***witch*** he is unable to do hard manuel labor" (8253)
"I am asking for your help for to locate my Son ***which*** he is in the ——" (8106)
"—— left Our home without Our Knoweledge or consent and Joined the . . . at —— ***witch*** he was only 18 Years old at time he . . ." (8258)

STANDARD ENGLISH

"balloon companies *which* are now . . ." (9031)
"at the rate of $25 per month, *which* includes heat and light" (8283)
"a house consisting of six rooms and bath *which* they own" (8303)
". . . give her entire pay to her mother *which* she does at the present time" (8081)
"the theft of an automobile for *which* indictments are probably still pending" (8017)
"I had some service in . . . shortly prior to 1905, of *which* I have no difinite record" (9055)
"he went off on a trip and has not returned since *which* time I have had no knowledge . . ." (8296)
"She hopes to keep enough of the money . . . to take care of her own funeral expenses . . . unless her grandson is discharged . . . in *which* event she will use this money to . . ." (8095)

VULGAR ENGLISH

"my correct date of birth *which* is September 28 . . ." (8070)
"one more effort *which* I pray will be successful" (8080)
". . . by disability of father *which* I consider is our case" (8080)
"to look after baggage *which* I left here" (8094)
"come home and give me aid *which* I believe he will" (8079)
"and the name in *which* my son inlisted under . . ." (8259)
"he got in through a lawyer for $21.00 *which* he had $6.00 to pay yet" (8218)

while

The function word *while* in the two uses of introducing a temporal clause and introducing a concessive clause appeared in both the Standard English letters and those of Vulgar English. As an adversative, however, it appeared in the Standard English materials only.

STANDARD ENGLISH

1. *Temporal*
"all his property was sequestered *while* he was in jail" (8296)

"*While* he was at home for the three months he never did a stroke of work" (8144)

2. *Concessive*

"*While* neither are here now; I think both can be located" (8014)

"The personnel of our Department . . . has been reduced *while* the number of students taking the course has increased over twenty per cent" (9051)

3. *Adversative*

"Plain surveying is used in surveying small areas and short distances *while* geodetic surveying is used in surveying large areas" (9003)

"The government does not especially need his services *while* from all indications his family does" (8073)

"the other countries of Europe were unprepared *while* Germany had been preparing . . . for the last forty years" (9017)

VULGAR ENGLISH

1. *Temporal*

"*While* he was on . . . duty he was making money enough to support me" (8230)

"my boy send her money to help her out *while* she lived" (8028)

2. *Concessive* (only one example)

"*While* he is pretty good some days others he is'nt able to go" (8251)

3. *Adversative* (no examples)

who

The function word *who* with its inflected forms *whose* and *whom* appears much more frequently in the Standard English materials than in those of Vulgar English (seventy nine instances in Standard English, forty seven in Vulgar English). As a matter of fact, only the form *who* appears in the Vulgar English letters; there are no instances of *whose* or of *whom.*

STANDARD ENGLISH

"his people *who* were becoming crowded" (9017)

"This brought on war with France *who* was in alliance with Serbia" (9017)

"on behalf of a Mrs. —— . . . *whose* son is at present . . ." (8294)

"—— is a native of Nevada, *whose* parents lived practically . . ." (9061)

"leaving a wife behind *whom* he was deserting" (8076)

"a neighbor *whom* we interviewed" (8002)

"let me know *whom* should be notified" (8075)

VULGAR ENGLISH

> "the poor old couple *hu* raised them" (8005)
> "Many reasons are given by Candidates *who* are seeking appointment . . ." (8057)
> "we did not know *who* to write to" (8038)

why

The function word *why* is used in the instances from Standard English most often to introduce an indirect question, as in the following examples:

> "I cannot understand *why* I was not notified" (9010)
> "I understand *why* they have become impatient" (9033)

At times the *why* joins its clause to a noun, as in the following:

> "setting forth reasons *why* I should not pay" (9032)
> "I see no reason *why* he cannot be made to send his mother a reasonable allowance" (8174)

In the instances from Vulgar English the function word *why* is also used to introduce an indirect question.

> "to find out *why* the people aint never discharge my son" (8001)
> "I dont see *why* that I must be the unlucky dog" (8039)
> "I wounder *why* yo Dont rite to me" (8179)

But there are among the Vulgar English instances a number in which the *why* seems to be a very loose connective with no trace of its usual significance equivalent to "for what reason." Instances of this sort appeared only in the Vulgar English letters.

> "but when I got here *why* she kep putting it off" (8243)
> "then when I called her up *why* she told me to . . ." (8243)
> "so when I got there *why* she had a Dective" (8243)

Some expanded function words with word groups

In the pages above, certain "compound" or expanded function words have been already pointed out and illustrated. These are such words as the expansions of *and,* as in *and also, and in addition, and still, and therefore, and so, and consequently, and for this reason, and by this action* (pages 217–221); the expansions of *as,* as in *as soon as, as long as, as much as, as far as, as quick as,* etc., *as if, as to whether, as to which, as to what* (pages 222–223); the expansions of *so* in *so that* and *so for this reason* (pages 226–227); and the strengthening of *after, though,* and *if* by *even* as in *even after, even though, even if,* as well as the strengthening of *since* by *ever* as in *ever since.*

Other combinations that seem to operate as units are *in as much as, in case, in the event that,* and *in order that.* Examples of these compound forms that occur only in the Standard English letters are the following:

> "*In as much as* I was on duty ——, it would seem that . . ." (9010)
>
> "*In case* there is a change in the diagnosis, a duplicate card is made out . . ." (9002)
>
> "*in the event that* we do not receive a reply within ten days we will take up . . ." (8299)
>
> "I desire to . . . *in order that* I may be near to my business interests" (9000)

From this survey of the function words with word groups the following statements can be made concerning a comparison of the uses appearing in the two sets of material examined.

1. There seem to be approximately the same number of the so-called "subordinate clauses" in Vulgar English as in Standard English. (Standard English, 994; Vulgar English, 959.)
2. *As* introducing a cause or reason appeared in both the Standard English letters and those of Vulgar English, but was much more frequent (two and one half times) in the Vulgar English materials.
3. *Like* as a conjunction appeared in both sets of material, but in the Standard English letters only in a construction without the verb.
4. *Since* introducing a causal clause appeared only in the Standard English letters. Introducing a temporal clause it appeared in both sets of material.
5. *So,* equivalent to a somewhat weak *therefore,* was used in both the Standard English materials and those of Vulgar English, but was very much more frequent in this use in the Vulgar English letters (five times as frequent). In the Vulgar English letters there appeared also some instances in which the *so* introduces a clause which seems simply to follow another as a matter of time sequence.
6. *That* introducing word groups appeared much more frequently in the Standard English letters. Especially was this true in respect to *that* as the introductory word for object clauses after such verbs as *say, know, think, wish,* etc. In contrast, in the Vulgar English materials there were many more such object clauses after these same verbs without any function word than appeared in the Standard English letters. (*That* with such object clauses, Standard English, 255;

Vulgar English, 103. Such object clauses without function word, Standard English, 47; Vulgar English, 129.)

7. *That* as a relative pronoun for "persons" appeared in both sets of material but much more frequently in Vulgar English.

8. *Why* as a very loose connective with no trace of its usual significance appeared only in the Vulgar English letters.

III. THREE MISCELLANEOUS FUNCTION WORDS

In addition to the function words used with nouns (the prepositions), those used with verbs (the so-called auxiliaries), those used with adjectives (the words of degree), and those used with word groups (the conjunctions), there are three other words whose uses as function words it is necessary to discuss. These are the words *it, there,* and *one.*

it

The word *it* has been used in a variety of ways throughout the history of the language. It is and has long been, for example, the form of the pronoun used as a substitute for neuter nouns, as in the following sentences:

> "I became interested in radio and have given *it* considerable study" (9029)
>
> "The room is poorly furnished and *it* is most disorderly" (8095)
>
> "The general court of which I am a member will have no further business before *it*" (9028)
>
> "knowing the angle of dip and allowing for *it*" (9037)
>
> "If I borrow one hundred and twenty dollars and send *it* to you . . ." (8274)
>
> "The mixture has done *its* useful work . . ." (9027)

This substitute word *it* not only stands for particular words in the context as in the preceding examples; it often represents a whole statement or the matter implied in a statement.

> "We cant even pay our way and I am going to prove *it* to you" (8005)
>
> "a reconciliation may be brought about if *it* is the will of the parties" (8296)
>
> "If this account has not been paid *it* is because the bill never reached . . ." (9057)
>
> "they took him and for over a week no one ever told me where he was. *It* turned me gray" (8201)
>
> "And as her husband expressed *it,* she is slowly dying with cancer" (8064)

"I would like to complete four years of this duty if *it* would not effect my chance of being . . ." (9064)

But the particular uses of *it* to which attention is especially directed here are those in which it operates as a function word to fill the requirements of our favorite sentence pattern.

a. it + verb + *that* (clause)

STANDARD ENGLISH

"*It* is very necessary that I have the above recommendations" (9027)
"*it* is believed that the training received at . . . would be a great help to me as a . . ." (9015)
"*it* does seem too bad that he should be dismissed" (9011)
"*it* may appear at first sight that to detail me to another station is an unnecessary expense" (9042)
"*it* is understood that there is no travel pay" (9029)
"*it* is only near the edges of the map that noticeable errors creep in" (9003)
"I first want *it* understood that I am not crying" (9033)
"I make *it* clear that there is no authority of this nature vested . . ." (8073)

VULGAR ENGLISH

"*It* is my earnest desire that you grant him a discharge" (8069)
"*It* is very necessary that we get him out" (8270)
"But *it* was only a couple of hours later that he left" (8288)

b. it + verb + (adjective) + *to* + infinitive

STANDARD ENGLISH

"*it* would be impossible to obtain others" (9010)
"*it* seems best to have him complete his . . ." (8139)
"*it* would be of no more expense to send me there" (9042)
"Was *it* correct to have drawn pay . . ." (9035)
"*it* is my desire to return to the . . ." (9001)
". . . is going to make *it* difficult in a financial way to get settled" (9033)
"If you think *it* is right to send him" (9018)
"I do not find *it* necessary to sign this one" (9022)
"I took *it* upon myself to talk with him" (8296)

VULGAR ENGLISH

"I must tell you *it* costs money to have all these things done" (8072)
"*it* will fall to him to help me" (8067)

"*It* cost me $25 dollars to get him home" (8288)
"He dont know what *it* is to stay away from Home" (8190)

c. it + verb + (adjective) + *for* + substantive + *to* + infinitive

STANDARD ENGLISH

"*it* would be impossible for them to raise sufficient funds" (8073)
"*it* would have been a most easy matter for him to accomplish" (9032)
"I also think *it* is somewhat dangerous for this woman to be living by herself" (8294)

VULGAR ENGLISH

"*it* is impossible for him to support me" (8129)
"*it* is for us stronger ones to help the weaker ones" (8038)
"*it* takes 6 Days for a letter to get to New York . . ." (8096)
"I think *it* would be better for him to be at home" (8113)

d. it + verb + clause (no introductory function word)

STANDARD ENGLISH

"The mental condition of the mother . . . is bad . . . and *it* is feared will become serious" (8065)

VULGAR ENGLISH

"*it* seems to me he is very young" (8167)

e. it + verb + *if* (clause)

STANDARD ENGLISH

"*it* would be of material assistance to him if his son . . . could be discharged" (8163)

VULGAR ENGLISH—NO EXAMPLES

f. Miscellaneous

STANDARD ENGLISH

"*it* was he who suggested that she write to . . ." (8095)
"Request transportation for myself, wife and infant daughter . . . from San Francisco to . . . , or if *it* be possible, by rail from . . . , Utah, to . . ." (9043)
"if *it* is not inconsistent with the exigencies of the service, I request that I be given assignment to . . ." (9028)
"I would appreciate *it* very much if you would let me know" (8075)
"*it* would seem as if I had received both a . . . and a . . ." (9018)

VULGAR ENGLISH

"*it* is a hart broken mother . . . hu has to suffer" (8005)
"if *it* was another man they would have got 1 month" (8039)

"if *it* is agreable I want him to come home" (8277)
"Hoping that you will look into this matter as soon as *it* is possible" (8270)
"I would appreciate *it* very much if I could have my Son home . . ." (8225)
"*it* look like I cant hardly stand for him to be away from me" (8204)
"*it* is so Hot here" (8096)
"*It* is getting so near Christmas" (8038)
"i suppose . . . would allow me some of his pay the way *it* stands now" (8281)

Some types of examples that appeared in the Vulgar English letters but not in those of Standard English:

"if *it* is any way that I can get him out I wish you would please let me know" (8021)
"Let me know if *it* is some one by that name and discription there" (8186)
"here is a fellow that was going away 8 day and got 15 years and another was gon 3 months and got 3 months in the guard hous that is the way they hand *it* to you" (8039)

The figures showing the number of instances for these various uses of the function word *it* are as follows:

TABLE XXXV

Varieties of construction	*Number of instances*	
	Standard English	Vulgar English
a. *it* + verb + *that* (clause)	51	4
b. *it* + verb + (adjective) + *to* + infinitive	22	6
c. *it* + verb + *for* + substantive + *to* + infinitive	8	7
d. *it* + verb + clause (no introductory conjunction)	2	1
e. *it* + verb + *if* (clause)	2	0
Total	85	18
f. Miscellaneous—other than those above	8	38

Although the actual number of instances of the function word *it* appearing in our materials is really not sufficient to justify statements of significant differences between the two sets of material, two facts should probably be indicated.

1. The use of *it* in the position of subject with the "logical" subject expressed in a *that*-clause or a *to*-infinitive after the verb appeared primarily in the Standard English letters. (Standard English, seventy-three; Vulgar English, ten.)

2. The use of *it* in the subject position and equivalent to *there* appeared only in the Vulgar English letters.

there

There as an adverb of locality or place is of rather frequent occurrence and may stand in any one of a number of positions in the sentence, but *there* as an unstressed function word occurs less frequently and is limited to the position that is usually the place of the subject substantive. In fact, its function seems to be simply to fill out the sentence pattern when the subject substantive is placed after the verb in a fact statement. Twenty six instances occurred in the Standard English letters and thirteen instances in those of Vulgar English.

STANDARD ENGLISH

"*there* is no other man on both lists" (9018)
"*There* were no written forms given . . ." (9052)
"If *there* were any instructions at all I do not recall them" (9052)
"In case *there* is a change in the diagnosis, a duplicate card is made out" (9002)
"he thought that *there* was a shorter route" (9012)
"nor was *there* any person on duty" (9010)
"*There* is $2.00 in improvement assessments" (8303)
"*there* was no material or funds available" (9040)
"*There* seems to be a chronic oedema . . ." (9006)

VULGAR ENGLISH

"*there* will be Six little orphans in the Street if my Son doesnt come back home soon" (8288)
"if *there* is any thing not wright let me know" (8135)
"Would you please find out if *there* was a man by the name of —— in . . ." (8310)
"would *there* be any trouble getting him out . . ." (8012)
"I want to know if *there* are a chance for me to get him out of . . ." (8090)

In the use of *there* as a function word no differences appeared in the practice of the two sets of material examined.[12] As indicated above, however, only in Vulgar English appeared the older

[12] See also pages 56 to 57.

use of *it* equivalent to the function word *there* as in "if *it* is any way that I can get him out please . . ." (8021), and in general the function word *there* seems to be more frequently used in Standard English, although the number of instances found in these particular materials furnishes no basis for any conclusion.

one

The word *one,* starting as the English lowest cardinal numeral, has developed in several ways. It still continues as a numeral, but has also produced (1) the indefinite article *a, an,* (2) the anaphoric pronoun as in "I could not get a car so I thought I would borrow *one*" (8030), "it is requested that the error be corrected if it is *one*" (9022), and (3) the independent indefinite pronoun as in "and for over a week no *one* ever told me where he was" (8201), "I do not think that *one* could expect to be cheerful and delighted with . . ." (9033). In addition to these uses there are those to be included here as function word uses.

"The decisive innovation was the use of combinations like *a good one.* This, I think, is to some extent like the use of *it* in *it rains* or in *I think it necessary to wait,* and like the use of *there* in *there was peace* or *let there be peace:* in all these cases a word becomes necessary because speakers are accustomed to have some word in that particular place: *it* and *there* take the place of a subject or of an object, and similarly *one* takes the place usually occupied by a substantive." [13]

As a function word, *one* is distinctly dissociated from the numeral.

"The dissociation from the numeral is especially clear, (1) when the pl. *ones* is used, (2) when *one* is preceded by another *one,* or *ones* by another numeral, (3) when *one* is preceded by *the* or a similarly definite word, for *one* is originally indefinite, as appears from the development of the indefinite article from a weakened form of *one.*" [14]

As a function word, *one* furnished a device for distinguishing number with such words as have no number inflection, as in the interrogative "Which *one* do you want?" "Which *ones* do you want?" or in adjectives, "the good *one,*" "one good *one*" "the good *ones,*"

[13] Otto Jespersen, *A Modern English Grammar* (Heidelberg, 1928–1931), Vol. II, p. 246. See also his complete discussion of "the prop-word *one.*" pp. 245–271.
[14] *Ibid.,* p. 251.

"two good *ones.*" It also provides a means for using a genitive inflection with words which do not have it, as in "We took that *one's* club away," "The little *one's* eyes filled with tears."

Only a few instances of *one* as a function word occurred in our materials, eight in the letters of Standard English and six in those of Vulgar English.

STANDARD ENGLISH

"I believe that the H—— home is a good *one*" (8296)
"I tried to give an analysis and a fair *one*" (9057)
"The resulting situation will be a difficult *one* for me to meet" (9056)
"I did purchase the material to make my area a liveable *one*" (9040)
"Do not mistake my position for *one* of criticism" (9000)

VULGAR ENGLISH

"I am nearly 50 years old with 5 little *ones* to support" (8187)
"He has doctored with quite a number but these are the last *ones*" (8052)
"it has his nerves affected so terrible and his limbs, especially the right *one* until he just drags that heel every step" (8052)
"I am pleading to you for his return home as there is a large family he being the oldess *one*" (8020)

X

THE USES OF WORD ORDER

As has been indicated above (Chapters IV and VI), the order of the words as they stand in a sentence has become for Modern English an important device to show grammatical or structural relationships. This device, *word order,* has, in English, especially since the fourteenth century, been in competition with the other devices, word forms or inflections and function words, for the expression of certain grammatical ideas. In this discussion of the uses of word order we shall not be concerned with the rhetorical or stylistic effects of word position—the force of an unusual arrangement of sentence elements or the so-called naturally emphatic positions within the sentence. Nor shall we attempt here a description of the so-called normal positions of the various grammatical elements of a sentence and the possible variations from those positions.[1] The purpose of this chapter is very definitely limited to an effort to set forth those grammatical ideas which in Modern English *depend upon word order for expression.* The development of these structural or grammatical uses of word order is still in progress in Modern English, and there is still considerable alternative practice and conflict of usage, so that it will be possible only to describe the chief patterns and tendencies

[1] A description of the normal positions of the various parts of speech and the exceptions to the usual positions has been the usual procedure of those grammarians that have treated the subject of word order in English. See, for example—

Henry Sweet, *A New English Grammar,* Part II (Oxford, Clarendon Press, 1898), ¶ 1759–1880.

E. Kruisinga, *A Handbook of Present Day English* (Utrecht, Kremenk and Zoon, 1915), Vol. II, pp. 458–489.

H. Poutsma, *A Grammar of Late Modern English,* Vol. I (Groningen, P. Noordhoof, 1904), pp. 245–348.

E. Maetzner, *An English Grammar* (tr. Grece, London, John Murray, 1874), Vol. III, pp. 535–573.

E. Einenkel, *Geschichte der englischen Sprache* (Strassburg, Karl J. Trübner, 1916), Vol. II, pp. 169–192.

and to note some of the exceptions to those patterns as we have done in the case of other types of grammatical apparatus.

The grammatical ideas that a language may express may be roughly divided into two types.[2] There are first what might be called the "essential or unavoidable" relational concepts, and there are, second, the "dispensable or secondary" relational concepts. If, for example, one is to say anything about a bear and a man in connection with the action of killing, it is essential and unavoidable that he indicate which one did the killing and which one was killed. All known languages express this sort of relationship (the so-called subject-object relationship) unmistakably. On the other hand, whether the killing took place in the past, the present, or the future; whether it was instantaneous or long drawn out; whether there were several bears, or two bears, or but one bear; and whether the speaker knew this fact of his own first hand knowledge or only from hearsay—these matters are of the "dispensable or secondary" type and may or may not be expressed. Languages differ greatly with respect to the extent to which their grammatical practices force the speakers to give attention to these points. A number of the North American Indian languages, for instance, compel the speaker to choose between the forms that indicate whether he is reporting what has been told him by some one else or matters that he himself has experienced. English verb forms compel the speaker to choose a present, past, or future form for his statements, even though he may want to express a general principle good for all time. In English, too, we are forced, in naming any concrete thing, to indicate a singular or a plural even though the matter of number is of no consequence. We must say either "What *man* came?" or "What *men* came?" when we use the noun. There is no common number noun form such as the convenient pronouns in "*Who* came?" and "*What* stood there?" English grammar, therefore, as does every other language, expresses the "essential and unavoidable" relationships and, in addi-

[2] For a stimulating discussion of "Grammatical Concepts" see Edward Sapir, *Language* (New York, Harcourt, Brace and Co., 1921), Chapter V, pp. 86–126. For the point made here see especially pp. 98, 99, 116. "We are thus once more reminded of the distinction between essential or unavoidable relational concepts and the dispensable type. The former are universally expressed, the latter are but sparsely developed in some languages, elaborated with a bewildering exuberance in others (p. 99)."

tion, its own particular set of the "dispensable or secondary" grammatical ideas.

In Chapters V and VI above we have seen the particular grammatical ideas expressed in English by inflections or the forms of words. These are, in Present-day English, chiefly number and tense—grammatical concepts that are clearly of the dispensable or secondary type. In Chapters VII, VIII, and IX are set forth the grammatical ideas expressed by function words. With verbs, these function words indicate especially precise times for the action or attitudes of the speaker toward the action, and therefore, also, in large measure, express grammatical ideas of the dispensable or secondary type. In this chapter (Chapter X) we shall find that the grammatical ideas expressed in English by word order are almost completely those that must be classed with the essential or unavoidable relational concepts. They are primarily those of the so-called "subject" and "object" relation and those that we include under the term "modification." [3] As a matter of fact, it might almost be fair to say that the history of the English language in respect to its grammar has in some large measure been a steady progress away from that type of language in which both "dispensable or secondary" grammatical concepts and "essential or unavoidable" ones are expressed by inflections or word forms, toward a type of language in which inflections are used for only the "dispensable or secondary" grammatical ideas, and word order for the "essential or unavoidable" grammatical relationships.

This point is so important in an attempt to grasp the structure of English that it will be worth while to set forth here certain parts of the historical evidence upon which it rests. Such a historical view will probably also furnish the best background against which to view the differences of Standard English and Vulgar English in the grammatical uses of word order which are to be presented later in this chapter.

The first of the essential or unavoidable grammatical relationships that all known languages express are the so-called "subject" and "object" relations. We shall not here enter the discussion of the meanings of the words *subject* and *object* as they are used in the grammars, nor shall we attempt to define precisely the content and the variety of the subject and object relationships. It is

[3] See below, p. 255 ff.

enough to say that, if we wish to speak of a thing and an action, it seems essential that we know whether the thing is conceived as the "starting point" or the "end point" of the action: [4]

The water wet the sponge.
The sponge absorbed the water.

The book lies on the table.
The table supports the book.

When the thing is grasped as the starting point of the action, we call it "subject," and when it is grasped as the end point of the action, we call it "object." In Old English practically all the grammatical relationships to which the language gave attention could be expressed by inflections and nearly all were so expressed. Some were expressed by function words, but none, so far as I know, actually depended upon word order for expression. The "subject" relationship was expressed by the nominative case form, and the "object" relationship was most frequently expressed by the accusative or the dative inflection (sometimes by the genitive).

It is true that in Old English in most cases there was no distinction of form in the nominative and accusative endings of the nouns themselves. But with these nouns there were used an inflected article and an inflected adjective, and these "agreeing" words most frequently had distinct forms to separate the nominative from the accusative. There were also many cases of two nouns used with a verb in which the number form of the verb clearly showed which noun was subject. As a matter of fact, in Old English less than 10 per cent of the instances lack these distinctive forms. Dative forms of the nouns were usually in themselves quite distinct.

The particular historical facts of significance for our purpose here concern (*a*) the position of those words which in Old English bore the accusative inflections—the "accusative-object," and (*b*) the position of those words which in Old English bore the dative inflection—the "dative-object." In both cases we are concerned only with those accusative-object and dative-object instances which did not involve the use of a preposition (function word). In examining the materials of Middle English and Early

[4] See Sapir, *op. cit.*, p. 98. See also above, Chapter VIII, pages 188–190 and especially note 57.

Modern English when the distinctive inflectional syllables of both adjectives and articles had been lost, we counted as accusative-objects or as dative-objects only those instances for which we had clear inflectional parallels in Old English.

In brief statements, then, the significant facts in the historical development of (*a*)—i. e., the position of those words which in Old English bore accusative inflections—seem to be the following:

1. In Old English the accusative-object could stand in any position. The order of the words seems to have no bearing whatever upon the grammatical relationship. The accusative inflection expressed the relationship completely. The following sentences each express the same relationship, that the "bear" is the "end point" of the activity, that it is the one that was "struck":

Se mann þone beran sloh.
Þone beran se mann sloh.
Þone beran sloh se mann.
Sloh se mann þone beran.

2. In Late Old English of about 1000 A. D., if the sermons of Aelfric can be taken as a fair representation of the language of that time, about 53 per cent of the accusative-objects appeared *before the verbs* and only about 47 per cent after the verbs.[5] Typical examples are

"and Crist to helle gewende and *þone deofol* gewylde"
(and Christ to hell went and *the devil* overcame)
acc.

"*gladne giefend* lufað God"
(a *cheerful giver* loveth God)
acc.

"ælc man . . . þe . . . *ðone oðerne* hyrwde"
(each man who *the other* despised)
acc.

"and butan se Ælmihtiga God *þa dagas* gescyrte"
(and unless the Almighty God *those days* shorten)
acc.

3. The change from the free position of the accusative-object either before or after the verb to the fixed position after the verb is indicated by the figures in Table XXXVI.[6]

[5] I am indebted to a number of my students for collecting many of the instances upon which these figures are based. We have tried to count all the examples in each of the texts examined.

[6] Not enough texts have been examined to take the figures as an accurate statement of the situation for the 1200 and 1300 dates. The figures for 1500, however, cover more than a thousand examples.

TABLE XXXVI

	1000	1200	1300	1400	1500
Accusative-object *before* verb	52.5%	53.7%	40 + %	14.3%	1.87%
Accusative-object *after* verb	47.5%	46.3%	60 − %	85.7%	98.13%

4. Almost by 1400 and certainly before 1500 the position following the verb had become the fixed position for the accusative object.

In similar brief statements, the significant facts in the historical development of (*b*)—i. e., the position of those words which bore the dative inflection, the "dative-object" [7]—seem to be [8] :

1. In Old English the dative-object like the accusative-object could stand in any position. Even when an accusative-object was also expressed, the order of the words in relation to each other and in relation to the verb seems to have no bearing upon the grammatical relationship. Typical examples are

"Cartaginenses sendon *fultum* (acc.) *Tarentinum.*" (dat.)

(Carthaginians sent *aid* [*to*] *Tarentinians*). *Orosius* 162. 8.

"*þam godan casere* (dat.) sende theodosie *ærend-gewrit.*" (acc.)

([*to*] *the good Caesar* sent Theodosia [*a*] *message.*) Ælfric *Saints* I. 536. 792.

"he asende his *apostlum* (dat.) *þone halgan gast.*" (acc.)

(he sent [*to*] his *apostles the Holy Ghost.*) Wulfstan I. 230. 27.

"Hi moston *him* (dat.) beran *unforbodene flæsc.*" (acc.)

(They were permitted [*to*] *him* to take *unforbidden flesh.*) Ælfric *Saints* II. 72. 91.

As a matter of fact, the words with the dative inflections could be changed into any other position in these sentences without altering

[7] In as much as the dative-object and the accusative-object are brought into contrast only where the two appear together, the statements 1 to 4 cover only an examination of those instances in which both a dative-object and an accusative-object appear.

[8] For most of the instances used here I am indebted to Dr. Frederic G. Cassidy whose dissertation deals with *The Backgrounds in Old English of the Modern English Substitutes for the Dative-Object in the Group Verb + Dative-Object + Accusative-Object* (Ann Arbor, University of Michigan, 1938).

the grammatical relationship now expressed and without doing violence to the patterns of Old English word order.

2. In the materials examined for Old English (900 A. D. to 1000 A. D.) we find the distribution of some 2,558 instances that is shown in Tables XXXVII and XXXVIII.

TABLE XXXVII

	Dative-Object BEFORE the verb		Dative-Object AFTER the verb	
	Number	Per cent	Number	Per cent
Nouns	95	27.6%	249	72.4%
Pronouns	492	48.7	518	51.3
Both together	587	43.4	767	56.6

TABLE XXXVIII

	Dative-Object BEFORE Acc.-Object		Dative-Object AFTER Acc.-Object	
	Number	Per cent	Number	Per cent
Nouns	249	64%	140	36%
Pronouns	674	82.8	141	17.2
Both together	923	76.6	281	23.3

3. The materials examined for Early Middle English (c. 1200 A. D.) show a clear (although not a violent) tendency to place the dative-object after the verb. The figures are given in Table XXXIX.

TABLE XXXIX

	Dative-Object BEFORE Verb		Dative-Object AFTER Verb	
	Number	Per cent	Number	Per cent
Nouns	26	23%	88	77%
Pronouns	218	43	288	57
Both together	244	39.4	376	60.6

4. Just as in the case of the accusative-object, by the early part of the fifteenth century, the position of a noun as dative-object [9] had become fixed. It was after the verb but before an accusative-object.

[9] It is perhaps unnecessary to remind the reader that our discussion here does not include the so-called dative-object with the preposition (function word). If the relationship is expressed by a function word, it does not depend upon word order.

The general situation then at the end of the fourteenth century and the beginning of the fifteenth was this. The fixed "object" position was *after* the verb and accusative-objects were distinguished from dative-objects by the fact that dative-objects (especially when nouns) preceded accusative-objects. Most important was the fact that by this time practically no nouns as accusative-objects or as dative-objects preceded the verb.[10] As a result the position before the verb, cleared of the presence of formally distinct accusative-objects and dative-objects, became *subject territory* and thus exercised its pressure upon the function of all the substantives that stood there.

Nouns which formerly stood before the so-called impersonal verbs as dative-objects with dative case inflection, now, with the case inflection gone, functioned as subjects wherever the verb forms permitted.[11]

"The knight liked it right noght"—*Tale of Gamelyn,* 52.
"This tale nedeth noght be glosed"—*Confessio Amantis,* VII, 3786.

Nouns following these impersonal verbs, which formerly were subjects with clear nominative case inflections, now, standing in object territory, tended to function as objects.

"Whan a wolf wanteþ [h]is fode, . . . of the erþe he et" (When to a wolf is lacking his food, . . . of the earth he eats)—*Alexander and Dindarus,* 860.

The functional pressure of the position before the verb as subject territory was so strong that dative-accusative pronoun forms were changed to accord with the pattern.[12]

"Me lakketh nothing" became "I lack nothing."
"Hem lacked a ladder" became "They lacked a ladder."
"Hem nedede no help" became "They needed no help."
"Me wæs gegiefan an boc" became "I was given a book."

[10] Pronouns, having distinctive case forms still appeared occasionally as dative-objects or as acccusative-objects before verbs.

[11] The examples printed by Willem van der Gaaf in his dissertation *The Transition from Impersonal to Personal in Middle-English* (1904) have been of great service. See also O. Jespersen, *A Modern English Grammar,* Vol. III (Heidelberg, 1927), 11.2–11.35.

[12] See also above pages 90–91.

Even the form of the verb itself was changed to agree with a substantive pressed by the fixed word order to function as subject. Compare, for example, Chaucer's "Wostow nought wel that it *am* I" with the following fifteenth century sentence: "It *is* I that am here in your syth" (*Coventry Mysteries*).

In general, then, in respect to the expression of the subject and object relations, the development in English has been away from inflectional devices which made it grammatically possible for subjects and objects to stand in *any* position among the words of a sentence, to the use of grammatically functioning fixed word order patterns which made the position before the verb, "subject" territory and the position after the verb, "object" territory.

Before attempting to describe more precisely the operation of the grammatical use of these positions in Present-day Standard and Vulgar English it is necessary to give something of the historical evidence concerning the development of the expression of the second of the essential or unavoidable relationships that all known languages express—the direction of modification.

If, for example, the qualities "red" and "big" are expressed at the time one is speaking of both a *man* and a *barn*, it is necessary to know to which of these two—the *man* or the *barn*—the qualities "red" and "big" are to be attached. It is essential that a language have some means of showing to which thing-words any quality-words belong. We must know what modifies what. There must be some device to show *the direction of modification.* We are here not concerned with the content of the modification nor with the various kinds of modification,[13] but solely with the develop-

[13] Some examples to illustrate the great variety of the kinds of modification are the following. It is not always easy to state the precise kind of relation that exists between the modifier and its headword.

fresh water
shallow water
muddy water
rain water
sea water
well water
drinking water
ice water

a young boy
an elevator boy
an errand boy
a cabin boy
a high school boy
one boy
a college student
a mathematics student
a hard student
a boy friend

drunken oaths
married life
a total stranger

a perfect stranger
a flat denial
liquid measure

a long sentence (i. e., The Judge gave the criminal)
utter darkness

(*Continued on next page*)

ment of the particular devices English has used for showing this essential and unavoidable relationship, called here the "direction of modification."

In Old English this relationship of modification (the character-substance or modifier-noun relationship) was indicated primarily by means of inflectional forms. Articles and adjectives "agreed" [14] with the nouns they modified; that is, they had endings that stood for the same grammatical relationships as those of the nouns to which they belonged. Thus in such a sentence as "on ænium oþerum mynstres þingum" [15] it is quite clear that *oþerum* must go with *þingum,* for the case form of both words is dative plural. That of *mynstres* is genitive singular so that *oþerum* could not be a modifier of *mynstres*. We could not, therefore, keep the Old English order of words if we wished to give the Modern English equivalent of this phrase, for in the Modern English phrase "in any other monastery's things" the word *other* modifies *monastery's*. We are compelled to say "in any *other things* of the monastery," for in Modern English *other* can be made to modify *things* only by being placed immediately before it.

In Old English, with the use of inflectional forms to show the direction of modification, it was quite possible to place modifiers either before or after their nouns or to separate them from their nouns by other words. Some examples are the following: [16]

"Comon þær scipu six to Wiht"
(Came there ships six to Wight) *Anglo-Saxon Chronicle* 897.

"Æþelwulfes suna twegen"
(Æthelwulf's sons two) *Anglo-Saxon Chronicle* 855.

---

an habitual liar
a grown-up party
a deaf and dumb teacher
the lost and found notices
the cotton trade
a gold mine
a new acquaintance
an insane asylum
a mental hospital
a psychopathic ward
a stone wall
a stony path
a rapid writer
a practical joker
an old friend

[14] See above pages 45–46.

[15] From the tenth century, *Benedictine Rule,* 95.14.

[16] For most of the examples used in my discussion here and for the figures on the post-position genitive following, I am indebted to Russell Thomas whose dissertation on *The Development of the Adnominal Periphrastic Genitive in English* contains a wealth of material.

"and ealle þara nytena frumcennedan"
(and all the animals' first born) = Mdn. Eng. "all first born of the animals." *Exodus* 133.5.

"Ge gesawon ealle þa mæran drihtnes weorc"
(Ye saw all the great lord's works) — Mdn. Eng. "Ye saw all the great works of (the) lord" *Deuteronomy* 214. 7.

"an lytel sæs earm"
(a little sea's arm) = Mdn. Eng. "a little arm of the sea." *Orosius* 28. 12–13.

"to ðæm Godes huse"
(to the God's house) = Mdn. Eng. "to the house of God." *Orosius* 94. 18.

"þone drihtnes þægen"
(the lord's servant) = Mdn. Eng. "the servant of (a) lord" Ælfric 184. 249.

Perhaps the progressive fixing of the word order pattern for modification can best be illustrated by the facts concerning the position of the inflected genitive modifying a noun. The inflected adnominal genitive has always been adjectival in its function and in Old English could, like the adjectives, stand either before or after the noun [17] it modified. In the Old English of Alfred (c. 900 A. D.), out of 2,247 instances, 1,175 or 52.4 per cent stood before the noun modified, and 1,072 or 47.6 per cent stood after the noun modified.

The figures in Table XL show the developing change in this situation.

TABLE XL

	c. 900	c. 1000	c. 1100	c. 1200	c. 1250
Before its noun	52.4%	69.1%	77.4%	87.4%	99.1%
After its noun	47.6%	30.9%	22.6%	12.6%	.9%

By the end of the thirteenth century the post-positive inflected genitive had completely disappeared. By this time the general word order pattern to express the direction of modification had become

[17] An example of such a post-positive genitive is the following from Aelfric: "þæt he and eall Israhela folc sceoldon offrian Gode *an lamb anes geares.*"

well established. Single word modifiers of the noun or adjective class preceding the nouns they modified remained in that position and became the usual practice, whereas single word modifiers of this class in other positions tended to be eliminated or to use a function word. With the loss of inflection this particular position before a noun became the grammatical device of Modern English to indicate adjunct relationship.

Just as in the case of the other grammatical patterns that have developed in English, there have continued to exist in our practice certain remnants of the older situation that have not yielded to the pressure of the newer pattern. Some of these uses are

a. Nouns in apposition
"William the Conqueror"
"Alfred the king" (The older "Aelfred cyning," in which no article was used with the second noun, has become the regular "King Alfred.")
b. Cardinal numerals as modifiers
"Chapter ten"
"Page three"
"in the year 1000"
c. Some petrified phrases
"God Almighty"
"Brother mine"
d. Modifying participles
"for the time being"
"the day following" (cf. "the following day")
"the money required" (cf. "the required money")
e. Some phrases borrowed from other languages—especially from French
"heirs male"
"the body politic"

With the functioning of this word order pattern to indicate modification without the need of inflection, there have appeared an increasing number of instances in which the genitive form is suppressed, resulting in a noun modifier with no formal indication, *other than position,* of its adjunct character.[18] Such, for example, are the following:

"a ten days leave"	"the company officers
"a six months course"	"the hospital gardens"
"a one day vacation"	"my business interests"

[18] See above page 43 and also C. C. Fries, "Some Notes on the Inflected Genitive in Present-Day English," *Language,* Vol. 14, 1938, pp. 121–133, especially pp. 128–130.

In fact, in Present-day English, position alone indicates modification, and nouns, both singular and plural, are freely placed before others as modifiers. The nature of the modification may be of the widest variety and often is extremely vague. The following examples are typical: [19]

"construction programs"
"flood control"
"flood control projects"
"senate appropriations committee"
"film explosion"
"farm crops"
"[attacks] Vandenberg plan"
"the present Works Progress administration system"
"benefit payments"
"war threat"
"state jobs"
"world war veteran"
"old-age insurance"
"appropriation bill"
"the federal old-age insurance program"
"the 22-member group"
"farm labor"
"the 2 per-cent payroll tax"
"real estate holdings
"securities salesmen"
"airplane factories"
"peace talks"
"the pump-priming bill"
"troop movements"

In line with this pressure of word order as a grammatical device to indicate modification is the strong tendency for the first of two adjectives modifying a noun to become a modifier of the second adjective—the word immediately following. In the expression "the dark green house" there is a strong tendency to regard *dark* as a modifier of *green* rather than of *house*. In "an icy cold drink" and "a blazing hot fire," *icy* and *blazing* tend strongly to be felt as modifiers of *cold* and *hot* respectively.[20]

In general, then, single word modifiers of the adjective and noun

[19] These examples were all taken from the first page of *The Ann Arbor News* for May 24, 1938.

[20] For the function word developing from this process, see above, Chapter IX, section I.

class have with the loss of their inflections, tended to hold a single fixed position immediately *preceding* the nouns they modified. This position, therefore, has tended to become the grammatical device of Modern English to displace inflections as the means of indicating the essential relationship of the direction of modification.

The situation with respect to word group modifiers, however, differs somewhat from that of the single word modifiers. Word group modifiers have become fixed in the position *following* the nouns they modify. The development of the periphrastic genitive is typical of this group. The periphrastic form of the genitive with *of* rose in frequency after the post-positive genitive had practically disappeared. The figures in Table XLI show the details of this progress.[21]

TABLE XLI

	Post-positive Genitive	*Periphrastic Genitive*	*Pre-positive Genitive*
c. 900	47.5%	.5%	52%
c. 1000	30.5	1.0	68.5
c. 1100	22.2	1.2	76.6
c. 1200	11.8	6.3	81.9
c. 1250	.6	31.4	68.0
c. 1300	.0	84.4	15.6

All word group modifiers of nouns, those phrases introduced by the function words called prepositions [22] and those clauses introduced by relative pronouns, tend to modify *the word immediately preceding*. It is the pressure of this pattern in spite of the logic of context that creates the humor in such sentences as the following:

"an old gentleman held a boy in his arms about the size of little Rawdon"

"The children will christen the battleship on Thursday that they built"

"Wanted: a piano by Richard Jones with a modern small case"

"The undersigned was given a physical examination for promotion by a Medical Board"

With the fixing of this position for modifying word groups, there has appeared an increasing number of modifying clauses with the

[21] See Thomas, *op. cit.*, p. 70.

[22] See above p. 119.

introductory function word relative omitted. The position itself serves without the pronoun to indicate the subordinate modifying function of the clause,[23] as in

"There is a man below wants to speak to you."
"This is the boy we spoke of."
"In the songs I love to sing."
"Those nice people I stayed with."
"What is it you are talking of?"
"I am not the madman you thought me."

Both in respect to the grammatical relation of modification just discussed and in respect to the subject and object relation dealt with earlier in this chapter, the development in English has been away from grammatically functioning inflectional devices and a variety of accompanying positions in the sentence to a loss of inflections with grammatically functioning fixed word order.

In Present-day English the situation in regard to the grammatically functioning fixed word order revealed by the letters examined for this survey seems to be as follows:

I. THE FIXED POSITIONS IN THE ACTOR-ACTION-GOAL CONSTRUCTION IN STATEMENTS

The grammatical significance of the fixed positions in the "actor-action-goal" construction in statements—the most common sentence type in English.

These positions concern the relations between substantives and verbs.

1. A single noun preceding the verb—a noun that has the full formal characteristics of a substantive (i. e., with possible determiners as well as inflection for number)—and is not preceded by an accompanying function word, nor inflected for genitive case, is the subject or the starting point of the actor-action construction.

STANDARD ENGLISH

"telegraphic *resignation* is not permitted" (9005)
"his *work* with both organizations redounded most favorably to his professional ability" (9005)

[23] For many examples of these "contact-clauses" from the sixteenth-century to Present-day English, see O. Jespersen, *A Modern English Grammar*, Vol. III (Heidelberg, 1927), pp. 132–153.

"My *duties* as Veterinary Inspector . . . take me to very remote places" (9004)
"The north *end* of a compass needle always tends to point down" (9003)
"Mrs. ——'s *remains* lie in the Army Morgue" (9003)
"the enlisted man's *parents* are in need of him" (8183)
"the mother's *affidavit* . . . has already been furnished" (8239)
"the month's *time* that I have lost has necessitated quite a lot of extra work" (9027)
"The *findings* of the board are forwarded in duplicate" (9002)
"the soldier's *father* returned to Italy" (8144)

VULGAR ENGLISH

"Many *reasons* are given by candidates" (8057)
"the *public* would not associate with Soilders" (8057)
"the *charges* against him are taking an auto" (8038)
"my *clouds* dont have those bright lineings" (8038)
"his right *name* is —— ——" (8033)
"my *Son* has enlisted" (8033)
"Of course a *man* can not go home unless . . ." (8026)
"this other *man* was still living" (8026)
"that poor *mother* has went and got a job" (8005)
"This boy's *father* is in the insane Asylum" (8077)
"his *parents* were both dead" (8211)
"my sons full *name* is —— ——" (8038)
"Sister Callie *boy* is in the U.S. Army" (8181)

2. Two such nouns preceding the verb—nouns that are equivalent or refer to the same person or thing—are the subject and an appositive, the first in order being the subject.

STANDARD ENGLISH

"The *mother Mrs.* —— is getting along nicely" (8017)
"*Mrs. M*——, the *grandmother,* informed our visitor" (8095)
"*Mr.* —— of —— ——, a constituent and a *friend* of long standing, was in my office" (8064)
"The *grocer, Mr.* —— verified the account" (8283)
"The *mother,* ——, is seemingly in good health" (8283)
"Her *son B*—— did not support her" (8144)
"her married *daughter, Mrs. P*——, acted as interpreter" (8144)
"*Captain* ——, a *graduate* of the University of Nebraska, is at present in Nebraska" (9050)
"the *Sears Roebuck Plant,* an immense new *structure* is being erected here" (8139)

Similar sentences from the Vulgar English letters are somewhat rare.[24] There were but twenty one instances in all and of these, ten are of the words "my son —— ——."

VULGAR ENGLISH

"My *son C—— L——* is in . . ." (8000)
"My *son L—— J——* is in . . ." (8032)
"My *son* —— —— is under age" (8042)
"Now my *son* —— —— is in confinement" (8052)
"My *Son* —— —— was Inticed to Join" (8100)
"About two months ago my *Son* —— —— enlisted" (8116)
"My *son* —— —— has been missing from home" (8115)
"My *son* —— —— Came up for clemency" (8153)
"My *son M—— L——* has Joined the . . ." (8162)
"My *Son* —— —— left home" (8176)
"—— —— my *son* joined the . . ." (8121)
"*Mr.* —— his *father* is a cripple" (8067)
"My *boy W—— S——*" (8194)
"the *soldier C—— L——*" (8025)
"his invalid *sister L—— P——*" (8028)

3. Two or more such nouns preceding the verb—nouns that do not refer to the same person or thing but are levelled by similar accent and/or function words—constitute a compound subject (two or more subjects).

STANDARD ENGLISH

"the *care* and *repair* of . . . vehicles at this station are under my supervision" (9052)
"the necessary *forms* and other *machinery* for operation was furnished by . . ." (8416)
"the *organization* and *work* of this office has increased ten foal" (9000)
"The *discipline* and *hygiene* of the . . . speaks for itself" (8415)
"their sanitary *conditions* and the *arrangement* of their quarters was very good" (8426)
"The *registrant* as well as his *dependents* were given an opportunity to appear" (8417)
"*Backsights* and *foresights* are approximately equal" (9037)

[24] The following type of structure appeared in the Vulgar English letters but not in those of Standard English:
"*Mr. R—— H—— he* can give you my name" (8025)
"My *son James he* left home" (8218)
"My *husband he* is 70 years old" (8272)
Although the pronoun subjects were very frequent in Vulgar English, only one appositive occurred with these pronouns:
"and *we* his *parents* want to get him out" (8165)

"My *experience* and *duties* with . . . have been very limited" (9019)

VULGAR ENGLISH

"My *Wife* & 2 *children* has got the Plegleory" (8179)
"The *father* and *mother* is dead" (8181)
"*D*—— *R*—— and *R*—— *R*—— is the Same Boy" (8151) [25]
"After 13 days *him* and this *man* . . . was found" (8026)

4. If two nouns precede the verb, stand next to one another, and are not levelled by accent and/or function words, but with only one possible determiner and that before the first noun, the second noun is the subject and the first a modifier of the subject.[26]

STANDARD ENGLISH

"A *base line* is the starting line from which . . ." (9037)
"*Register cards* are made for all cases" (9002)
"*Map projection* is a method of . . ." (9003)
"My *war experience* has all been . . ." (9015)
"the *exhaust valve* opens" (9027)
"*Government quarters* are not available there" (9030)
"The *family quarters* at present used are . . ." (9030)
"*Flying training* is desired" (9061)
"The *condemnation suits* are being tried" (9062)

The only instance from the Vulgar English materials of a subject noun so modified is the following:

"my *soldier boy* has been in . . ." (8028)

5. A single noun following the verb—a noun that has the full formal characteristics of a noun and is not preceded by an accompanying function word or inflected for genitive case, if this noun refers to the same person or thing as the subject noun—is an identifying noun—a so-called predicate nominative.

STANDARD ENGLISH

"This soldier is a *toolmaker*" (8081)
"The family were fine *people*" (8283)

[25] An interesting example is the following in which but one person is referred to but in respect to his two capacities—as husband and as father:
"my *Husband* and his *father* is unable to support the Family" (8052)

[26] Such modifying nouns may also be attached to any of the "objects" after the verb. Whether before or after the verb, the modifying noun causes no confusion in the matter of the relations between the verb and the substantive. It is touched here in order to be excluded.
"I have had *business dealings* with them" (8004)
"draw any *pay envelope*" (8002)

"the incident was an *accident*" (9043)
"the actual time consumed was five *days*" (9034)
"a diagnosis of chronic appendicitis was the final *outcome*" (9006)
"my folks have been American *citizens*" (9036)
"one cause was the *desire* of . . ." (9017)
"the time would be a distinct *advantage*" (9058)
"the authority establishing the second hospital might be a division *surgeon*" (9002)
"the only means of support is *$15.00* weekly compensation insurance" (8260)

VULGAR ENGLISH

"the writer is a *soldier*" (8057)
"Many candidates are *men* who . . ." (8057)
"J—— S—— is a poor *boy*" (8063)
"We have always been good *parents* to our children" (8074)

6. Such a single noun following the verb, if it does not refer to the same person or thing as the subject noun, is the object—the end point of the "action." [27]

STANDARD ENGLISH

"The family . . . pay *rent*" (8283)
"The grocer . . . verified the *account*" (8283)
"Examination of Mrs. —— about July 1st shows no *improvement*" (8266)
"the defendent had left the *jurisdiction* of the court" (8296)
"Mrs. —— did *housework* for . . ." (8240)
"The grandmother earns some *money* by canvassing" (8095)
"Congress passed a *law* that . . ." (8183)
"the Act of Congress should not receive a different *interpretation* now" (9030)
"P—— M——'s brother and sister meet all necessary *expenses*" (8027)

[27] In this group I should also put the following:
"The boys are taught the fundamental *principles*" (9017)
"the son may be granted the *discharge*" (8240)
"their request would be given *consideration*" (8160)
"the undersigned was given a physical *examination*" (9054)
"any which are lacking to complete my record will be given my prompt *attention*" (9027)
It is less certain whether the following should also be included here:
"Alimony was denied the *wife*" (8296)
"personal quarters are furnished the *officers*" (9030)
"Quarters were furnished such *officers*" (9030)
"The custody of the children was denied both the *father* and the *mother*" (8296)

VULGAR ENGLISH

"James had no written *consent*" (8218)
"My son James he left *home*" [28] (8218)
"that poor mother . . . got a *job* to help keep the family" (8005)
"any mother would Sign any armory *paper*" (8005)
"my clouds dont have those bright *lineings*" (8038)
"another got 3 months in the *gard house*" (8039)
"he did not realize the *responsibility*" (8173)
"ever one knows me *condition*" (8171)
"we need the *boy*" (8121)
"he passed the *examination*" (8021)
"we herd *nothing*" (8049)
"you almost immediately see a *change*" (8063)
"He walked the *streets* for weeks" (8080)

7. Two such nouns following the verb—nouns that do not refer to the same person or thing as the subject noun, but do themselves each refer to the same person or thing as the other—are a "direct" object and a "result" object or so-called "object complement" after such verbs as *call, make, elect, appoint, consider*. After other verbs they are direct object and appositive, the first in order being the direct object.[29] Only one instance appeared in the Standard English materials—and that with a pronoun for the first "object."

"The community considers *him* a *liability*" (8017)

The following are the only examples to appear in the Vulgar English materials:

"He named *his self Roy*" (8151)
"that leaves his *name J—— J—— F—— M*" (8101)

8. Two or more such nouns following the verb—nouns that do not refer to the same person or thing as the subject noun and do not themselves each refer to the same person or thing as the other, but are levelled by accent and/or function words—are a compound accusative-object ("direct" object)—i. e., several objects.

[28] One might question the including here of this sentence "My son . . . left *home*," and not such expressions as "The boy came *home*," "My son returned *home*," "The boy went home," etc., and in the form of the sentence as it stands there may be no difference between the two types. But with *home* in the first sentence any of the "determiners" are possible, *the, a, this, that*, etc., whereas in the others such determiners are not possible and the noun thus lacks the full formal characteristics of a substantive. This fact is also true of such "time" nouns as the following:

"*Yesterday* the man went to work"
"He will come home *next week*"

[29] Such a sentence as "My son was baptized J—— J—— M——" (8101) I should classify with those in 5 above.

STANDARD ENGLISH

"The children need *shoes* and *underwear*" (8260)
"Mrs. —— has several *sons* and *daughters*" (8240)
"his mother needs his *support* and *comfort*" (8294)
"Mr. —— leaves a *widow* and a *girl* of 11 years and the *son*" (8137)
"The father owns a small *house* and two *acres* of land" (8064)
"The family owe a grocery *bill* of $50 and a bread *bill* of $18.00" (8283)
"The mother needs his *companionship* more than the *$5.00* per month" (8064)

VULGAR ENGLISH

"we could pay our *rent* and *Bills*" (8233)

9. Two such nouns following the verb—nouns that do not refer to the same person or thing as the subject noun, and do not themselves each refer to the same person or thing as each other, and are not levelled by accent and/or function words—are a dative-object ("indirect" object) and an accusative-object ("direct" object)—the first in order being the dative or "indirect" object.[30]

STANDARD ENGLISH

"$5.00 per month will do his *mother* more material *good*" (8174)
(Most of the instances appear with a pronoun as "indirect" object.)
"Miss V—— . . . has written *you* the enclosed *letter*" (8144)
"some of the . . . could tell *you* the *results*" (9033)
"the expense of . . . has cost *me* considerable *money*" (9033)
"This error has caused *me* trouble and *annoyance*" (9007)
"all the districts have afforded *him opportunities*" (9023)

VULGAR ENGLISH[31]

"—— get my *son* a *release*" (8233)
"the . . . offices . . . tells his *son* all the nice *things*" (8005)
"—— pay the *government* whatever *expenses* then . . ." (8251)
"I sent S——'s *captain* an *afidavit*" (8037)
(Other instances appear with a pronoun as "indirect" object.)
"the goverament will pay *them* an *allotment*" (8258)
"I wrote *you* a *letter*" (8274)
"I am dropping *you* a few *lines*" (8288)
"he sends *me* $8.00 *dollars*" (8233)
"you fine *me* my *reference*" (8044)

[30] See examples given in note 27 above for sentences in the so-called passive voice in which such a dative-object or accusative-object has become the subject. See also Chapter VIII, section L.

[31] The kind of constructions for which examples are given in note 27 above did not occur in the Vulgar English materials.

"you will grant *him clemency*" (8153)
"cause . . . *anybody* any *trouble*" (8100)

The application of the statements given above [32] to the following series of sentences in which the position of the word *sentinel* is the chief difference will probably help in setting forth the significance of word order as a device for showing these particular grammatical relationships.

a. The sentinel and a man stood by the box.
b. The sentinel, a man, stood by the box.
c. The man, a sentinel, stood by the box.
d. The sentinel man stood by the box.

[32] For convenience the statements are here brought together in summary.

The word order pattern for the nouns of the actor-action-goal construction:

1. A single noun preceding the verb—a noun that has the full characteristics of a substantive (i. e., with possible determiners as well as inflection for number), that is not preceded by an accompanying function word, nor inflected for genitive case—is the subject or the starting point of the actor-action construction.

2. Two such nouns preceding the verb—nouns that are equivalent or refer to the same person or thing—are the subject and an appositive, the first in order being the subject.

3. Two or more such nouns preceding the verb—nouns that do not refer to the some person or thing but which are levelled by similar accent and/or function words—constitute a compound subject (two or more subjects).

4. If two nouns precede the verb, stand next to one another, and are not levelled by accent and/or function words, but with only one possible determiner and that before the first noun, the second noun is the subject and the first a modifier of the subject.

5. A single noun following the verb—a noun that has the full formal characteristics of a substantive and is not preceded by an accompanying function word or inflected for genitive case—if this noun refers to the same person or thing as the subject noun, is an identifying noun—a so-called "predicate nominative."

6. Such a single noun following the verb, if it does not refer to the same person or thing as the subject noun, is the end point of the action or object.

7. Two such nouns following the verb—nouns that do not refer to the same person or thing as the subject noun, but do themselves each refer to the same person or thing as the other, are a "direct" object and a "result" object or a so-called "object complement," after such verbs as *call, make, elect, appoint, consider.* After other verbs they are "direct" object and appositive, the first in order being the direct object.

8. Two or more such nouns following the verb—nouns that do not refer to the same person or thing as the subject noun and do not themselves each refer to the same person or thing as the other, but are levelled by accent and/or function words—are a compound accusative ("direct") object—i. e., several objects.

9. Two such nouns following the verb—nouns that do not refer to the same person or thing as the subject noun, and do not themselves each refer to the same person or thing as the other, and are not levelled by accent and/or function words—are a dative-object ("indirect" object) and an accusative object ("direct" object), the first in order being the dative or indirect object.

10. If two nouns follow the verb, stand next to one another, and are not levelled by accent and/or function words, but with only one possible determiner and that before the first noun, the first noun is a modifier of the second and the second may be either 5 or 6 above.

e. The man sentinel stood by the box.
f. The man stood a sentinel by the box.
g. The man stood by the sentinel box.
h. The man stood by the box sentinel.
i. The man made the sentinel a box.
j. The captain made the man a sentinel.

In *a* there are two nouns preceding the verb—nouns with the full formal characteristics of a substantive, nouns that are not accompanied by such function words as *of, by, at,* etc. and that do not refer to the same person or thing, but are levelled by the function word *and*. These nouns are therefore a compound subject (two subjects). (See statement 3, page 263.)

In *b* and *c* there are two such nouns before the verb which are equivalent or refer to the same person or thing. In *b,* therefore, *sentinel* is subject and *man* is appositive. In *c man* is subject and *sentinel* is appositive. (See statement 2, page 262.)

In *d* and *e* two nouns precede the verb, stand next to one another, are not levelled by a function word, but they have only one determiner and that before the first noun. In *d,* therefore, *man* is subject and *sentinel* is a modifier of *man*. In *e, sentinel* is subject and *man* is a modifier of *sentinel*. (See statement 4, page 264.)

In *f* two nouns follow the verb, but the relation of *box* is indicated by the function word *by* accompanying it, leaving only *sentinel* as the noun whose relationship is indicated by word order. This noun as it stands here in a sentence isolated from other context may be in either of two relationships. If it refers to the same person or thing as the subject noun, it is a "predicate nominative" or identifying noun. (See statement 5, page 264.) If it does not refer to the same person or thing as the subject noun, it is "object." (See statement 6, page 265.)

In *g* and *h* two nouns follow the verb,[33] stand next to each other, are not levelled by a function word, but they have only one determiner and that before the first noun. In *g, sentinel* is a modifier of *box* and in *h, box* is a modifier of *sentinel*. (See statement 4, page 264.)

In *i* two nouns with the full formal characteristics of a substantive follow the verb. They do not refer to the same person or thing

[33] The fact that they are preceded by the function word *by* has no bearing upon our immediate problem here, for we are making a statement concerning their relation to each other, not concerning the relation of either one to the verb.

as the subject noun, they do not themselves each refer to the same person or thing as each other, and they are not levelled by function words such as *and* or *or*. Therefore, *sentinel* is the dative-object ("indirect" object) and *box* the accusative-object ("direct" object). (See statement 9, page 267.)

In *j* two nouns with the full formal characteristics of a substantive follow the verb. They do not refer to the same person or thing as the subject noun, but they do themselves each refer to the same person or thing as the other. Therefore, *man* is accusative-object and *sentinel* is a "result" object ("object complement"). (See statement 7, page 266.)

The chief differences between the practice in the Standard English materials and that in the Vulgar English materials are

a. The Standard English materials contain many more *nouns* in the subject and object relation than do those of Vulgar English. The Vulgar English letters use pronouns in these relations primarily.

b. Only one noun modifier of a subject appears in the Vulgar English materials as against some thirty instances in the Standard English letters. (See page 264.)

c. The so-called "object complement" construction seems to be very rare. There was but one instance in the Standard English letters and none in those of Vulgar English. (See page 266.)

d. The word order method of indicating a distinction between a dative-object ("indirect" object) and accusative-object ("direct" object), although used in both groups, is much more frequent in Standard English. About twice as many instances appeared in the Standard English letters as in those of the Vulgar English group. (See pages 92, 267, and 268.) Vulgar English seems to use more frequently the function words *to* and *for* to express this grammatical relationship.

e. Aside from the four points here noted there seem to be no differences in the practices of the two social groups in these uses of word order to show the relations of nouns and verbs.

II. THE FIXED POSITIONS IN THE MODIFIER-NOUN (CHARACTER-SUBSTANCE) CONSTRUCTION

As shown above (pages 259 and 260) single word modifiers of the noun and adjective classes, in general pattern, immediately precede the words they modify, but word group modifiers (so-called "phrases" and "subordinate clauses"), in general pattern, immediately follow the words they modify. The following statements seem to represent the situation.

1. A single word with the formal characteristics of an adjective [34] preceding a noun is a modifier of that noun. This is an exceedingly common type of construction. In the Standard English letters there were 1,413 instances. The exceptions to this pattern—the cases in which a single word modifier followed the noun—were comparatively rare, for there were but seventy six in all. In other words, of the 1,489 instances with single word adjective modifiers of nouns, 94.9 per cent immediately preceded the noun and 5.1 per cent immediately followed. Examples of this common pattern of modification, widely various in respect to the kind of relation existing between the two elements, are the following:

"*favorable* action" (8234)
"*personal* quarters" (9030)
"*practical* work" (9052)
"*foreign* service" (9028)
"*regular* channels" (9061)
"a *delightful* man" (9003)
"*reasonable* precautions" (9032)
"my *sincere* desire" (9000)
"a *nervous* breakdown" (8002)
"the *proper* officers" (8076)
"my *proper* station" (9036)
"his *legal* guardian" (8114)
"his *physical* condition" (8283)
"the *total* amount" (9032)
"the *young* man" (9023)
"*sterling* character" (9038)

Examples of such single word modifiers in a position after the noun are of the types shown in the following groups:

STANDARD ENGLISH

a.

"no travel pay or allowance *available*" (9029)
"no funds *available*" (9040)
"the best physical condition *possible*" (9066)
"of the information *available*" (9061)

b.

"a young man, *industrious* and *trustworthy*" (9039)
"a man, *straight* and *truthful*" (8060)

[34] The chief formal characteristic of an adjective is the inflection (or the function word) of comparison.

c.

"some . . . post not far *distant*" (9043)
"a young man—strictly *temperate*" (9038)

d.

"the best information *obtainable* from her" (8095)
"at some institution not *familiar* to me" (9050)
"on the list *eligible* for duty" (9042)
"the temperament *suitable* for . . ." (9028)
"the time *necessary* for accomplishing this" (9040)
"all expense *incident* to the transfer" (9059)
"six children *dependent* upon her" (8189)
"one *worthy* of trust" (9029)

e.

"two weeks *ago*" (8095)
"seven years *ago*" (8144)

f.[35]

"for the time *being*" (9017)
"for a week *following*" (8002)

g.[36]

"any further information *needed*" (8283)
"discharges of the nature *requested*" (8073)
"any papers *attached*" (9035)
"of injuries *received*" (9027)
"the procedure *used*" (9032)
"the actual time *consumed*" (9034)
"the examinations *required*" (9012)

h.

"to have its date *corrected*" (9036)
"in having this resolution *passed*" (9036)
"have this matter *checked up*" (9057)
"to have her son *discharged*" (8023)
"have the papers *prepared*" (8160)
"had her hand *caught*" (8095)

[35] There were, however, eight times as many instances of this kind with the adjective preceding the noun.
"the *following* statement" (9019)
"the *resulting* benefit" (9042)
"the *outstanding* bills" (9040)
There is, of course, no such parallel for the example "for the time *being*."

[36] Here again there were many more instances with the adjective preceding the noun—three times as many.
"the *required tests*" (9050) (9036)
"the *designated* place" (9043)
"the *returned* requisitions" (9040)
"the *inclosed* resolution" (9036)
"the *attached* order" (9061)
"the *desired* report" (8299)

In the Vulgar English materials there were fewer adjective modifiers all told, and a number of the types illustrated above did not appear. There were 479 in all. Of these, 458 or 95.6 per cent were of the common pattern, immediately preceding the noun and twenty one or 4.4 per cent following the word modified.

Examples of the common pattern showing something of the variety of relation involved are

"a *weak* heart" (8117)
"his *younger* brother" (8141)
"in *good* health" (8127)
"a *good* worker" (8074)
"a *steady* worker" (8080)
"your *kind* attention" (8104)
"a *nervous* wreck" (8080)
"an *honorable* discharge" (8288)
"a *foolish* thing" (8080)
"my *earnest* desire" (8288)
"a *critical* condition" (8080)
"to a *local* post" (8082)
"*unfortunate* circumstances" (8084)
"his *Baptismal* certificate" (8000)
"his *crect* age" (8000)
"my *correct* date of birth" (8070)
"my *sole* support" (8034)
"*financial* aid" (8034)
"the *open* air" (8063)
"the *proper* application" (8063)
"an *early* date" (8261)
"*last* week" (8288)
"*continual* use of liquor" (8080)
"*Regular* hours" (8063)
"a *existing* vacancy" (8082)
"the *following* reasons" (8036)
"he enlisted as a *single* man" (8012)

Examples of such single word modifiers in a position after the noun are of the types shown in the following groups but are rare in the Vulgar English materials. (For convenience of comparison the groups are given the same letters as are the groups of the Standard English materials. At the end a miscellaneous group (*i*) is added of instances unlike any that appeared in Standard English.)

VULGAR ENGLISH

a.

"that will be time *inough*" (8080)
"anything *wrong*" (8118) (8005) (8135) (8201)

b.

"a poor boy without education *undevelop*" (8063)

c. No examples

d.

"he was making money *enough* to support me" (8230)

e.

"about 6 years *ago*" [37] (8030)
"some few days *ago*" (8135)
"two months *ago*" (8116)

f. No examples

g.

"the duties *assigned*" (8063)
"the last *seen* of him" (8115)
"an affadavitt *sworn* to by me" (8101)
"all mail *un called for*" (8149)

h.

"he has had his leg *broken* twice" (8032)

i.

"is crying himself *sick*" (8053)
"it turned me *gray*" (8201)
"he was found *dead*" (8094)

"on his way *back*" (8117)

"leave us *all*" (8288)
"take care of them *all*" (8288)
"mad with us *all*" (8181)

2. If two nouns stand next to one another, and are not levelled by accent and/or function words, but with only one possible determiner and that before the first noun, the first noun is a modifier of the second. These noun adjuncts with no formal indication, other than position, of their modifying function are very frequent in the Standard English materials. There, there are 412 in all, but in the Vulgar English letters there are only 111—approximately only one fourth as many in an equal amount of writing.

[37] For many the pressure of the word order pattern is such that *years* is felt to be a modifier of *ago*.

In these noun adjunct constructions the relations between the modifier and the noun are even more various than between the adjectives and the nouns they modify. (Shown above note 13.) Often the relationship is very loose and hard to define. This variety of relationship is especially marked in the instances from Standard English.[38] In order to illustrate this variety a fairly large number of examples are included here.

STANDARD ENGLISH

"a *school* teacher" (8060)
"the *school* year" (9031)
"*sea* level" (9037)
"my *victory* medal" (9018)
"the *promotion* list" (9022)
"*examination* papers" (9035)
"a *summer* camp" (9034)
"at *target* practice" (9014)
"the *home* conditions" (8137)
"our *home* address" (9040)
"a *home* visit" (8240)
"my *leave* order" (9050)
"*longevity* pay" (9050)
"my *household* effects" (9056)
"the *newspaper* clipping" (9057)
"the *reparations* problem" (9057)
"my *college* course" (9058)
"at *government* expense" (9058)
"a *transportation* request" (9052)
"my *freight* allowance" (9058)
"*blanket* roll" (9060)
"the *condemnation* suits" (9062)
"a *work* statement" (8303)
"a *bread* bill" (8283)
"the *store* bill" (8002)
"the *land* contract" (8081)
"the *family* physician" (8283)
"*army* life" (8027)
"a *funeral* bill" (8027)
"*business* dealings" (8004)
"no *business* training" (8137)
"the *company* store" (8002)
"any *pay* envelope" (8002)
"my *business* interests" (9000)
"a *leave* status" (9001)
"a *compass* needle" (9003)
"the *hospital* fund" (9002)
"the *hospital* gardens" (9002)
"*janitor* service" (8260)
"a *cataract* operation" (8207)
"*labor* conditions" (8207)
"*beauty* culture" (8095)
"the *immigration* law" (8144)

VULGAR ENGLISH

"his *boy* chums" (8018)
"for *Doctor* bills" (8288)
"a *silk* mill" (8079)
"my *mason* work" (8067)
"to *church* school" (8067)
"a *home* parole" (8052)
"his *home* town" (8038)
"my *soldier* boy" (8028)

[38] The process of these noun adjuncts seems to me to be the same as that underlying the formation of compounds. In fact it is hardly possible in many instances to draw a line bounding the compounds and separating them from these free syntactical groups. Accent and specialization of meaning set off many clear cases, but there is a wide band of borderline cases. Frequency of a particular combination often leads to the phonetic and semantic features characteristic of a compound. For our purpose no sharp line of demarkation is either necessary or desirable. See also the attitude expressed concerning "compound function words" on pages 114–118 above.

"my *Gardine* papers" (8025)
"the *coal* mines" (8005)
"his *Baptism* certificate" (8000) [39]
"no *birth* certificut" (8254)
"the *county* farm" (8133)
"the *prothonotary* office" (8157)
"*blood* pressure" (8235)
"*lung* trouble" (8171)
"*automobile* machinist" (8173)
"at *Judgment* day" (8181)
"the *licence* bureau" (8186)
"*peace* times" (8250)
"her *grocerie* store" (8251)
"his *life* work" (8251)
"the *air* army" (8274)

3. In some of the modifier-noun (character-substance) constructions there appeared two or even more modifiers for a single noun.

a. These multiple modifiers when levelled by accent and/or function words operate as do the simple single word modifiers. The following examples are illustrative:

"*strong and beautiful* children" (9012)
"*sanitary and healthful* habits" (9012)
"*due and diligent* care" (9032)
"an *honest and honorable* boy" (8060)
"her *physical and mental* comfort" (8294)
"*agricultural and mechanical* arts" (9058)
"an *easy, accurate* manner" (9037)
"a *robust, active* physique" (9009)
"*a restless, roving* disposition" (8139)
"*honest, honorable, straight* men" (8060)

b. Often, however, multiple modifiers are not so levelled, and then the pressure of the word order pattern for indicating the direction of modification shows itself, for wherever the lexical meanings of the words permit, each modifier tends to modify the unit immediately following.[40]

"in *reasonable good* health" (8017)
"a *little rented* house" (8142)
"*excellent moral* character" (9009)
"*high moral* character" (9005)
"an *absolute bona fide* statement" (8267)
"*more varied* service" (9028)

This tendency shows itself also where the second modifier is a noun adjunct.[41]

[39] Compare "his *Baptismal* certificate" from the same letter (8000).

[40] For a discussion of this process in the development of function words with adjectives, see above, Chapter IX, section I.

[41] Often, of course, the noun adjunct and its head word tend to become a single unit (almost a compound) which the adjective modifies.

"the *present school year*" (9031)

"all *regular army* captains" (9034)
"a *special service* school" (9024)
"his *foreign service* tour" (9061)
"a *successful flying* officer" (9028)
"the *ninth corps* area" (9064)

Where several noun adjuncts occur in order, the rule of immediate contact for modification seems to have no exceptions.

"a *beauty culture* parlor" (8095)
"a *street car* accident" (8093)
"the *street rail-way* company" (8095)
"*gas engine* laboratory" (9052)
"*air service* instructor" (9031)

In line with this tendency, also, the ordinal numerals and such words as *next, last, past,* appeared invariably before other adjective modifiers.

"the *next* two years" (9064)
"the *last* forty years" (9017)
"the *past* ten years" (9039)
"the *first* regular opening" (8143)
"the *last* few times" (8002)
"the *next* upward stroke" (9027)

In the Vulgar English materials there were only about a dozen examples all told of multiple modifiers in the character-substance construction. These were all like those of Standard English shown under (3 *a*) above or like those just indicated with the words *next, last,* etc.

"*each* and *every* day" (8005)
"his *old Blind* father" (8121)
"a *true loyal* citizen" (8235)
"a *nice honest quite* boy" (8187)
"a *fine big honest* lad" (8288)
"the *last 8* years" (8115)
"the *last 6* month" (8168)

4. In the case of word group modifiers of nouns, i. e., the so-called prepositional phrases (the function words with nouns discussed above, pages 108 and 127) and the subordinate modifying

"his *entire College course*" (9041)
"some *important business matter*" (9016)
"the *present labor conditions*" (8207)
"a *local cigar factory*" (8144)

clauses, the fixed position has become that immediately following the word modified. In other words a prepositional phrase or a subordinate clause in general pattern modifies the word immediately *preceding*.

a. The actual numbers of the prepositional phrases used as modifiers of nouns that immediately precede them correspond very well with the numbers of simple adjectives preceding the nouns they modify.

In the Standard English materials there are 1,258 and in the Vulgar English letters 490.[42] These in every case except one follow immediately the nouns they modify.

Examples are

"the information *at hand*" (8260)
"a reconciliation *between him and his wife*" (8296)
"a journey *by transport*" (9053)
"a divorce *from bed and board*" (8296)
"a course *in trigonometry*" (9027)
"carelessness *on my part*" (9040)
"the personal care *of this son*" (8023)
"in your letter *to her*" (8234)
"experience *with horses*" (9015)
"a widow *without means*" (8023)

The one instance in which the whole context proves that the phrase cannot modify the preceding noun is the following:

"The undersigned was given a physical examination for promotion *by a medical board*" (9054)

It is in just such a case as this, however, that the actual use of word order to indicate the direction of modification makes itself felt, for even here the reader is pressed to take the phrase "by a medical board" as a modifier of the word *promotion* in spite of the logic of the context. But there are a certain number of instances (sixty seven in the Standard English letters and sixty six in the Vulgar English materials) in which a word group modifier following a noun could just as well, according to the logic of the context, be considered a modifier of the verb, inasmuch as phrase modifiers of verbs are much less fixed in their positions.

[42] The number of simple adjectives preceding nouns was 1,413 in the Standard English letters and 479 in those of Vulgar English. See above pages 271 and 273.

Some examples are

"I have no interest *in the matter*" (8260) (8139)
"I received a letter *from the Adjutant General*" (8160)
"I am maintaining a place of abode *at Ashville*" (9030)
"a company . . . made satisfactory records *at target practice*" (9014)
"There is on hope *for her*" (8064)

In all these instances, however, both those from Standard English and those from Vulgar English, the phrase can be taken in accord with the pattern as a modifier of the noun which it follows.

b. The situation with respect to the position of subordinate clause modifiers of nouns is much like that of the prepositional phrase modifiers, although with marked differences. As indicated above, the general pattern holds that such a clause modifies the noun immediately preceding. In the Standard English materials there are 338 such clauses as against fifty eight that do not immediately follow the noun they modify. Of all the subordinate clauses modifying nouns, 86 per cent follow immediately the noun modified; 14 per cent have other words intervening, usually a phrase modifier of the same noun. Examples of the general pattern in which the clause is a modifier of an immediately preceding noun are

"a neighbor *whom we interviewed*" (8002)
"people *who know the father*" (8002)
"the community *where he lived*" (8017)
"various papers *which were requested*" (8027)
"within a few miles of B—— *where I live*" (8060)
"all products *that are generally raised* . . ." (8060)
"the circumstances *in which they are situated*" (8064)

Of the 338 instances in this general pattern twenty seven or 8 per cent omit the function word to introduce the subordinate clause. Position without function word is sufficient. Examples are

"The only decision *I can find*" (9063)
"The time *I would spend there*" (9058)
"This is the first time *anything of this nature has happened to me*" (9057)
"from the time *he was a small boy*" (9029)
"the period *they can best receive training*" (9012)
"any news *you can give me*" (8075)
"the money *she now has on hand*" (8095)
"doing the best *he could*" (8296)

Examples of those clauses that do not immediately follow the noun they modify are

"my verbal *request* made to you *that I be transferred*" (9062)
"all *officers* on duty at training camps *who arrive as I did*" (9060)
"my *application* for transfer to —— *which was submitted* . . ." (9053)
"the above mentioned *letter* from —— *which said* . . ." (9050)
"many *officers* in this camp *whom I rank* . . ." (9042)
"I purchased a new *automobile* from this company *for which I paid them cash*" (9033)
"There is *nothing* in the Act *that justifies the conclusion*" (9030)
"a qualified *officer* of the United States Army *who will be acceptable to the* . . ." (9029)
"for any *position* of trust or otherwise *that he might apply for*" (9029)
"our chief of staff had some *ideas* with respect to —— and —— *which could hardly be considered as in accord with* . . ." (9000)
"The *$5.00* per month *which he is sending to*" (8064)
"Mrs. —— has two other *sons*, aged 18 and 20 years, *who are living with* . . ." (8142)
"they will have the *papers* prepared *that you require*" (8160)
"the sister has made *affidavit* to that effect *which I am enclosing*" (8234)
"The family occupy a *house* consisting of six rooms and bath *which they own*" (8303)

In the Vulgar English letters fewer clauses were used as modifiers of nouns—214 in all. Of these 207 or 92 per cent follow immediately the noun they modify; 8 per cent have other words intervening.

Examples of those clauses that immediately follow the nouns they modify are

"any trouble *whitch might set me Back*" (8281)
"a favor *which I promised*" (8265)
"the name *in which my son enlisted under*" (8259)
"my husband —— —— *who is now in* . . ." (8230)
"our son *who left home*" (8193)
"the place *where my son was born*" (8107)
"people *that have known us*" (8074)

Of the 207 instances in this general pattern, sixty five or 31 per cent omit the function word to introduce the subordinate clause.

Examples are

"The income *my husband gets*" (8265)
"whatever expenses *they had*" (8251)
"the information *you request*" (8242)
"ony thing *you wont to know*" (8179)
"an oll the Sister *he got in World*" (8112)
"what more Proof *I can give you*" (8072)
"I guess my clouds dont have those bright lineings *some folks tell about*" (8038)
"with the abuse *I haft to take*" (8205)
"the work *his step father followed*" (8218)
"That $25. *I had to borrow . . .*" (8288)

Examples of those clauses that do not immediately follow the nouns they modify are

"There is also four *children* in the family *who are too young to work*" (8270)
"relate a few *facts* to you *that I am sure you have not . . .*" (8080)
"get my Gardine *papers* from the Clerk at the County seat *that was made to years ago*" (8025)
"I heard tha was a rection *officer* at Lynchburg *that run around with* ——" (8045)
"I have sent the two last *doctors* certificats *that have tended on him*" (8072)

In brief summary, the most noteworthy facts concerning the uses of word order in respect to the modifier-noun (character-substance) relation are the following:

a. As a pattern, single word modifiers precede the nouns they modify. In spite of the fact that there are about three times as many adjective modifiers in the Standard English materials as in those of Vulgar English, the actual proportions of those that precede to those that follow are remarkably close. (Standard English, 1,489 instances; 94.9 per cent precede their nouns, and 5.1 per cent follow. Vulgar English, 479 instances; 95.6 per cent precede their nouns, and 4.4 per cent follow.)

b. The free use of the noun adjunct seems to be much more characteristic of Standard English than of Vulgar English. Four times as many instances appeared in the Standard English letters and in these same letters the types of relations between the modifying noun and its head word show much more variety.

c. Standard English uses multiple modifiers much more frequently than does Vulgar English. Only eleven instances all told appeared in the Vulgar English materials and these were all either of two or three levelled adjectives or of such words as *last* with a numeral.

d. As a pattern, word group modifiers (the so-called prepositional phrases and the subordinate clauses) modify the nouns immediately preceding them. Of the prepositional phrases there is only one instance, and that is in Standard English, in which the phrase, according to the context, could not modify the immediately preceding noun. There are, however, about an equal number of instances in both the Standard English letters and those of Vulgar English in which the phrase, although immediately following a noun it could modify, might also logically modify the verb preceding that noun. Of the subordinate clause modifiers, a larger proportion do not immediately follow the noun they modify but have other words intervening. In practically all cases these intervening words are a phrase modifying the same noun. In many of these cases, too, there is some pressure to feel the clause as a modifier of the noun of the phrase it immediately follows in spite of the logic of the context. Here again, in spite of the fact that the number of the clause modifiers in the Standard English letters is nearly twice that of the clause modifiers in the Vulgar English materials, there is a remarkably similar proportion of those that immediately follow their nouns in each case. (Standard English, 396 in all; 86 per cent immediately follow the nouns they modify, 14 per cent have other words intervening. Vulgar English, 214 in all; 92 per cent immediately follow the nouns they modify, 8 per cent have other words intervening.)

e. The omission of the function word to introduce the modifying clause when that clause immediately follows the noun it modifies is much more frequent in the Vulgar English materials than in those of Standard English. In these cases, position without the function word seems to be sufficient. In the Standard English letters, only 8 per cent omit the function word, whereas in the Vulgar English materials 31 per cent omit the introductory function word.

XI

SOME INFERENCES FROM THIS STUDY FOR A WORKABLE PROGRAM IN ENGLISH LANGUAGE FOR THE SCHOOLS

Much labor has, in recent years, gone into the investigations of the so-called "common errors" in the English of pupils in the hope of thus determining the particular errors which school children most frequently make and then of building a program of drill that will effectively eliminate them.[1] Although one may justly insist that the technique employed in collecting these "errors" has been so loose as to make inaccurate and unreliable the conclusions of most of these investigations, yet some significance attaches to the fact that they do reveal a striking similarity of results. The same categories of "errors" appear with the highest counts in all the studies. Charters insists also that

> ". . . the similarity of frequencies in errors in cities widely distributed geographically indicates that a large proportion of the errors of school children are national rather than sectional errors." [2]

These facts offer clear evidence that there is a common body of material in these so-called errors to which teachers direct attention over the whole country. The published language usage tests [3] furnish additional ground for this same conclusion, for practically all of these tests cover approximately the same items. In other words, the so-called "incorrect" English of the pupils in our schools, as determined by error counts and language tests, consists of a rather limited body of items that appear to be the same for all sections of the United States.

[1] See above pp. 20–21, notes 5 and 6.

[2] *Sixteenth Yearbook* of the National Society for the Study of Education (Bloomington, Ind., Public School Publishing Co., 1917), p. 110.

[3] See the list in Rollo L. Lyman's *Summary of Investigations Relating to Grammar, Language and Composition,* pp. 112–114, 129, 130.

The same "error" items appear not only in all parts of our country, they also turn up in about the same proportions in *every grade throughout the elementary school, the high school, and the college.*[4] In some cases the studies of language errors show that the errors actually increase in number and proportion in the later grades after teachers have made an attack upon them and the study of grammar has begun. After finding that pronouns were "used incorrectly more frequently in Grade VIII than in the lower grades," the authors of one study raise the following question:

"Is the present teaching of pronouns leading to a more confused state of mind in the eighth-grade child than existed when he was in the third grade and was entirely unconscious of the rules of grammar governing the use of such words?"[5]

As a matter of fact, any one who makes a thorough survey of the published studies of the language errors of those who attend our schools and colleges is forced to the conclusion that the teaching efforts that have been and are now directed toward the elimination of these so-called errors are largely ineffective and futile.[6] In these efforts, the study of "grammar" has at times been exceedingly prominent; at others it has been abandoned as useless.[7] Most of those who have recently expressed themselves concerning the curriculum in English have taken the point of view that the school study of grammar is of very little use in dealing with the matter of language correctness. The following statement is typical:

[4] See the studies of "persistence of errors" summarized in Lyman, *op. cit.*, pp. 77, 78, 97–104. Compare also L. J. O'Rourke, *Rebuilding the English-Usage Curriculum* (Washington, 1934), p. 7. "The findings show that the average increase in mastery, from one grade to another, is very slight."

[5] See Isabel Sears and Amelia Diebel, "A Study of the Common Mistakes in Pupils' Oral English," *Elementary School Journal,* Vol. 17, pp. 44–54.

[6] "More time is being spent in the high-school English classes of America today upon grammar and usage than upon any other single phase of instruction. Daily checking of what was going on in classrooms from Seattle to Richmond, Virginia, and from Los Angeles to Cranston, Rhode Island, established that fact in 1932. It is further substantiated by similar data from daily visitation in fifty representative towns in New York State in 1936."—Dora V. Smith, "English Grammar Again," *English Journal,* Vol. 27, 1938, pp. 647, 648.

For additional evidence concerning the process to which pupils are subjected see also S. A. Leonard, "How English Teachers Correct Papers," *English Journal,* Vol. 12, 1923, pp. 517–532.

[7] See J. C. Tressler, "Is Grammar Dead?" *English Journal,* Vol. 27, 1938, pp. 396–401; Reed Smith, "Grammar: The Swing of the Pendulum," *English Journal,* Vol. 27, 1938, pp. 637–643; and Dora V. Smith, "English Grammar Again," *English Journal,* Vol. 27, 1938, pp. 643–649.

"Because scientific investigations have failed to show the effectiveness of grammar in the elimination of usage errors, it is not here organized for that purpose." [8]

It is the point of view of this report that *a study of the real grammar of Present-day English has never been used in the schools* and that the conclusions concerning its effectiveness relate only to the type of "grammar" that has been tried. The "grammar" hitherto used in the schools has been either the logical analysis of sentences and "parsing," most often illustrated by the various methods of diagramming, or a learning of rules and definitions which were assumed to be the measures of correct language.[9] As indicated in the first two chapters of this book, this use of grammar assumes that the problem of language usage is a simple one of *correct* forms and *mistakes* which can easily be separated according to the rules. The teaching efforts that have been devoted to this type of grammar have therefore been directed toward making pupils "conscious of the rules" by which to determine correctness.

In the light of the principles which underlie our investigation this customary use of "grammar" is fundamentally unsound. First, language usage cannot thus be separated into two simple classes. Instead, our usage presents a complex range of differing and changing practices which must be understood in relation to the feelings of an indefinite number of social groups. Second, sensitiveness to usage—a richness of assimilated experience through which one becomes

[8] W. W. Hatfield, *An Experience Curriculum in English* (New York, D. Appleton-Century Co., 1935), p. 228. See also the studies that deal with the problem of whether a knowledge of grammar actually "functions," as listed or summarized in the following:

a. Dora V. Smith, *Instruction in English,* United States Department of the Interior, *Bulletin,* 1932, *No.* 17, National Survey of Education, *Monograph No.* 20, p. 35.

b. Dora V. Smith, "The Contributions of Research to Teaching and Curriculum Making in English, July, 1934, to July, 1937," *English Journal*, Vol. 27, 1938, pp. 295–311.

c. Harry N. Rivlin, "The Present Status of Research in Functional Grammar," *English Journal,* Vol. 27, 1938, pp. 590–597.

[9] See, for example, W. W. Charters, *Teaching the Common Branches* (New York, The Macmillan Co., Rev. ed., 1924), pp. 96, 98, 115.

"Grammar consists of a series of rules and definitions. . . . Since . . . ninety-five percent of all children and teachers come from homes or communities where incorrect English is used, nearly everyone has before him the long hard task of overcoming habits set up early in life before he studied grammar in school. . . . Such people are exposed to the ridicule of those who notice the error, and the only way in which they can cure themselves is by eternal vigilance and the study of grammar."

aware of the suggestions attaching to words and constructions because of the circumstances in which they are commonly used—is the only condition upon which good English can be won. All the effort which goes to make one *conscious* of "rules of grammar" serves to deaden this sensitiveness to one's speech environment and to turn one's attention away from the only source of real knowledge.

This book, therefore, presents a *grammar* of Present-day American English that differs from any that has yet been tried in the efforts to deal with the language practices of students. It contains no rules and definitions of correct English and it is not a closed handbook of usage. It does, however, attempt to provide the starting point for a workable program in English language for the schools by its method and materials.

1. In method it presents an outline of the three important grammatical devices which Present-day English uses (forms of words, function words, word order) and the purposes for which they are employed. This grammatical outline is in reality a sketch to guide observation and to furnish a basis for the classification and interpretation of the language phenomena observed. The outline is filled out in some detail with the facts observed in a definite body of material that was carefully selected as representative of the practices of certain social groups. In details, the sketch presented here is very much limited, and needs, therefore, to be constantly checked, corrected, and supplemented by actual observations upon other bodies of language material.

2. In method, too, this sketch attempts to give some proportion to the description of the grammar of Present-day English by the use of quantitative information. Many of the generalizations appearing in English grammars actually express or imply quantitative judgments—judgments of absolute or relative frequency. Most of these depend upon general impressions rather than upon an attempt carefully to calculate the frequency of actual instances in any body of material. Here every example of each grammatical item discussed was recorded so that its relative frequency in the body of material here examined could be indicated. For a teaching program it seems worth while to know, for example, the nine words that account for 92 per cent of all the instances of prepositions used and the twelve words that account for 93 per cent of all the instances of

conjunctions; that only forty six verbs have different forms for the past tense and past participle and that less than 5 per cent of the instances of plural nouns have forms other than the "s" pattern.

3. In materials, this book attempts to find those language items in which Standard English and Vulgar English differ. As a matter of fact, if the letters here examined can be regarded as characteristic of these two groups of users of English, there are many details of language practice to which drill is given in our schools, items that are discussed or condemned in our handbooks of usage, which are not matters of distinction between the practices of Standard English and Vulgar English. Here it has been assumed that the obligation resting upon the schools is to teach the knowledge of and the ability to use the "standard" English of the United States. But for a workable program, the teaching must deal with real Standard English, that which is actually used in conducting the major affairs of our country, and not with grammatical usages that have no validity outside the English classroom. From the materials examined here it seems clear that the following items, for example, are not matters of difference between Standard English and Vulgar English. They all appear to be used with some frequency in the Standard English materials.

a. *None* with plural verb
b. The indefinites *everyone, everybody,* etc., with a plural reference pronoun or a plural verb separated from the indefinite by other words
c. The use in accord with the pressures of word order of the case forms of the six pronouns which still retain dative-accusative forms
d. The use of the indicative form in non-fact clauses
e. *As* introducing a causal clause and *so* equal to a weakened *therefore*
f. The noun adjunct

4. In its materials, also, this study seems very clearly to show that the point of primary attack in a program of English language for the schools should be in striving to develop a knowledge of and practice in using the *wide resources of the language.* Over and over again in the preceding chapters it appeared that the differences between the language of the educated and that of those with little

education did not lie primarily in the fact that the former used one set of forms and the latter an entirely different set. In fact, in most cases, the actual deviation of the language of the uneducated from Standard English grammar seemed much less than is usually assumed, and in practically all instances was in the direction of greater conservatism. Vulgar English uses many forms that were common in the older stages of the language and that Standard English has given up.

The most striking difference between the language of the two groups lay in the fact that Vulgar English seems essentially poverty stricken. It uses less of the resources of the language, and a few forms are used very frequently. *Get,* for example, in its many senses appears in both the Standard English and the Vulgar English materials, but it is employed ten times as frequently in the Vulgar English letters as in those of Standard English. *So* as a weak *therefore* occurs in the Standard English letters as well as in those of Vulgar English, but it is used six times as often in the Vulgar English materials as in those of Standard English. On the other hand, the "expanded" form of the function word with substantives,[10] an expansion which amounts to an analysis and emphasis of the precise meaning relationship involved, occurs only one third as often in the Vulgar English letters as in those of Standard English. In vocabulary and in grammar the mark of the language of the uneducated is its poverty. The user of Vulgar English seems less sensitive in his impressions, less keen in his realizations, and more incomplete in his representations. It would seem to be a sound inference from the results of our study that perhaps the major emphasis in a program of language study that is to be effective should be in providing a language experience that is directed toward acquaintance with and practice in the rich and varied resources of the language. Here again observation of actual usage seems the most important method, and the tools of observation absolutely essential.

A program of English language teaching in the schools, if it is to have any chance of dealing effectively with the language of pupils, must start from the following points of agreement:

[10] See above, pages 115–117.

A. We must agree upon the kind of English which it is the obligation of the schools to teach.

The social pressure which makes Standard English the obligation of the schools [11] applies primarily to informal English—the language of the polite conversation of cultivated people, of their familiar letters and everyday discussions—rather than to formal literary English. We may not like many of the constructions that characterize the language of "well-bred ease," and we may even wish that we could change the many illogical expressions that are old as well as those that have been and are being newly created. This was the hope of those that urged the setting up of an authorized academy "to correct and fix" the English language from Edmund Bolton in 1617 to Jonathan Swift in 1712. To "provide a definite standard for the English language," to "prune it of its crudities" and its "false syntax," and to "bring it into method" expressed the aims of an increasing number of the writers of grammars in the eighteenth century. In spite of all their efforts and the huge expenditure of teaching time and resources in the schools, there is hardly a single item of the grammar of our language that has been affected. Our language has been and is changing constantly, but these changes do not come from the practices of the uneducated nor from the foreigners in our midst and, more important than anything else, the direction of those changes seems *not* to be affected by the efforts of the writers of handbooks and of school teachers. In spite of the teaching hours devoted to *lie* and *lay,* for example, the displacing of the preterit *lay* and the past participle *lain* by the "weak" verb form with dental suffix, *laid* goes steadily on. We may not like it, but we can do absolutely nothing effective about it.

Johnson, after seven years of work on his *Dictionary,* writes the following:

"Those who have been persuaded to think well of my design, require that it should fix our language, and put a stop to those alterations which time and chance has hitherto been suffered to make in it without opposition. With this consequence I will confess I flattered myself for a while; but now begin to fear that I have indulged expectation which neither reason nor experience can justify. When we see men grow old and die at a certain time one after another, from cen-

[11] See above, pages 11–15.

tury to century, we laugh at the elixir that promises to prolong life to a thousand years; and with equal justice may the lexicographer be derided, who, being unable to produce a single example of a nation that has preserved their words and phrases from mutability, shall imagine that his dictionary can embalm his language, and secure it from corruption and decay, that it is his power to change sublunary nature, or clear the world at once from folly, vanity and affectation. With this hope, however, academies have been instituted, to guard the avenues of their languages, to retain fugitives, and repulse intruders: but this vigilance and activity have hitherto been vain; sounds are too volatile and subtile for legal restraints; to enchain syllables and to lash the wind, are equally the undertakings of pride, unwilling to measure its desires by its strength." [12]

The experience of at least two hundred years shows that we cannot hope to change the practices of a language; we can only help students to learn what those practices are. Social pressure will necessarily support a particular set of speech habits, and a language program to be effective must have the active support of real social pressure. But it cannot be an imaginary social pressure as has so often been the case in the attempt to foster a school-mastered speech; it must be the vigorous social pressure of a living speech, the forms of which can be constantly verified upon the lips of actual speakers. For our schools we can muster real social pressure for the learning of actual, living, *informal* Standard English.

B. We must agree to base our teaching upon an accurate, realistic description of the actual practices of informal Standard English and eliminate from our language programs all those matters of dispute for which there is any considerable usage in informal Standard English.

The body of this book (Chapters V to X) has thus attempted a tentative sketch of the grammatical practices characteristic of informal Standard English. This sketch was based upon a limited body of material consisting of some three thousand letters and therefore covers proportionately only an exceedingly small volume of present English usage. From the point of view of grammar, however, many items appeared with considerable frequency and furnish sufficient evidence from which to conclude that many matters to which our teaching now gives time can be safely omitted from our

[12] Samuel Johnson, *English Dictionary* (1755), Preface.

programs. It would seem to be a waste of time and resources—a waste that is harmful in the light of the great many important things to be taught—to strive futilely to eliminate from the speech of our pupils practices that our sketch shows to be fairly frequent in informal Standard English. We need not set ourselves positively to teach these practices; we need only ignore them for more important matters. To be effective a language program must be cleared of every item that is not so definitely a practice of Vulgar English that it carries the connotations of that particular social group.

C. We must agree to stimulate among our pupils observation of actual usage and to go as far as possible in giving them a practical equipment for this purpose.

From the time of the introduction of English as a subject of study in the schools teachers as well as pupils have habitually turned their attention away from an observation of the facts of actual usage to "authority." Like Lord Chesterfield they wished for a dictator,[13] and the school grammars and dictionaries in a practical way did fulfill that office. But these grammars with their rules that were in part the rules of Latin grammar and in part the results of "reason" did not and could not provide the tools of an effective language program. Even if the subject of English could command much more of the pupil's time than it does now, it would be impossible to train the pupil in all the specific language items he would need throughout his life. To be really effective a language program must prepare the pupil for independent growth, and the only possible means of accomplishing that end is to lead him to become an intelligent observer of language usage. If we would have him observe intelligently the facts of the language usage about him, he must acquire the necessary tools; he must become thoroughly familiar with the three types of devices which our particular language uses to indicate

[13] Lord Chesterfield, in his well known letter, published in 1754, the year before Johnson's *Dictionary* appeared, wrote as follows:

"It must be owned that our language is at present in a state of anarchy; and hitherto, perhaps, it may not have been the worse for it. During our free and open trade, many words and expressions have been imported, adopted, and naturalized from other languages, which have greatly enriched our own. . . . The time for discrimination seems to be now come. Toleration, adoption and naturalization have run their lengths. Good order and authority are now necessary. But where shall we find them, and at the same time the obedience due to them? We must have recourse to the old Roman expedient in times of confusion, and chuse a dictator. Upon this principle I give my vote for Mr. Johnson to fill that great and arduous post."

grammatical ideas. He must know the usual grammatical uses in English of word forms or inflections, of function words, and of word order. It is in these respects that the various sets of language habits differ, and only in so far as the pupil can thus refer any given usage to the pattern has he the equipment necessary to make intelligent observations and decisions for himself. It is upon *grammar* in this form that is new in the schools that the hope of a workable program of English language teaching rests.

INDEX

[All references are to pages. Subject entries are in roman; particular words or groups of words are in *italics;* and authors and titles are in CAPITALS AND SMALL CAPITALS. Letters in parentheses thus *in regard(s) to* indicate variations.]

THE NATIONAL COUNCIL OF TEACHERS OF ENGLISH

211 WEST SIXTY-EIGHTH STREET, CHICAGO, ILLINOIS

PUBLICATIONS

Issued by special committees of the National Council of Teachers of English under the direction of the Publications Committee:

John J. DeBoer — Homer A. Watt
Stella S. Center — Neal M. Cross
Holland D. Roberts, *Chairman*

Reading for Fun (elementary book list)
Compilation directed by Eloise Ramsay
Books for Home Reading (for High Schools)
Leisure Reading (for Grades Seven, Eight, and Nine)
Compilation directed by Stella S. Center and Max J. Herzberg, Committee Co-Chairman
Good Reading (for Colleges)
Compilation directed by Atwood H. Townsend, Committee Chairman
Current English Usage, Sterling Andrus Leonard, Committee Chairman
Guide to Play Selection, Milton Smith, Committee Chairman
The Teaching of College English, Oscar James Campbell, Committee Chairman
Photoplay Appreciation in American High Schools, William Lewin, Committee Chairman
An Experience Curriculum in English, W. Wilbur Hatfield, Committee Chairman
A Correlated Curriculum, Ruth Mary Weeks, Committee Chairman
Teaching High School Students to Read, Stella S. Center and Gladys L. Persons
War and Peace, An Anthology, compilation directed by Ida T. Jacobs
Film and School, Helen Rand and Richard Byrd Lewis
Facts About Current English Usage, Albert H. Marckwardt and Fred G. Walcott
Conducting Experiences in English, Angela M. Broening, Committee Chairman
Educating for Peace, Ida T. Jacobs, Committee Chairman
American English Grammar, Charles C. Fries

OFFICIAL ORGANS

The English Journal and *College English* for Colleges and High Schools
Editor, W. Wilbur Hatfield, 211 West Sixty-Eighth Street, Chicago, Illinois